GUESTS WITHOUT GRIEF

ENTERTAINING MADE EASY FOR THE HESITANT HOST

PAULA JHUNG

A FIRESIDE BOOK
PUBLISHED BY SIMON & SCHUSTER

FIRESIDE
Rockefeller Center
1230 Avenue of the Americas
New York, NY 10020

Designed by Susan Hood

Manufactured in the United States of America
10 9 8 7 6 5 4 3 2 1

Library of Congress Cataloging-in-Publication Data
Jhung, Paula.
Guests without grief: entertaining made easy for the hesitant host / Paula Jhung.
p. cm.
"A Fireside book."
Includes index.
1. Dinners and dining. 2. Entertaining.
TX737.J47 1997
642'.4—dc21 96-49538
CIP

ISBN 0-684-81884-1

PRAISE FOR PAULA JHUNG'S *HOW TO AVOID HOUSEWORK*

"In this witty book, Paula Jhung shows us how to deal with the inescapable reality of daily house maintenance—efficiently and unobsessively."

—Alexandra Stoddard, author of *Creating a Beautiful Home*

"An amusing, easy-to-read book full of advice . . . shrewd . . . Practicality and humor blend to make this book both useful and entertaining."

—*The Boston Book Review*

"Experienced housekeepers will identify with this inspiring book. The time to read it is now."

—*Portland Oregonian*

"Paula Jhung has some nifty solutions on how to keep your home looking good without doing a lot of cleaning."

—*Encinitas Blade Citizen*

"I was intrigued and delighted when *How to Avoid Housework* crossed my desk. Paula Jhung is a woman after my own heart."

—Nancy Romanenko, *Asbury Park Sunday Press*

"This is an anti-housework bible that's packed with tips and secrets."

—*Sacramento Bee*

"This breezy upbeat book will gladden slatterns everywhere."

—*Publishers Weekly*

"Down-to-earth advice."

—*Booklist*

"Paula Jhung has pulled together a whole book of nifty tips to help the 'cleanliness challenged' have a house that even a mother-in-law could love."

—Rosemary Brewer, *The Atlanta Constitution*

"Helpfully humorous housecleaning advice."

—*The Dallas Morning News*

"Jhung outlines all you need to know to keep ahead of Mr. Grime."

—*Palm Beach Post*

"Jhung uses a mix of anecdotes, humor, and advice."

—*Los Angeles Times*

"Witty . . . overflows with realistic ways to become smarter at organizing, cleaning, and preserving everything in and around your home."

—*Bridal Guide*

To my mother, Catherine Finlayson,

Who loved the company but hated the complications

CONTENTS

INTRODUCTION: REVELATIONS OF A RELUCTANT HOST

I'm no party pundit. I've won no host-of-the-year awards. In fact, I've long had a love/hate relationship with entertaining. I love the company, but hate the work.

I grew up in a large family whose social life revolved around weddings and wakes. There was little company because there was never the budget, know-how, or, with six kids and assorted relatives living in a highly disorganized house, a presentable setting. Besides, my mother reasoned, who needed company when we had our own crowd?

When I struck out on my own, I determined to change all that. I wanted to be a woman of the world who knew how to mix the perfect martini, whip up a gourmet meal, and live in a place that would dazzle my guests. But being basically lazy and often broke, I had to learn how to do it all at someone else's expense.

So where does one go to learn how to cook, serve, *and* see the world? The friendly skies, of course. As a flight attendant, I learned how to cork champagne and dish out pâté in the front cabin, as well as keep the masses happy with peanuts in the back. I also became expert in dealing with meal shortages, burned prime rib, and the testiness of coffee-splattered passengers.

When I tired of the glamour of red-eye flights and white-knuckle landings, I went back to school to study interior design. Here I discovered that texture, color, and presentation worked as well in a room as it did on a plate. Then motherhood taught me about realistic expectations, making do, and birthday parties from hell.

Still, I struggled as a host. I'd read books and magazines on entertaining only to feel depressed and inadequate, since my surroundings and spreads never measured up to what was depicted in those glossy guides. When I did work up my nerve to have people over, I'd spend days knocking myself out cooking and cleaning, only to feel strung out and resentful by the time my guests arrived. Hardly the welcoming host.

I needed a reality check. After a little introspection and a lot of observation, I came to realize that it isn't a glittering setting or great food that makes a visit fun, it's the attitude of the host. The best of them are more interested in their guests' well-being than in the effect their homes, food, or personalities are making. They're relaxed; therefore, their guests relax, too.

Besides, doing things *too* well can backfire. Case in point: Years ago, I had a friend who worked herself into a frenzy organizing elaborate soirees, filled with live music, fantastic decorations, and fabulous food. People loved her parties, but they seldom reciprocated. She thought the people in her circle were lazy. Intimidated was probably closer to the truth. Who has the guts or the energy to compete with someone who entertains so spectacularly that our own attempts pale in comparison?

Fortunately, today's hospitality standards are more in reach. And contrary to the well-meaning advice of celebrated overachievers, we do not have to hand-embroider the bedsheets, fold the napkins into origami, and stuff petits pois with Beluga caviar. The casual approach is in, as well as simplicity, understatement, and an overall relaxation of formalities. As a lazy host, my time—and maybe yours—has come.

Someone once said, "Part of the joy of living is having and entertaining friends." I think most of us would agree as long as we can entertain without the time, money, and hassle that are so often part of the package. What I've aimed to do on the following pages is lighten and brighten that package with work-saving tips, doable flourishes, and ways to make guests feel that they never want to leave, as well as providing the diplomatic secrets of making sure they do.

Entertaining *can* be entertaining for even the most reluctant host.

TEN BENEFITS OF HOSTING

It may be more fun to be the visitor than the visitee, but there are advantages to playing master of ceremonies:

1. *The guests are handpicked. How often do we go somewhere where we like everyone?*
2. *We get to serve what we like to eat. Control in the kitchen means no gastronomic risk in the dining room.*
3. *Rank has its privileges. Being in charge offers more opportunity for cruising and schmoozing, since we can butt into, and exit, conversations with relative grace: "What's a nice guy like you doing in a place like this?" "Oops, I think I hear the timer."*
4. *There's a place to go. We're not left out when the world seems to be partying on the celebrated occasion, be it New Year's, Halloween, or our own birthdays.*
5. *Entertaining scores popularity points. Everyone wants to get chummy with a party giver. Years ago, my four-year-old daughter, Lisa, brought this point home when she disarmed the nursery school bully by asking, "Do you want to come to my birthday party?" The fact that her birthday wasn't for another six months didn't seem to faze either of them.*
6. *It's an ego trip. Guests praise our cooking, our homes, and our efforts, whether we deserve the accolades or not.*
7. *Social skills increase. When we're plugged into the computer, the phone, and the television most of the day, people skills* need *polishing.*
8. *Hosting is healthy. A Stanford University study shows that cultivating a network of friends is linked to higher levels of immunity.*
9. *It beats the blues. It's hard to feel sorry for ourselves when we're concentrating on the welfare of others.*
10. *Hospitality begets hospitality. We keep in touch with the people we care about, and with any luck, we'll get invited to their shindigs.*

THE PROCRASTINATOR'S GUIDE TO EXCUSES

Do you recognize any of these descriptions?

The Perfectionist: *"When I paint the house, redecorate the living room, and take that cooking class, I'll have people over."*
The Overdoer: *"The last party I had nearly killed me. I'm not throwing another one for at least a decade."*
The Domestically Challenged: *"I can't have anybody over; no one would be able to find the sofa under all that laundry."*
Nervous Nellie: *"I get so high-strung, I make everyone uncomfortable."*
The Drone: *"I don't even have time to call my friends, let alone have them over."*
The Poverty-Stricken: *"I can't afford to have people over, I'm so broke."*
The Mooch: *"Who needs to entertain when my friends are so good at it?"*

PART I

SURROUNDINGS

CHAPTER 1

SECRETS OF A COMPANY-CLEAN HOME

Forget the wining and dining, the hardest part of entertaining is having a presentable home; especially when kids, pets, and messy housemates keep things in a perpetual state of disorder.

As a veteran in the war against housework, I'd like to share some strategies on preventing dust, dirt, and clutter, as well as making the place *look* a lot cleaner than it really is.

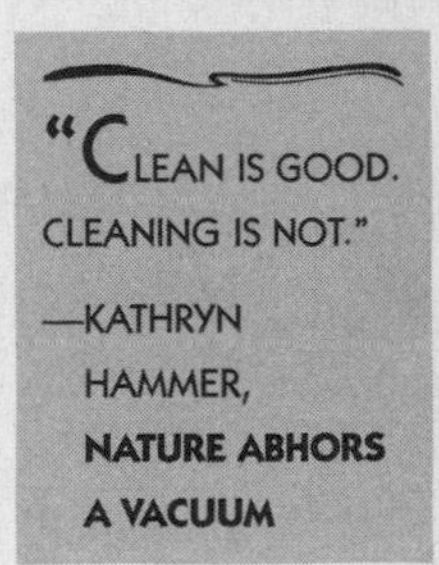

"CLEAN IS GOOD.
CLEANING IS NOT."
—KATHRYN
HAMMER,
NATURE ABHORS
A VACUUM

KEEPING UP APPEARANCES

- Furnish for living, not for show. Pale carpets, delicate fabrics, and fragile furnishings create worry and intensive care, while well-worn woods, softly faded fabrics, and other practical materials are less demanding and easier to live with.
- Undecorate. Too much furniture and too many knickknacks make a home hard to keep clean, while clear surfaces, open space, and a few choice accessories are easier to keep tidy and give a sense of serenity. Understatement simplifies living.
- Scoop and stash. Devote a few minutes at the beginning or end of

every day to putting away out-of-place items. Set the kitchen timer, then play beat the clock.

- Primp. Get in the habit of a daily spruce-up by plumping up the sofa cushions, pinching off brown houseplant leaves, and straightening pictures, lampshades, and chairs. Hand grooming is more gratifying and much easier than hauling out the major equipment.
- Make it easy. Encourage neatness in the kids by providing plenty of reachable shelves, color-coded bins for sorting, and lots of sturdy wall hooks.
- Make it convenient. Keep bowl, tub, and glass cleaners in the bathroom, attach an extension cord to the vacuum cleaner, and have a good-sized wastebasket in every room.
- Play tough. As an ophthalmologist and mother of five children under twelve, Joan Kaestner has to keep a semblance of order in her family's lives. She and her husband, Reed, regularly spot-check rooms and dock allowances for out-of-place items. They also keep one room off-limits to toys and snacks.

MASTER THE ART OF CAMOUFLAGE

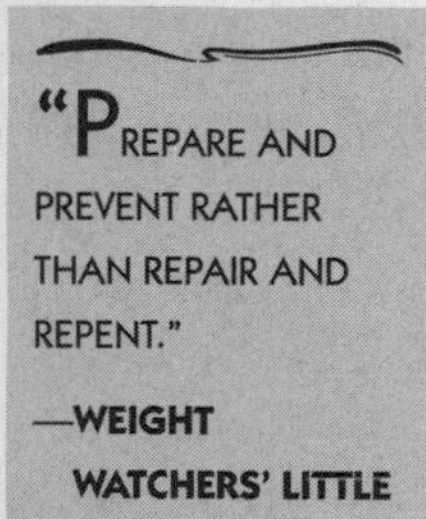

"PREPARE AND PREVENT RATHER THAN REPAIR AND REPENT."
—WEIGHT WATCHERS' LITTLE BOOK OF WISDOM

- Think about how an area is used, then use color and pattern to camouflage the inevitable. Sponge-painted or stipple-painted walls hide dents and smudges. Densely patterned rugs and fabrics conceal spots and stains. Heavily grained woods disguise dust, dings, and wear.
- Some areas just naturally breed disorder, so keep a decorative screen close by. Houston writer David Jameson screens his messy desk from the living area with a set of stained and louvered bifold doors. Interior designer Giselle Covelli covered three two-by-six boards with leftover rolls of pricey Scalamandré wallpaper, then hinged them together to divide her dining area from her home gym. Coco Chanel added depth, dimension, and stash space to her Paris apartments with elegant Coromandel screens.
- If hard water is a fact of life, buy frosted drinking glasses to hide the mineral film, and keep a porcelain cup on the bathroom counter.
- Hang colorful printed towels in the bathroom. Pure white terry won't stay that way when there are dirty little hands in the house.

WHAT WE CAN GET AWAY WITH

- *Unlaundered sheets on the bed*
- *A mountain of wash in the laundry room*
- *Baskets of ironing*
- *Crud under the refrigerator*
- *Gunk in the oven*
- *Dust on the table legs*
- *Lint on a light carpet*

WHAT WE PROBABLY CAN'T

- *Stains on the glassware*
- *Dust on the coffee table*
- *Crumbs on the sofa*
- *Hair in the bathroom sink*
- *Ring around the toilet bowl*
- *Spots on the tablecloth and napkins*
- *Spinach between the teeth*
- *Taco sauce on the T-shirt*

CLOBBER CLUTTER

- Choose freedom over sentimentality. Souvenirs, school papers, and most other rembrances of things past spawn more work and frustration than they do fond memories. We don't need "things" to conjure up good times.
- Play photographer. If you can't bear to part with dusty corsages, first-grade artwork, and A+ compositions, either take a snapshot or videotape the artist describing his or her work.
- Rather than spending big bucks on yet another organizing system, learn to live with less. "The issue is not 'How can I organize?'" said *Time Management for Dummies* author Jeffrey Mayer. "It's 'What can I get rid of that's slowing me down?'"
- Get in the habit of putting things back immediately. Tossed clothes and other wayward items must be dealt with eventually, so we just double the work by leaving them where they fall.
- Ideally, everything should be in its place, but if there's too much everything, and too few places, stash the overflow in decorative cardboard boxes. Stacked and labeled, they can house everything from office and school supplies to out-of-season clothing.
- Get real about reading. Too many subscriptions to newspapers, magazines, and book clubs generate guilt and frustration when we can't keep up. It's better to buy or borrow reading material when there's time to read it rather than dealing with an overwhelming pile of pulp.

- Keep a trash can in the garage or on the front porch and toss unwanted mail before it has a chance to take root inside the house. If you're lucky enough to have a PO box instead of home delivery, take advantage of post-office recycling cans. I junk at least half of my mail at Uncle Sam's.
- Place an attractive tray or basket wherever the mail usually lands. A container corrals an otherwise sprawling pile of mail, and makes it easy to move when company comes.
- Divide and conquer mail as soon as possible. Segregate bills in a desk folder. Stack reading material next to a comfy chair. Post appointments, invitations, and reminders where they'll be easily seen.
- Keep a large shopping bag by the back door and regularly deposit outgrown, unloved, and otherwise unused items. Take them to a consignment shop or, better yet, to a shelter where they'll do some good.
- Place a labeled box for each child by the back door so they have a place to dump their books, balls, and other "in & out" equipment.
- Toss other people's clutter into a remote area. Teacher Francine Stoppler rounds up her kids' clutter in a big trash bag and tosses it into the farthest reaches of their basement crawl space. "It's dark and spidery back there, so the kids are motivated to pick up after themselves regularly," she says.
- Give them their space. Professional organizer Harriet Schechter, author of *More Time for Sex,* uses a similar method, tossing her husband Henry's droppings into his home office, which she dubs "The Pit." "You can hear him rustling around in there looking for things," says Schechter, "sort of like a large rodent."

"YOU SHOW ME A WOMAN WHO DOES NOT HAVE A JUNK DRAWER AND I'LL SHOW YOU A WOMAN WHO LAUNDERS HER LINT."

—ERMA BOMBECK

- Note, don't nag. One spouse of a slob found the pen mightier than the tongue. On his dropped underwear, she scribbled on a sticky note, "Help! I've fallen and I can't get up." On his socks, she stuck, "My feet left me, please walk me to the hamper." On the dirty dishes, "Thanks for the snack—the Roach Family." "It's helping," she claims. "At least I no longer sound like a shrew."
- Free closet space by buying quality, not quantity. Europeans are known for buying a few good classic outfits they update with colorful silk scarves, ties, and other interchangeable accessories. When there's less stuff jammed in a closet, there's less embarrassment hanging visitors' things.
- We can control, but not obliterate, everyday clutter, so keep a drawer,

a shelf in a cupboard, or a space under a skirted table in reserve as a place to stash in an emergency.

- Make sure the stash space is safe. According to a story in the *San Diego Union-Tribune,* a woman hid a bottle of wine, from which she was drinking, in the oven when her pastor paid a surprise visit. The next day, as the oven heated up for the Thanksgiving turkey, the bottle exploded, blew open the door, and sprayed burgundy all over the kitchen.

"MEN FANTASIZE ABOUT HAVING A HAREM, A GROUP OF WOMEN THAT FULFILLS ALL THEIR WISHES. WOMEN DON'T FANTASIZE ABOUT HAVING A MALE HAREM. THAT'S JUST MORE MEN TO PICK UP AFTER."

—**RITA RUDNER'S GUIDE TO MEN**

DEFLECT DUST

- Keep windows closed on windy days, especially in a city, a desert, or in an agricultural area.
- Seal windows and doors with weather stripping.
- Hang machine-washable window curtains and sheers to filter out dust.
- Change furnace and air-conditioning filters winter and summer. A season of heating and cooling mucks up filters, so when blowing air hits a dirty filter, dust flies throughout the home.
- Pledge to Endust. Furniture polishes typically contain oils that act as a magnet to dust. But an annual coat of wax or, better yet, a permanent coat of polyurethane needs nothing more than a quick swipe with a barely damp rag.
- If the piece is teak, use a product made especially for it. Woodworker Sam Waterhouse recommends allowing the product to seep into the wood for a few hours, then buffing it till there's no dust-drawing residue.

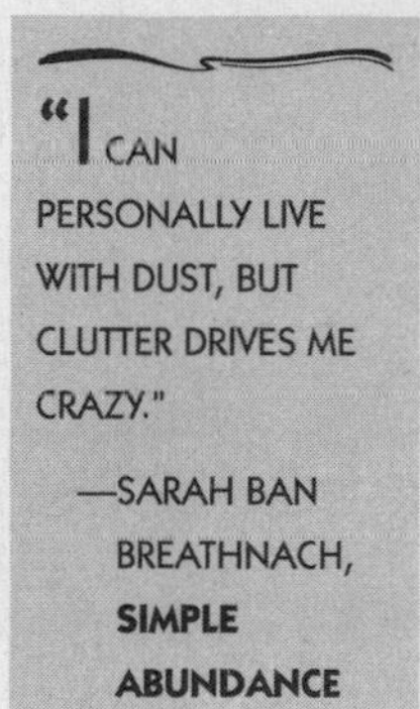
"I CAN PERSONALLY LIVE WITH DUST, BUT CLUTTER DRIVES ME CRAZY."

—SARAH BAN BREATHNACH, **SIMPLE ABUNDANCE**

- Ban in-house smoking. Cigarette, cigar, and pipe smoking blacken household surfaces the same way they blacken lungs.
- Plug in a purifier. Allergy sufferers have discovered a bonus to clearing the air electronically: less dusting. We don't need to wheeze and sneeze to enjoy the dust-busting benefits of scrubbed air.

PRACTICE PREVENTION

- Lose the shoes. Many countries throughout the world leave the dust, dirt, and germs of the streets outside where they belong. By getting the household in the habit of leaving "outside shoes" in the basement, by the back door, or other main point of entry, we save ourselves the hassle of chasing down and cleaning up a roadful of dirt. (If you have any doubt, wipe the sole of your shoe with a damp paper towel the next time you come in from outdoors.) Guests are exempt, since it's the household that generates most of the muck.
- Confine dining. Snacks eaten everywhere make for spills, spots, and stains throughout the house. Make it a rule that all food is eaten over a counter, table, or other surface that can take it.
- Keep bugs and vermin in check by cleaning up food spills, taking out the trash daily, and caulking cracks and holes that lead out to the wild.

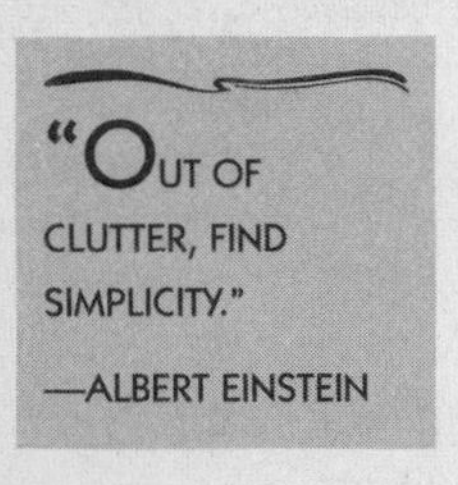
"OUT OF
CLUTTER, FIND
SIMPLICITY."
—ALBERT EINSTEIN

- Flip on fans. Bath and kitchen exhaust fans suck up moisture, odors, and grease before they get a chance to work their way into the walls and fabrics.
- Hang a weighted shower curtain to protect the bathroom floor from faucet-generated floods.
- Avoid tub ring by replacing bar soap with an equal mix of Calgon, baking soda, and Epsom salts. Store it with a scoop in a pretty container. The blend leaves the skin *and* the tub smooth and scum-free.

GET HELP

- Hire a cleaning pro to come in regularly, or at least before an event. There's a definite sense of security in being able to have guests just after the house has been professionally cleaned.
- Know you're not alone. According to a Roper Starch Worldwide poll, one in six Americans hired cleaning help last year, up from one in ten a decade ago.
- Be resourceful. Help doesn't have to come from an expensive cleaning service. Good freelancers can be found through the references of friends and at university employment agencies. Even baby-sitters and grass cutters can be drafted to do some of the dirty work.

RED ALERT

You just got home from work, the place is a shambles, and guests are arriving in less than an hour. While the wine is chilling and dinner heating, round up the troops, and mount the following plan of attack:

> "HOUSECLEANING IS LIKE CHEKOV; IT STARTS SLOW AND THEN IT TAPERS OFF."
>
> —HENRY ALFORD, **NEW YORK TIMES**

- Quickly scoop up wayward debris in a laundry basket. Put it where it belongs if there's time, hide it if there isn't.
- Concentrate cleaning where it shows. The coffee table, bathroom sink, mirror, and toilet are under closer scrutiny from guests than the dust bunnies under the sofa, the unmade beds, or the mountain of wash in the laundry room.
- If there's no time to dust, throw a tablecloth over a dusty and finger-smeared coffee table. A twenty-four-inch to thirty-six-inch square is perfect on most rectangular tables when it's placed on the diagonal.
- Close the doors to hopelessly messy rooms.
- Stash toiletries in a basket or shopping bag under the bathroom sink.
- Close the shower curtain.
- Change or reverse the towels.
- Empty overflowing wastebaskets.
- Change the cat litter.
- Open a window and air out the place.
- Spray a little pine- or lemon-scented all-purpose cleaner in the air.
- Wash up, put on a clean something-or-other, and run a comb through your hair. Your appearance is more important than your home's.
- Cop an attitude. If you are caught completely off guard when you come home to find your in-laws lurking in the kitchen or the preacher parked in the parlor, settle them in with a beverage, and take a few minutes to make the necessary sanitary adjustments. Then relax. It is more important to concentrate on our guests' well-being than on the impression our surroundings are making. The days of pretending we live in a *Leave It to Beaver* set are over. According to lifestyle writer Michael Walsh, "We're becoming far less self-conscious about our homes and are more willing to let visitors and guests see the way we really live." It's about time.
- Console yourself. Only the obsessive-compulsive always live in perfectly pristine surroundings,

> "WITH MY INVITATIONS, I SEND DIRECTIONS AS A GUIDE, BUT MY HOUSE IS SUCH A MESS, THEY NEED A MAP FOR INSIDE."
>
> —PHYLLIS DILLER

and we all know how much fun *they* are to visit. Besides, studies show that most people feel more comfortable among a little disarray than a not-a-thing-out-of-place room. Lived-in can be the most welcoming look of all.

WHEN A MESS IS BEST

When Bill and Donna Ridgeway added a wing to their new house, they threw a "Help Us Survive Remodeling Party." "There was so much dust, we knew cleaning was fruitless, so we went with the theme, and threw a lot of drop cloths around," said Donna. Galvanized buckets held the drinks, ladders the snacks, and a plank on sawhorses the chili and salads. "It was the first time I didn't worry about immaculate surroundings," said Donna. "It was liberating for me and apparently for our guests. Everyone was so loose."

CHAPTER 2

FAST FIXES FOR FRAZZLED ROOMS

Clean is one thing, but when the walls are scuffed, the furniture frayed, and company is on its way, we need help fast. We're not talkin' budget-breaking, time-consuming face-lifts here, but easy makeovers that deliver a lot of bang for the buck.

PLAY PICASSO

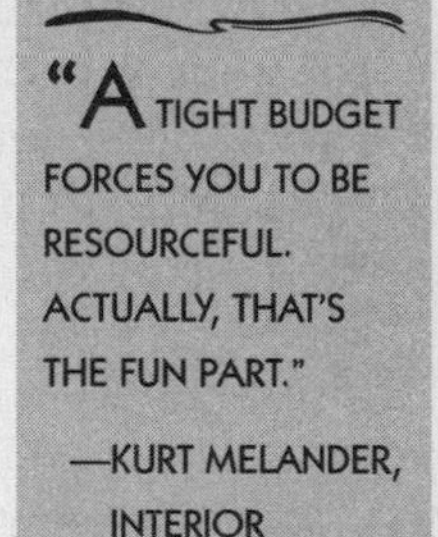

"A TIGHT BUDGET FORCES YOU TO BE RESOURCEFUL. ACTUALLY, THAT'S THE FUN PART."
—KURT MELANDER, INTERIOR DESIGNER

- When there is no time to scrub or cover scuffed-up walls, touch up spots in the original color using a small artist's brush or a cotton-tipped swab. I always keep small labeled jars of leftover paint on hand for emergency use.
- If there's only a bit of the original paint left, match it up by dipping a business card, Popsicle stick, or cardboard scrap into the paint can. Bring it to the paint store for a perfect match.
- If the original can of enamel is long gone, paint the lower third of the wall, the part that gets the most abuse, in a coordinating or contrasting shade. Add a chair rail made from stock molding or a narrow wallpaper border to separate the two tones.
- When walls are truly hopeless, sponge-paint them with watered-down latex in a slightly lighter or darker tone. Faux-finishes special-

HOW WE SEE OUR HOMES

When Self *magazine polled readers on how they felt about their homes, 13 percent saw it as a pit stop, saying they were so busy, they seldom spent time there. Seventeen percent looked at it as a showpiece—a place that's fun to jazz up. Eighteen percent called it a retreat—a place to get away—while 43 percent described it as a nest—a place to enjoy family and friends.*

One respondent described her ideal home as a place "cozy enough to be healthy and dirty enough to be fun."

ist Gary Williams gave a stone-washed denim look to worn navy walls simply by sponging thinned white paint over the existing color. "There are more challenging techniques, but anyone can quickly master white over color," said Williams. "The original shade shows through, but the white glaze brightens it up and hides a few sins." If the results are more faux pas than faux finish, they can simply be painted over.

- Dab on the color-wash in small sections with a sea sponge, or pull small random chunks out of a synthetic sponge for a finish with texture and depth.
- Resuscitate bleached-out upholstery fabric by painting the surrounding walls a deep, rich color. A decade ago, one New York designer did up an old-money living room with blue and green chintz fabrics against pale yellow walls. Rather than change the upholstery, he simply repainted the walls deep green, which made the fading fabric spring back to life.

"A WELL-WORN SOFA IS WONDERFUL. IT MEANS PEOPLE HAVE BEEN HAVING A GOOD TIME."

—MARIE KINNAMAN, INTERIOR DESIGNER

SPRUCE UP THE SOFA

- Gift wrap it. Maybe the sofa and armchairs have seen better days, but they can regain their youth with slipcovers. After years of scarcity and cheesy design, ready-made covers are chic, cheap, and plentiful again at linen shops, department stores, and in home furnishing catalogs. The style and fit are looser, giving the room a relaxed look.

- Salvage a grody sofa or chair by tossing a good-sized quilt, shawl, or other glamorous throw over the whole thing. I'm rather attached to an old camel recliner that is long overdue for an upgrade. Until I get around to it, I dress it for company by draping a cream-colored, soft cotton throw over it.
- Consider a rug as a cover. In her book *Shortcuts to Great Decorating,* interior designer Mary Gilliatt shows a kilim rug draped and tucked over a threadbare sofa. Freud also draped his famous couch with Oriental rugs. The look is lush, but make sure the rug is pliable and soft.
- Add pizzazz by buying a few ready-made throw pillows, or buy a couple of down pillow forms and cover them with an affordable amount of fabulous fabric. Give them quick-change reversibility by backing them with contrasting velvet, suede, or silk.
- If sofa cushions have the imprint of one too many couch potatoes, beef them up with new foam or feathers. English designer Diana Phipps puffs up tired cushions with feathers from sale-priced down bed pillows. In her book *Affordable Splendor,* Phipps explains that feathers mold to the body when leaned against, instead of aggressively leaping back like foam.
- Feather implants are messy and best done in a small bathroom or laundry room. Just rip open a fist-sized hole in the pillow, grab a handful of feathers and transplant them from donor to patient.

THE COMPANY COUCH

Home-grown couch potatoes take note: America's Research Group, a consumer survey organization for the furniture industry, says how much we spend on a sofa relates less *to how much we coddle the family and* more *to how often company calls.*

A survey of 16,064 respondents found that those who entertain at home three times a year or less spend no more than $535 for a sofa. If they entertain three to five times a year, they average $683. If they entertain six to nine times a year, they pay $915. And the real party animals who entertain ten or more times a year fork over approximately $1,500 to impress their guests.

COVER A CRUDDY TABLE

- The dining room table is one place we want to shine, since it's where everyone eventually gathers. If the top is hopelessly wronged and there's no time or desire to haul out the sander or chemicals, simply cover it with beautiful fabric or a ready-made tablecloth.
- Give a lightweight tablecloth body by placing a slightly shorter cloth underneath. Use a ready-made cloth as liner or cut it from a bedsheet or plain muslin. No need for hemming.
- Top it all with glass. A glass top not only holds the fabric in place, it also protects it and the table from spills, burns, and other minor mishaps. Ready-made glass tops are available in limited sizes from home and hardware centers. If a custom-cut piece is needed, make sure the glass is at least one-quarter-inch thick for strength, has polished edges, and is cut slightly smaller than the tabletop so it doesn't get bumped to oblivion. A quarter-inch recess from the edge is about right.
- Cover a small side table with a square silk scarf over a floor-length, solid-color cloth, and top it with glass.
- Disguise an abused coffee table with a large mirrored tray, or top it with a cut-to-fit cushion and use it as an ottoman.

CHEER-UP CHAIRS

- Loose seat cushions on occasional chairs can be recovered easily. If the cushion sits within the frame, simply pop it out, stretch and staple the new fabric over the old, then squeeze it back into the frame.
- Expand your options with dressmaker fabric. It's cut narrower and is generally cheaper than upholstery goods. Just make sure it has enough body and weight to hold up under sliding bottoms and falling food.
- Play up the country look by simply letting a peeled finish be, or enhance it further with a crackle glaze. Author, designer, and master of distressed finishes Tricia Guild believes we're comfortable around humble furniture the same way we're comfortable around humble people. Both are approachable and easy to live with.

ADD A SCREEN

Whether it's painted, papered, or covered with fabric, a decorative paneled screen not only hides a chronically messy spot, it also can:

- conceal a damaged wall
- hide pipes, vents, and unused radiators and air conditioners

- screen a portable coat rack
- seal off a drafty fireplace or window
- cozy up a seating area in a large room
- make a dressing area in a studio apartment or den/guest room
- create a headboard
- hang on a wall as art

Few furnishings add so much form and function at so little cost.

SALVAGE A FLOOR

- Get creative with rugs. Beautiful area rugs have flooded the market the past decade, so prices are down and quality is up. Rugs not only animate a room, they cover stains, worn spots, and protect the flooring below as well.
- Come clean. An electric carpet shampooer rents for around $20 a day, but an easier, more thorough, though more expensive solution is to have carpets professionally steam-cleaned. Either way, give them at least twenty-four hours to dry before company tromps all over them.
- Buff, don't wax. A dull wood floor may look as if it needs rewaxing, but it often just needs a once-over with a buffing machine.
- Hide behind a can of paint. Cover up wood or vinyl floors beyond salvation under a coat of heavy-duty deck paint, or stencil or splatter-paint on the worst areas.

"REFINISHING FLOORS IS NONSENSE. FLOORS ARE EITHER FINISHED OR THEY AREN'T. IF YOU CAN SEE INTO THE BASEMENT THE FLOOR IS UNFINISHED."

—P. J. O'ROURKE, **THE BACHELOR HOME COMPANION: A PRACTICAL GUIDE TO KEEPING HOUSE LIKE A PIG**

BRIGHTEN A BATHROOM

A bathroom not only gets a lot of wear, it also comes under private perusal from guests.

- Touch up a chipped and stained sink, tub, and toilet with a porcelain-repair kit.
- Remove stains from wallpaper with an art gum eraser.
- Blast away hard-water stains on a shower door with full-strength distilled vinegar.
- Turn threadbare towels into cleaning cloths and replace them with thick and luxurious new ones.

- Wash the shower curtain with a few towels in the machine, adding a cup of vinegar to the rinse cycle.
- Paint or replace a discolored toilet seat. Since harsh chemicals can yellow it, keep it pristine with a mix of vinegar and water.

JAZZ UP A KITCHEN

- Buy a new tablecloth to match or coordinate with window coverings and seat cushions.
- Replace battered cabinet knobs and handles with beautifully designed new ones.
- Rejuvenate a scratched butcher-block counter by scrubbing it with a soapy steel wool pad and rubbing in a little vegetable oil.
- Buy new linen towels and pot holders so guests aren't grossed out when they volunteer to take the turkey out of the oven or dry the dishes.

ALTERED STATES

"I come from the kind of family where my mother kept an extra roll of toilet paper on the tank in the back of the toilet, and it had a little knit hat with a pompom on it. I didn't know if the purpose of this was so people wouldn't know that we had an extra roll of toilet paper or because my mother felt even toilet paper is embarrassed to be what it is. The toilet paper had a hat, the dog had a sweater, and the couch arms and back had little fabric toupees to protect them. I never felt the need to try drugs growing up. My reality was already altered."—Jerry Seinfeld

GET FRESH

- Dump dying houseplants. We get so used to having these terminal cases around, we hardly see them, but they hint of an unhappy home life.
- Chuck fading, dusty, and cobwebby dried-flower arrangements. They're not meant to last forever.
- Use fake greens and flowers sparingly, and display them well above eye level in opaque containers. Clear glass is a dead giveaway for waterless impostors.

- Add life to a room with a large, healthy potted tree. Place it in a decorative container and nestle a small, trailing plant like a pothos or ivy at its base. A ficus, schefflera, or palm will add drama and lushness, especially if it's lit from below with a can light.
- Consider a few easy-care flowering plants like kalanchoes or bromeliads for color.
- Pick or purchase a big bouquet of seasonal flowers. One of the best things about flowers and plants is they take the focus off the less attractive features of a room.

WAKE-UP WALLS

- Join the local art museum and borrow prints free, or at a nominal cost.
- Check out the art cooperative at the local university or art school where reasonably priced originals can be purchased from budding talent.
- Enlarge and frame favorite snapshots. Black-and-white shots are effective when matted in white or gray and surrounded by white, black, or clear frames. Any collection looks best when all the frames are simple and consistent.
- Browse used bookstores for old volumes of framable maps, architectural drawings, botanical prints, and other appealing illustrations. Have mats cut to fit them into ready-made frames.
- Hang pictures so their centers are equal to the average person's eye level or about five feet six inches from the floor. If they're to be hung above a sofa, table, or other piece of furniture, position them so they sit just above the object.
- Trace the outline of the frames on newspaper or grocery sacks to get an idea of how they'll fill the space before attacking the wall with a hammer.
- Position a collection of pictures so either all the tops or all the bottoms align.
- Hang a framed mirror to catch the light, add depth, and reflect a view from a window.
- Keep large pictures and mirrors hanging straight by attaching at least two hangers on the back of each side rather than one in the middle.

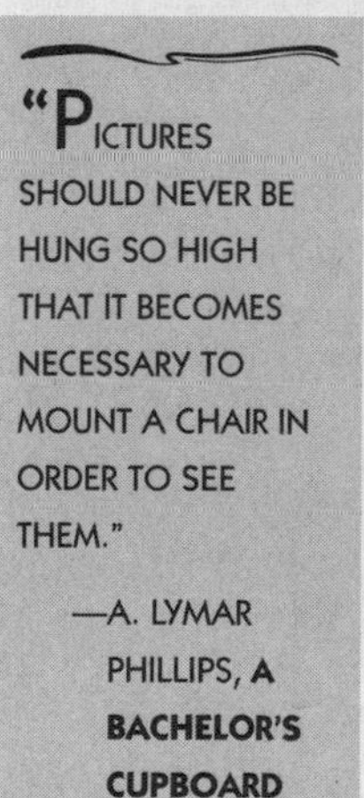
"PICTURES SHOULD NEVER BE HUNG SO HIGH THAT IT BECOMES NECESSARY TO MOUNT A CHAIR IN ORDER TO SEE THEM."

—A. LYMAR PHILLIPS, **A BACHELOR'S CUPBOARD** (1906)

GUSSY UP THE GUEST ROOM

- Freshen a clean but musty comforter by hanging it outside on a sunny day.
- Make a padded headboard by having the lumberyard cut a rectangle or arch of fiberboard or plywood. Staple cotton batting, then fabric (a matching sheet works well) over it, and attach it to the wall with L-shaped corner braces.
- Repair a tiny tear in a paper or vinyl window shade with clear nail polish.
- Sponge-paint a yellowing window shade to match the walls or stencil it using real leaves as patterns.
- Weave grosgrain ribbon through plain matchstick blinds to match or coordinate room colors.
- Tie back curtains with wired taffeta ribbon.
- Line drawers with scented paper.
- Paint the inside of the closet in a room-coordinating color. I once painted the inside of a guest closet lavender in a Wedgwood-blue room and hung seafoam green, French blue, and violet satin hangers inside. It's my only closet that looks better open than shut.

> "YOUR HOME IS A FORM OF SELF-EXPRESSION. IT DOESN'T LIE. WEAR IT LIKE A GREAT COMFORTABLE COAT THAT MAY HAVE A HOLE IN THE ELBOW."
>
> —PETER JENSEN, WRITER

TIDY THE OUTSIDE

- Make sure the outside entry lights are working and pick up toys and tools so no one makes a grand entrance stumbling up or down the walk.
- Check out solar-powered outdoor lights for pathways and steps. They're inexpensive, easy to install, and go on and off automatically.
- Put the pooper scooper into action if there are pets in the picture. My husband and I used to pay our daughter Kelley a nickel a poop so we didn't have to deal with it.
- Sweep the front entry and place a pot or two of bright flowering plants by the front door.
- Add color to a summer patio with flower-coordinating pillows and cushions.

CHAPTER 3

SETTING THE STAGE

By using a little psychology, we can set up our surroundings so we don't have to work so hard at playing host. In fact, we can pretty much control the mood and how well people interact by the way we arrange the furnishings, adjust the lighting, and plump up the comfort level.

Most of the following ideas for creating an inviting background work as well for big bashes as they do for small gatherings. They also make the home more livable for the inmates long after visitors have left.

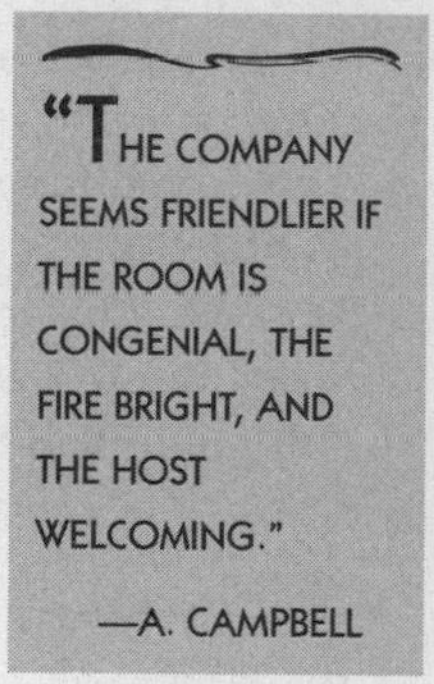

"THE COMPANY SEEMS FRIENDLIER IF THE ROOM IS CONGENIAL, THE FIRE BRIGHT, AND THE HOST WELCOMING."
—A. CAMPBELL

SOCIALIZE THE SPACE

- Pull a lineup of furnishings away from the walls, and arrange sofas and chairs into tight conversational groups. "I like all the chairs to talk to one another and to the sofas," says interior designer Mario Buatta, "instead of those parlor car arrangements that create two Siberias." Furniture must relate for people to communicate.
- Aim for the rough shape of an arc when arranging conversation areas. Anthropologist Margaret Mead observed that people feel most comfortable at slight angles rather than side by side or directly facing each other. A few chairs set at an angle also gives a room a more relaxed look.
- An L-shaped seating arrangement with sofas and chairs perpendicu-

lar to each other is another cozy grouping that opens up the room to traffic flow. Just make sure traffic runs past it, not through it, so it feels protected.

- Since people like to huddle, define conversation areas in a big room with area rugs, freestanding folding screens, or a row of potted trees. Sociological studies show the larger the room, the closer people like to sit together.
- If the front door opens directly into the living room, give the space a sense of shelter by separating the two areas with a folding screen, a table, or a chest.

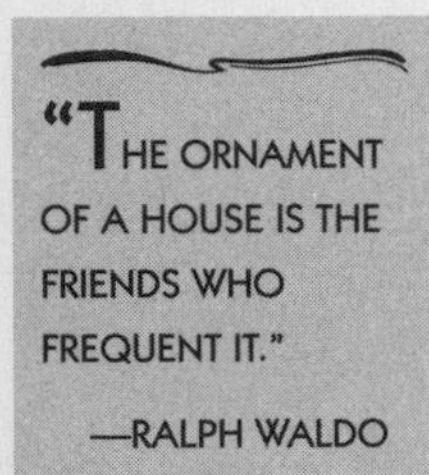

"THE ORNAMENT OF A HOUSE IS THE FRIENDS WHO FREQUENT IT."
—RALPH WALDO EMERSON

DIRECT TRAFFIC

- Lay out drink, conversation, food, and activity areas in a wide circle. Guests walk in the front door, for example, and the bar is on the left, the living room is in the center, and the food is on the right. In her book, *When Good People Throw Bad Parties,* author Terri Mandell explains that circles are natural migratory patterns, giving guests a chance to see and greet everyone as they move about.
- Provide plenty of space around the bar since this is where the crowd congregates. I once made the mistake of setting up the bar in the hallway to the bathroom. It turned into bottleneck city.
- If it's a rambling house, contain the party to a specified area, so small groups don't become isolated from the action.
- Remove obstacles: towering stacks of books, floor-level electric cords, and rickety chairs and tables.
- If the dining table is moved out from under the chandelier, hook the fixture close to the ceiling so there are no bonked noggins.

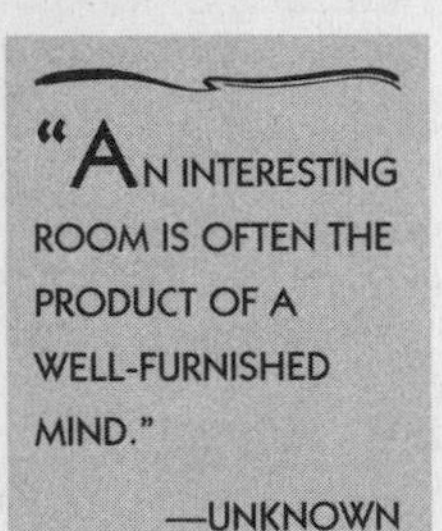

"AN INTERESTING ROOM IS OFTEN THE PRODUCT OF A WELL-FURNISHED MIND."
—UNKNOWN

- Have plenty of empty floor space for people to move around easily. Traffic lanes should be a minimum of two feet.
- Find a point of interest that draws people in and group furniture around it. A window with a view is a natural focus, as is a fireplace. If a room lacks a focal point, a table laden with food and drink will pull 'em in every time.

FRIENDLY FURNITURE

- When it's time to replace the old stuff, up the comfort level by buying overstuffed sofas and chairs with high supporting backs, fat rolled arms, and deep squishy cushions. Toss around a few plump throw pillows for good measure.
- Keep conversation flowing with flexible seating. In her book *Decorating for Comfort,* interior designer Teri Seidman writes, "People in the heat of conversation often rearrange your furniture, pulling their own chairs and moveable tables closer to another person or even to the warmth of the fireplace." Make it easy by attaching casters to ottomans and upholstered chairs, and use lightweight side chairs and fat floor cushions.

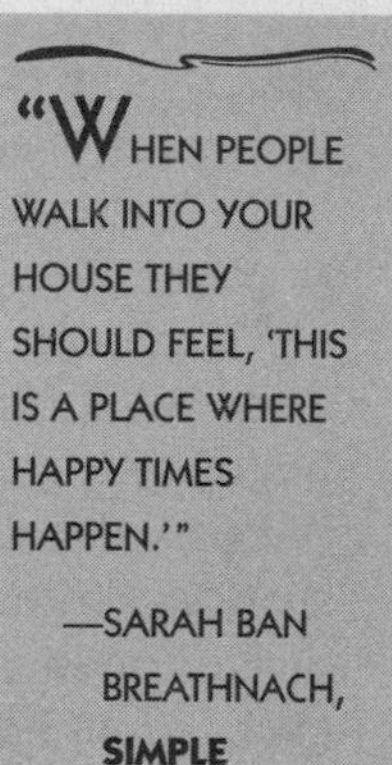

"WHEN PEOPLE WALK INTO YOUR HOUSE THEY SHOULD FEEL, 'THIS IS A PLACE WHERE HAPPY TIMES HAPPEN.' "
—SARAH BAN BREATHNACH,
SIMPLE ABUNDANCE

- Don't worry about seating everyone at a large party. A lack of chairs encourages mingling.
- Provide space to set down a glass or a plate next to every seat with either an end table, coffee table, shelf, or raised hearth. A set of lightweight nesting tables takes up little room, but provides plenty of landing space when needed.
- Unless it's a Super Bowl, video, or some other tube party, camouflage or move the TV to the bedroom so no one is tempted to turn on their daily dose.
- Invest in a good-looking game table and chairs. People feel most comfortable with what sociologists call "defensible space" in front of them.
- Consider a round dining table. A circle pulls everyone into the conversation, discourages formality, and seats odd numbers of people gracefully.
- Think of new uses for old furniture. A desk by day, for instance, can hold a buffet by night. A plant stand can hold a champagne bucket. A couple of file cabinets can be topped with a plank and cloth and used as a sideboard. "Don't be afraid to move things around to suit the occasion," advises Marie Kinnaman, an interior designer who specializes in using what's on hand.

"EVERY HOUSE NEEDS THREE CHAIRS: ONE FOR SOLITUDE, TWO FOR FRIENDSHIP, AND THREE FOR COMPANY."

—UNKNOWN

TANTALIZE WITH TEXTURE

- Counteract high touch with high tech. As *Megatrends* author John Naisbitt says, "The more high tech in our society, the more we will want to create high touch environments, with soft edges balancing the hard edges of technology."
- Toss a fuzzy mohair throw, a puffy quilt, or a woolly blanket over the arm or the back of a sofa or chair for an inviting look with a cozy feel. "Most people make the mistake of carefully folding a throw over the arm of the furniture," says Marie Kinnaman. "It's much more dramatic if it looks like it's artfully flung."
- Contrast plush velvet, buttery soft leather, fuzzy suede, and crisp cotton against mellow old wood, polished stone, and smooth tile.
- Add sparkle to softness with brass, crystal, and silver. Place these sparklers where light reflects and multiplies the effect.
- Strive for something dull, something bright, and something light in every room.

LIGHT YOUR FIRE

Few things in life are more inviting than the civilizing warmth of a crackling fire. So if you've got it, baby, flaunt it.

NINE STEPS TO A FRIENDLY FIRE

1. *Light the fire about a half hour before guests arrive so it only needs an occasional poke or log to keep it going.*
2. *Open the damper a few minutes before lighting to warm the chimney and create the needed draft of oxygen.*
3. *Get things going with a good supply of kindling on the grate: balled-up black-and-white newspaper, bone-dry twigs, or resiny pinecones.*
4. *Stagger three or four medium-sized seasoned and split hardwood logs over the kindling so fire-feeding oxygen flows freely around them.*
5. *Keep a brick on the grate to create air space between the logs.*
6. *Use a long wooden fireplace match to spark the fire without burning the fingers.*
7. *After the fire takes, add bigger logs, shoving them back against the wall so the heat radiates to the smaller logs and into the room.*
8. *Don't let the fire get too low. Otherwise, newly added logs won't catch readily and may sputter and smoke.*
9. *Close the screen so flying sparks don't land in anyone's hot toddy.*

- Make cooking part of the entertainment by roasting chestnuts over the fire in a perforated chestnut pan, popping corn in a long-handled corn-popping basket, or toasting marshmallows with long metal skewers. If the firebox is big enough, add a grill for meat and a swinging iron arm for a pot of stew.
- Invest in a cast-iron fireback, a decorative plate that leans against the rear wall of the firebox to shield it from excessive heat, hide cracked masonry, and reflect the fire's warmth back into the room.
- Consider burning fruit or nut woods like apple, peach, and walnut for a delicious aroma and brilliant flames.
- If it's too warm for a roaring fire, cluster candles on the grate for a flickering glow without the accompanying heat.
- Lay branches of evergreens and clusters of hard berries on the grate between use for a pretty effect. (Burn dried evergreens sparingly, if at all—they're explosive.)

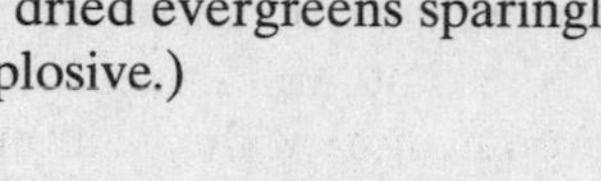

> "STIR THE FIRE . . . WHEEL THE SOFA ROUND . . . AND LET US WELCOME PEACEFUL EVENING IN."
>
> —WILLIAM COWPER

WARM UP WITH COLOR

- Pure white walls seem to expand space, but can be icy. Consider painting walls a warm vanilla instead.
- If you'd like a bit more color and a lot more warmth, paint the living room apricot, sunny yellow, or deep russet.
- Sponge the walls two or three tones for extra richness and depth. Ivory over tangerine, for example, will give a peaches-and-cream effect. Sponging also tones down a blaring color.
- Tint the ceiling a rosy, sunset tone. It'll cast a flattering reflection on the people below.
- If the ceiling is sky-high, bring it down to an intimate level with a rich persimmon, creamy caramel, or any warm shade that works with the color of the walls, floors, and furnishings.
- Hang rose, peach, or sunny-yellow translucent shades or sheers to warm northern light.
- Warm up a cool room with touches of geranium, coral, or shrimp-colored accessories.
- Slipcover impractical white or overly formal upholstery with warm,

> "THE WARMTH OF THE COLORS IN A ROOM MAKES A GREAT DEAL OF DIFFERENCE BETWEEN COMFORT AND DISCOMFORT."
>
> —ARCHITECT CHRISTOPHER ALEXANDER, **A PATTERN LANGUAGE**

medium-toned fabrics in stripes, dots, batiks, plaids, or other people-practical prints.

LIGHT THE WAY

Many of us under- or overdo when lighting for company. An underlit home is not only gloomy, it's risky, since guests can trip over thresholds and stumble down steps. I once attended a morning meeting in a house with little natural light on an overcast day. I don't know if the host was saving electricity or trying to hide the dust, but the lack of light was depressing. I'll take well-lit dust over moody blues any day.

Then there are the gatherings at which all the lights, including the kitchen fluorescents, burn brightly through the night. We may not walk into walls, but we all look ghastly under the clinical glare.

The idea is to create atmosphere without jeopardizing safety.

- Turn off the overheads and turn on the lamps. Pools of lamplight are more intimate and encourage conversation.
- At least three floor, table, and wall lamps are recommended for the average-sized living room, more if the walls are deeply colored.
- Buy lamps with three-way switches to control light levels.
- Warm a room in a softly reflective glow by bouncing light off ceilings and walls with sconces and torchères.
- Use a diffuser if there is a wide opening at the top of the shade of a lamp to cut the glare and remove the flying saucers on the ceiling.
- Make sure unshaded bulbs don't shine in anyone's eyes. Simple floor lamps with shallow triangular or shell-shaped shades are attractive and space-savvy, but their half-naked bulbs glare if you are seated.
- A room lit from below eye level seems friendlier. Try a floor canister or two placed between a piece of furniture and the wall, or nestle one in the base of a large plant to cast leafy shadows on the walls and ceiling. Just make sure to hide the bulb so it doesn't blind.
- Use the appropriate wattage for the fixture, since anything higher could overheat and start a fire.
- Highlight a favorite picture by aiming a strategically positioned floor canister on it, making sure the picture glass doesn't cause a glare.
- Replace pure white lampshades with cream-colored ones for a warmer glow, or consider opaque shades that cast circles of golden light below them.
- Unscrew the fluorescent bulb in the bath or powder room, and place a small lamp on the counter. "When you have a beautifully lit party, then a guest goes into the powder room, turns on the light, and says,

'Oh, my God! Is that what I look like?' it's hard to get back in the party mood again," says architectural and interior designer Van-Martin Rowe. "It's important to keep the light of the bathroom at the same level as the party."

- Leave the light on in the bath or powder room, so no one has to fumble with the switch.
- Draw the draperies after the sun sets to close off large expanses of cold, dark glass.
- Make the most of natural daylight by hanging a large mirror to reflect a window.

CANDLEPOWER

- A room full of the gentle flicker of candlelight is as romantic as it is flattering. Encase the candles in glass globes, stemmed glasses, or some other safe enclosure.
- Place votive candles strategically around the room. But use common sense. I placed votives throughout our new walnut bookshelves for one party and ended up with round black burns on the shelf above each candle.
- Set candles on a silver or mirrored tray in front of a mirror to double the dazzle.
- Cut long wicks or they'll burn the candle unevenly.
- Back up candles with dim lamplight. The idea is to romance guests, not keep them in the dark.
- Stock up on candles at pre- and post-Christmas sales.
- Consider oil lamps. Teacher and artist Lani Freymiller, whose rustic California home has been featured in numerous shelter publications, prefers their soft light to candles. "There's always a cross-breeze in our house and I was forever cleaning up candle wax," says Freymiller. "Oil lamps, however, are clean-burning, can be used inside and outside, and you can control the amount of light with the wick."

SPECIAL EFFECTS

- Thread strings of tiny white Christmas lights through the branches of a large potted tree. I strung lights through a large ficus last Christmas and moved it to the dining room. I like the combination of candlelight, dimmed chandelier, and the tiny white lights so much, I'm using it year-round.
- Go Hollywood. Los Angeles lighting designer Jason Harlow illuminates artwork with a framing projector, a device that produces a

custom shape and beam size that exactly frames an object. "It gives a piece depth and drama," says Harlow. "And makes it seem to float."

- Showcase treasures. Take a tip from interior designer and author Alexandra Stoddard and install tiny strip lights under the lip of display and bookshelves to highlight collections.

OUTDOOR LIGHTING

- If you have a yard, make it function as another room in warm weather and provide pretty views from the inside year-round with accent lighting. Lighting designers create outdoor rooms by treating fences and bordering hedges as walls, and trees as ceilings, softly bathing them in light. They then highlight attractive features like a colorful flower bed or a beautifully sculpted tree. The best part of night lighting is that you only see what you want to see. The weed patch, the homemade fort, and the yellow doggy spots are left in the dark.
- Use at least two lights to bring out a tree's dimension. Using only one light may give a flattened, cartoon effect.
- Tie tiny white Christmas lights to the limbs of bare or leafy trees. One California homeowner strings his enormous old patio oak with over six hundred bulbs. Every fifth bulb flashes, giving the effect of a light breeze wafting through the limbs.
- Weave tiny Christmas lights around the rail of a deck, the top of a fence, or the underside of a patio umbrella.
- Line walkways and patios with votive candles or luminarias. A luminaria is an open paper bag filled with a layer of sand and a fat candle. They're traditionally used for Christmas in the Southwest, but they're pretty and practical in any locale year-round.
- Suspend glass globes of candles from a tree's branches. Hanging globes can be found at garden centers and through home supply catalogs.
- Light up the night with citronella candles. The sharp lemon scent repels bugs. Choose the smaller size, since the big, clay-potted jobs often have thick wicks that smoke and burn too quickly.
- Check out fiber optics: light-embedded flexible strips that are skinny enough to squeeze into cracks and crevices. They look like starlight emerging from improbable places like stairs, arbors, fountains, and pools. Fiber optic light is expensive and tricky to install, but cheap and energy-efficient to operate.
- Use dimmers throughout the yard. They set the mood with a twist of a switch.

SOFT SOUNDS

> "STUFFED DEER HEADS ON WALLS ARE BAD ENOUGH, BUT IT'S WORSE WHEN THEY ARE WEARING DARK GLASSES AND HAVE STREAMERS AND ORNAMENTS IN THEIR ANTLERS BECAUSE THEN YOU KNOW THEY WERE ENJOYING THEMSELVES WHEN THEY WERE SHOT."
>
> —ELLEN DEGENERES

- Have enough soft elements to absorb the noise of rattling dishes, high-heeled shoes, and shrill laughter. Soft upholstery, dense rugs, and heavy draperies muffle noise like a layer of snow on a city street.
- Make the kids keep the volume of the TV, video games, and boom box down in the family room while you're entertaining in the living room. Or, better yet, buy the kids earphones.
- Set the mood with music. Play soothing sounds like George Winston or Ray Lynch during drinks and dinner to relax guests. Plug in jazzier stuff for games and entertainment, then play Wagner or lullabies as a subtle reminder to go home. Just make sure the music sets the stage, not dominates it.
- Load up the CD player with discs before guests arrive so you don't have to give music a second thought.
- Consider hiring a musician through the music department of a local university for a good-sized party. There's something special about the live sound of a tinkling piano, a Spanish guitar, or a heavenly harp. Limit it to the first hour or two. Once conversations take over, the music can't compete.
- If it's a big bash, either invite all the neighbors or tone down the music at 11:00 or 12:00 P.M. on the weekends, earlier on weeknights.

SCENTS AND SENSIBILITY

- Air out the place before guests arrive. Fresh air is the most pleasant fragrance and it'll dissipate stale house odors.
- Subtly scent rooms with fragrant flowers, or place a big bowl or basket of good-quality potpourri on a low shelf or on the floor under an end table. As the room warms with the arrival of guests, the fragrance rises. I like Aromatique's Smell of the Tree in winter, Splendor in the Bath, in summer, and Ralph Lauren's Thoroughbred most anytime.
- If the crowd is large and the room small, scent the air with green apple. According to the Smell and Taste Treatment and Research Foundation, the fruit makes a space seem more spacious, while the smell of charcoal-grilled meat gives people a closeted feeling.

- Hang tiny bags of herbs and spices or potpourri in front of heating vents.
- Fool guests into thinking you've been baking all day by simmering pickling spice on a back burner or baking a teaspoon of cinnamon in a low oven.
- Custom-scent fat candles with a drop of essential oil (found where quality potpourri is sold) in the pool of melting wax around the wick.
- However the home is scented, use a light hand. No one wants to feel they're trapped behind a perfume counter.

THE SMELL OF SEDUCTION

What turns a man on? A sniff of expensive perfume? The interior of a new Porsche? The smell of freshly laundered sheets?

"Try donuts," suggests the staff at the Smell and Taste Treatment and Research Foundation.

The Chicago-based institute measured the penile blood flow in hundreds of male subjects as they sniffed everything from spring blossoms to aged leather. But, as the old saw goes, the way to a man's heart, or perhaps libido, is through his stomach. Donuts, pumpkin pie, black licorice, and cinnamon buns sent the blood racing.

Director Alan Hirsch, M.D., isn't sure why the smell of food is such a turn-on, but he has a theory: "Our distant ancestors wandered around independently but would congregate at points of food kills, where they would have the greatest chance of finding a mate," he says. "If my theory is correct, then food odors may increase female sexual arousal as well. We're currently testing."

If the thought of dabbing a little eau de ribs behind the ears or pillowcase isn't appealing, consider dousing the house with Realm, a unisex perfume developed at the University of Utah. Though other scientists may be skeptical, Realm's researchers claim their scent is the first made with synthetic human pheromones, chemicals that arouse the opposite sex.

DETAILS

- Put away fragile porcelain, glassware, and anything precious, so no one freaks if something gets broken.
- Choose function over formality. Everyone is more at ease when a home is decorated with sturdy furnishings and practical materials.
- Seek out muted, almost faded-looking fabrics for furnishings and

windows. They not only make the room look more comfortable, they also age more gracefully than bright, clear colors that can fade into unfortunate shades.

- Collect books. There's something reassuring about a wall full of slightly worn, well-read volumes.
- Keep a few fun publications out on a table to thumb through so guests have something to do with their hands, as well as to draw others in. The *Far Side* series, *The Book of Questions, The Encyclopedia of Bad Taste,* or a provocative art book are good launching pads for conversation.
- Don't get carried away with pillows. If guests have to move them every time they snuggle into a sofa or chair, they've lost their purpose. Put cause before effect.
- Turn down the heat. A house full of warm bodies heats up a room quickly.

CHAPTER 4

THE LIVABLE DINING ROOM

The dining room is a dying room in most homes. It sits there day after day like a white silk suit in the back of a closet; nice to look at, but too fussy to bother with except for the most formal occasions. When the room *does* get pressed into use, there are protective pads to drag out, layers of linens to iron, and a stash of silver to polish.

We need to make it less starchy, more comfortable, and easier to use, so feeding company doesn't require major behind-the-scenes staging.

"GO LOW MAINTENANCE OR YOU'LL NEVER REALLY USE YOUR DINING ROOM."

—VAN-MARTIN ROWE, ARCHITECTURAL AND INTERIOR DESIGNER

THE BIG PICTURE

- Most homes have a good-sized living room with an adjoining smaller dining room. If the latter is hopelessly small, and the former underused, consider switching the furniture in the two rooms. Breaking bread, playing Scrabble, or just arguing about politics around the table is more satisfying than primly balancing a teacup over the parlor sofa any day.

THE TABLE

- The best table accommodates everything from dripped dip to spilled cider. If you're just starting out or are ready for a change, look for an old, well-worn model that already has the history and patina of use.
- If shopping for a new table, look for a tile top or a tough wood like hard rock maple or black walnut. Black walnut is so strong and shock-resistant it's used in rifle and shotgun stocks. Maple takes a beating as bowling lanes, school desks, and tool handles.
- Avoid a clear glass top since it scratches and shows dust. Besides, couples can't kick each other under it, if one commits a social blunder.
- Choose a wood top that's either burled or heavily grained so dings and scratches are hard to detect and easy to touch up.
- Protect a wood top with a coat of polyurethane. Polyurethane comes in various protective grades from the heaviest "bar-top" to a wipe-on "tung-finish." Wax gives some protection, but it stands up poorly to moisture.
- Hide a hopeless top. Many of the finest restaurants have scarred and ugly tables hiding under linen and glass. Simply drape the table with fabric and top it with a piece of cut-to-fit glass. Preserve a good table the same way.
- When shopping for a new table, measure to see if there's enough room between the apron of the table and the chair seat for guests to cross their legs. Ten to fourteen inches is usually sufficient. Also check the apron for smoothness, so stockings don't snag and knees don't splinter.
- Keep the geometry simple. Rectangular, square, and round tables are the most space-savvy. We lose place-setting space when we get into oval, hexagon, and octagon shapes.

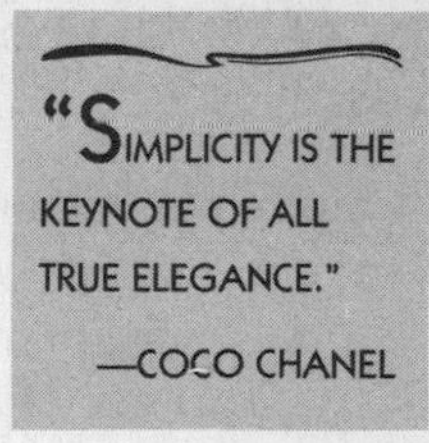
"SIMPLICITY IS THE
KEYNOTE OF ALL
TRUE ELEGANCE."
—COCO CHANEL

- Look for a round table that comes with curved leaves that plug into the edges, to preserve the circle. Most extensions turn a round table into a less practical oval one.
- To determine how big a table the room can take, allow at least thirty-three inches from the table edge to the wall, sideboard, or cabinet for chair clearance.
- Improvise. Magazine editor Alicia Berkley has barely enough room for a sofa, let alone a dining table in her tiny Manhattan studio. So she stenciled a thirty-eight-by-sixty-four-inch sheet of plywood in room-coordinating colors, and hung it on her hallway–living room wall. When she entertains, she simply tops a card table with the board, pulls it over to the L-shaped sofa, then places folding chairs

on the other side of it. "It's perfect for six," she says. "But I've squeezed as many as eight around it."

> "NEVER LOSE SIGHT OF THE FACT THAT IT IS THE FOOD THAT IS THE IMPORTANT THING, AND THAT YOUR TABLE SETTING AND DECORATION SHOULD COMPLEMENT RATHER THAN SUBMERGE IT."
>
> —TERANCE CONRAN

- Expand. Before we could afford a bigger table, my husband had the lumberyard cut a pair of plywood semicircles that we hinged together and placed on top of our table for six. Topped with a big round cloth made from a king-sized sheet, it sat eight comfortably and more or less securely. We only decided to upgrade a few years ago after a guest slammed his fist on the plywood edge (to make a point, not because he hated dinner), sending dishes and dinner skyward.
- Store table extensions out of the cold and damp to prevent warping.
- Two tables are sometimes better than one. Two identical rectangular tables, when placed apart, are good for drinks on one and a buffet on the other. Pushed together, they make a large square for a sit-down dinner. Butted end to end they form a long formal board when you want to play duke and duchess at opposite ends. After the party's over, use one as a desk, the other for dining.

"WOULD SOMEONE PLEASE TURN UP THE HEAT?"

A few of the hedonistic aristocrats of eighteenth-century France had dining rooms designed so the table disappeared between courses into a butler's pantry below. The idea was that guests could cavort as they wished away from the prying eyes of servants. The grandnephew of Cardinal Richelieu, for example, frequently invited freethinking and well-endowed guests to intimate nude dinners. "His servants," according to historian William Harlan Hale, "were models of discretion."

CHAIRS

- Chairs need to be comfortable, solid, and light enough to push back from the table. "If it's a bad chair, it's a bad meal," says architectural and interior designer Van-Martin Rowe, who prefers armchairs at every setting. "They're comfortable, easier to push out of, and more egalitarian," says the designer. "Why should only the host get the comfortable chair?" Armchairs can also be used at a desk, in the bedroom, and throughout the house.
- Test-drive a potential chair when shopping. Rowe suggests leaning forward in it, reaching, and tilting back to make sure it's stable. "It also needs to be able to slide under the tabletop without worrying about amputating a finger," he says.
- Chair seats should be at least eighteen inches deep to accommodate beams and thighs, and sixteen and one-half to seventeen and one-half inches off the floor, so the average arm easily reaches across the table and the average foot rests firmly on the floor.
- Consider something other than the traditional dining chair. One family replaced their wooden Windsor chairs with fully padded office chairs that swivel, tilt, and cradle the body. "No one wants to take coffee in the living room anymore," says Mary Milentich. "They just burrow in at the table all evening."
- Select chairs with loose bottom cushions, so there's a good and bad side. "Flip them over for the child or adult who hasn't quite mastered fork to mouth, or the uncle who sloshes wine as he toasts," suggests Van-Martin Rowe.
- If existing chairs have "vertabreaking" spindle backs, tie on back cushions up to the comfort level.
- Choose chair fabrics that clean easily and camouflage inevitable spills. Dense prints, leatherlike vinyls, and soil-releasing fabrics are the most practical around food and drink. Van-Martin Rowe, for example, recently used a top-quality Naugahyde in a pleasing rainbow of colors for a household with young children. "I let the children pick their own color, so the chair acts as a place card," says Rowe. "The palette gives a colorful, more casual approach."
- Consider slipcovers. Some manufacturers offer tailor-made slipcovers with their fully upholstered dining chairs.
- Spray fabrics with a fabric protector like Scotchgard. Test the spray first on an unobtrusive spot, and reapply after every third cleaning.

THE SIDEBOARD

That Jurassic china cabinet that does little more than show off the dishes is still around, but practical types have moved it out of the dining room and put it to use as a book or display case elsewhere. They've replaced it with a heat- and marproof sideboard that holds side dishes, dessert, and anything else that is part of the meal. A good-sized sideboard not only accommodates a buffet service, it also makes a formal dinner easier, since fewer kitchen trips are needed.

- If there's no room for a traditional sideboard, add a long, narrow table or install a shelf. Designer Jane Trudeau created a collapsible sideboard for a tiny dining space with a piece of plywood hinged to the wall. She covered the hinged side with a polyurethaned poster, and topped the utility side with tile so it could handle hot pots and cold drips.
- Leave well enough alone. I found a beautiful but marred sideboard at a consignment shop years ago that I planned to refinish. But when I realized it would further crack and peel from the sunny window above it, I decided to top the worst of it with a cotton runner and leave the rest in its worn glory. A wise decision, as it turned out, since a leaking vase of flowers made it look even more antique.

LIGHTING

- For optimum lighting and pleasing proportion, string the chandelier so its bottom is between thirty-six and forty-two inches from the tabletop. Many chandeliers hang too high.
- Place the chandelier and other incandescent lights on separate dimmers to control the light level and mood. Even a klutz can easily and safely install a dimmer switch.
- Don't rely on the chandelier to provide all the lighting. Candles, sconces on the walls, or lamps on the sideboard add to the magic.
- Brighter isn't necessarily better. I recently replaced a 40-watt with a 25-watt bulb in a wall sconce. The effect is softer, prettier, and more atmospheric.
- Never underestimate the power of candlelight. Candles cast rooms and complexions in a flattering glow. Buy them in bulk and use them generously around the room.
- Stock up on solid beeswax candles. They're well worth the extra cost since they're slow-burning, nearly smokeless, and drip inside their well, not on the table.

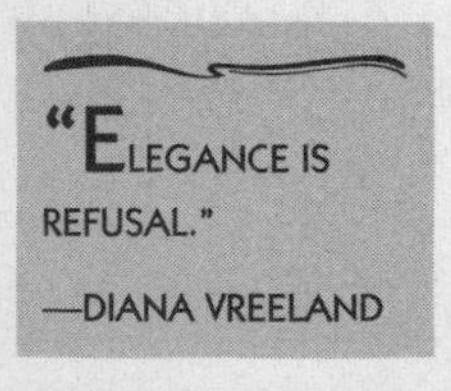
"Elegance is refusal."
—Diana Vreeland

- Stick with white or ivory candles. They blend with everything and are always in good taste.
- Refrigerate candles before lighting so they'll burn longer.
- Falling candles can flambé a tablecloth. Firmly plant them in their holders with candle adhesive or florist's clay. Or hold a match to a candle's bottom till the wax softens enough to wedge it into its holder.
- Collect decorative boxes of wood matches from restaurants. Wood matches are much easier to light than paper ones.

THE FLOOR

- A bare floor under a dining room table may be practical, but a rug looks luxurious, feels cozy, and absorbs noise. The trouble is, a dining room rug also absorbs everything that's spilled on it. So go with the flow and lay a rug with a dense design and in colors that represent the four major food groups. With its intricate patterns and rich jewel tones, a rug with a traditional Persian design is perfect. There are also some fabulous contemporary rugs on the market that are masters of camouflage.
- The art of camouflage is nothing new in dining rooms. The ruling classes of ancient Greece and Rome had artisans line their dining floors with mosaic tiles to mimic spilled morsels and crumbs. This witty, three-dimensional art form even had a name: *asaroton,* meaning "unswept" in Greek. The effect was so realistic, it was hard to detect the actual from the decorative droppings. Create your own artistic crumbs by splatter-painting a hardwood floor with heavy-duty deck paint.

EQUIPMENT

If we take the advice of the experts, we need an arsenal of fancy equipment to throw even the humblest dinner party. But as a devotee of the simple life, I've discovered it just ain't so. In fact, the fancier the stuff, the harder hosting can be.

I'm a sucker for white Battenberg-lace table linens, for instance, but it used to take me so much time to iron them before a party, I'd think twice before I'd invite anyone over. Since I've wised up, I cover my table with no-iron, poly/cotton blends, and I don't seem to have offended anyone yet.

I also now stick to "one-size-fits-all glasses," no longer fretting over what my white wines, red wines, brandies, and soft drinks are going to wear. I've learned there's more beauty in simplicity than show, and certainly less work.

TABLECLOTHS

- Choose easy-to-clean, little-iron, cotton/polyester tablecloths in deep shades or intricate prints.
- To avoid a skimpy look, make sure the cloth has at least a nine-inch drop from each edge of the table. A forty-by-seventy-two-inch table, for instance, needs a sixty-by-ninety-inch cloth. A forty-two-inch round table needs a seventy-inch cloth. Save floor-length cloths for stand-up buffets and bars, since they're risky around chair legs and people's feet.
- If you prefer the look of high-maintenance linen, limit it to a topper or runner over the easy-care cloth. Toppers also protect a good cloth or hide a spotted one, and can be rolled off between courses to reveal clean linen or gleaming wood below.
- Place a square topper over a round table. It has a more graceful effect than a round one, especially if the corners drape at least eight inches over the edge.
- Consider placing a white lace topper over a deeply colored cloth. The tone shows through the cutwork, and the rich color is less apt to show stains.
- Forget placemats when trying to squeeze in extra settings. Table runners or unadorned cloths are the best bet. A runner looks prettiest when it's a little shorter than the tablecloth.
- If someone spills wine or whatever on the cloth, mop it unobtrusively with a napkin and place a serving dish over it so the perpetrator won't feel guilty throughout dinner.
- Stock up on a few vinyl-covered cloths for outdoor use. They can even go formal inside when covered by an elegant topper.
- Folding antique linens weakens the fibers. Loosely roll them around poster mailing tubes found in office supply stores.

NAPKINS

- Look for napkins in colorful prints that coordinate china, linens, and flowers. Prints also camouflage food and wine stains.
- Make sure napkins are soft, absorbent, no-iron, and generously sized to fit any lap.
- Napkin rings originally served the practical purpose of identifying family linens to cut down on laundering. Today, they are purely dec-

orative, so use them only if space allows. Author and style setter Barbara Milo Orbach believes, "A table setting is a great opportunity for personal expression, but unnecessary clutter makes guests feel nervous and uncomfortable."

INVITING THE ANGEL OF DEATH

For centuries, hosts had servants carefully fold and tightly screw linens into specially designed presses so folds were sharp and uniform when laid out. But creases had to be perfect, since it was believed that if a crimp formed a small rectangular "coffin," the Grim Reaper would soon claim one of the diners.

By the nineteenth century, Victorian hosts avoided all possibility of alarm by rolling their cloths around specially designed tubes.

Smooth, perfectly creased, or slightly "coffined," anything goes today. The only person likely to die (of embarrassment) is the host, when someone moves that strategically placed platter hiding that big, ugly stain.

FANCY FOLDINGS

Napkin folding was not only a respected art form in the seventeenth century, it was also a well-paid profession. At the court of Louis XIV, the napkin artist heavily starched his linens and then folded them into fantastic shapes resembling birds, fish, and even major buildings. In 1668, Samuel Pepys wrote in his celebrated diary that he was "mightily pleased with the fellow that came to lay the cloth and fold the napkins, which I like so well, as that I am resolved to give him 40s to teach my wife to do it."

After the French Revolution, life, manners, and table settings became simpler, so the napkin-folding profession died out.

By the time Emily Post came to the table in the 1920s, she proclaimed "very fancy foldings are not in good taste." Post particularly abhorred the practice of tucking a roll in the folds of a napkin, since the bread invariably landed on the floor when the napkin was spread on the lap. She dictated that napkins should fold flat and be placed "on the top of the plate, never on the side."

Rules have loosened considerably since, but fancy flourishes can complicate the service. A napkin bursting from a goblet, for instance, means no water or wine can be poured till napkins are out of the glass and onto the lap. Unless there is help, or the party is small, that's an awkward time for a host to pour the beverages.

TABLEWARE

- Dust off that stash of fine china. Despite having a cache of fine porcelain, I know of a woman who always rents or borrows dishes for every party she gives. She says she wouldn't dream of risking her "wedding porcelain," so it sits behind closed doors waiting for, presumably, nothing short of a coronation.
- Since fine china is made from nonporous clay, and is fired at extremely high temperatures, it's less likely to stain, crack, and chip than everyday earthenware. Providing there is no gold trim, most porcelain and bone china are also dishwasher-safe.
- When shopping for new dinnerware, consider classic white. Embossed, etched, or plain, it's an elegant canvas for food, and blends beautifully with other china as well as all combinations of linens and flowers.
- If you do prefer color and pattern, keep it simple. An elegant border of red, green, or yellow accents food colors beautifully, but large, busy patterns and confetti colors make every meal look like goulash.
- Seek out crescent-shaped salad bowls. They take up less space on the table, since they hug the dinner plate.
- Keep serving pieces simple. We don't need fish-shaped platters, tomato-like tureens, and ceramic-rabbit salad bowls to remind guests of what they're eating.

"TO MANY VICTORIANS, NOTHING WAS MORE IMPORTANT THAN GENTILITY, EVEN IF ACHIEVING IT MEANT BEING VULGAR."

—WILLIAM HARLAN HALE, **THE HORIZON COOKBOOK AND ILLUSTRATED HISTORY OF EATING AND DRINKING THROUGH THE AGES**

GLASSWARE

- Buy oversized wineglasses for red and white wines, sparkling water, juice, soft drinks, and even cold soups and desserts. Purists may disagree, but the old rules about a different-sized glass for every drink are passé.

- Select glasses whose tops taper slightly inward, so oenophiles don't slosh as they swirl.
- Choose clear and plain stemware over the colored and faceted. Colored glass obscures the beauty of the grape, and depressions and engraving collect hard-to-remove stains. Classic simplicity is always beautiful.
- Steer clear of long-legged stemware. It may look elegant, but it has a high mortality rate.
- Don't invest in glassware so expensive that you'll have a cow if someone drops it.
- Have chipped crystal reground at a glass-cutting shop.
- Store glassware and china so they're easy to retrieve and put back.

VINTAGE MAIDENFORM

Legend has it that Marie Antoinette had wineglasses molded in the shape of her breasts. However, no one seems to know whether they were 32A champagne flutes, 36B red-wine goblets, or 40C brandy snifters.

SILVER

- A full set of sterling isn't necessary for today's entertaining. In fact, a trend among practical brides is to forgo silver in favor of easy-care stainless and alloys. But if you've got it, use it. Silver cutlery, trays, and other serving pieces add sparkle to a setting and can transform the mundane into the marvelous. Besides, the more silver is used, the less it tarnishes.
- Sterling is nearly solid silver with a bit of copper and antimony added for strength, hardness, and durability. Silver plate is silver-coated base metal, and the best has a thick coating and a highly defined pattern. Look for a wear warrantee when buying.
- Think twice before choosing an overly elaborate silver service. Depressions and embellishments are tarnish collectors.
- Frequent use is a good way to avoid silver tarnish and an elegant way to dine through life. According to Reed & Barton, silver can even be washed in the dishwasher as long as:

1. no other metals are washed with it,
2. it's washed with a powdered detergent rather than a residue-leaving liquid,
3. a rinse agent like Jet Dry is used in hard water,
4. the heat drying cycle is on so it dries quickly and thoroughly.

- Never use newspaper, plastic, or tissue for storing silver. Wrap it in tarnishproof flannel instead.
- Brighten silver with polish-impregnated fabric gloves. They're easier to use than rags and cream, and are available in many dining room, jewelry, and department stores.
- Select from three sizes of sterling flatware: "dinner setting"—the largest and most expensive; "place"—the most versatile; and "luncheon"—the smallest and least expensive. Any one of the three is appropriate and interchangeable at all meals and functions.
- Cut initial buying costs by supplementing sterling place settings with other metals. A combination of gold, silver, and pewter on a table is often more interesting than a perfect match.
- If you have a large stash of silver flatware, rotate it each time it's used so settings get the same amount of wear, remain tarnish-free, and take on the soft patina of use.

CHAPTER 5

THE ENTERTAINING KITCHEN

A kitchen that can turn out a meal for a couple or a crowd doesn't have to be large, stocked with trendy equipment, or look like a spread from *House Beautiful.* All it really needs is organized work space, decent lighting, and a few basic tools.

SO MANY APPLIANCES, SO LITTLE TIME

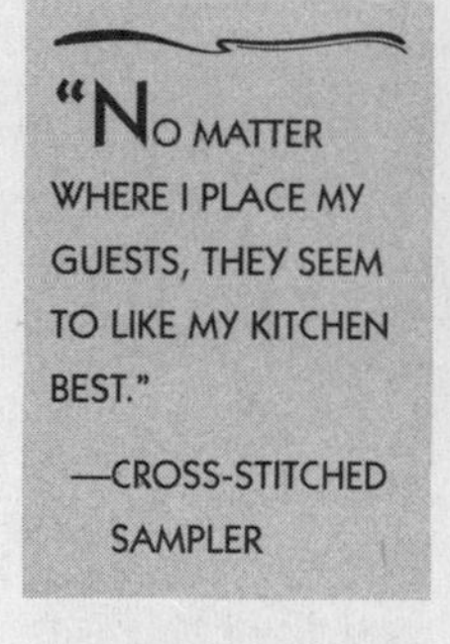

"NO MATTER WHERE I PLACE MY GUESTS, THEY SEEM TO LIKE MY KITCHEN BEST."
—CROSS-STITCHED SAMPLER

All those new gizmos meant to make entertaining easier often have the opposite effect. The cappuccino machine means we have to serve a fancy brew. We wouldn't dream of serving bakery buns when we have a bread maker. And that pasta machine pressures us into impressing guests with chili-studded, basil-scented, heart-shaped ravioli.

More often than not, these "conveniences" slow us down, clutter us up, and generate guilt when we don't use them. So before plunking down cold cash for the next hot fad, consider a *U.S. News & World Report*/CNN poll that found one in five Americans owns a fondue pot, but only 1 percent has actually used it in the last five years. It's the same story with sandwich presses, yogurt makers, and hot-dog cookers. All are either rusting in appliance graveyards or are taking up valuable space in the dark recesses of cabinets.

However, there *are* legitimate time-savers out there. The three many hosts find indispensable are:

1. the food processor—a racehorse of slicing, dicing, and shredding,
2. the blender—perfect for pulverizing a frozen cylinder of juice, whipping up a batch of margaritas, or shaking up a fruit smoothie,
3. the microwave—good for heating up made-ahead dishes, and quickly turning frost into a feast.

TOOLS

Like small appliances, many kitchen gadgets are space and time wasters. According to testing by Consumers Union, items like microwave crispers and passive defrosters just don't work. So it pays to cast a wary eye on the latest so-called timesaving gizmo. However, most cooks agree the following are worth their keep:

- Colander. It's handy to have a couple of them: one for draining pasta, the other for rinsing raw poultry and fresh vegetables. I find the kind with a long, horizontal handle the handiest.
- Dutch oven. A versatile pot for boiling pasta, simmering soups and stews, and even roasting a whole chicken.
- Steamer. With its ingenious folding sides, a metal steamer can fit into most pots. Use it to cook vegetables quickly and evenly, and to gently simmer hard-cooked eggs.

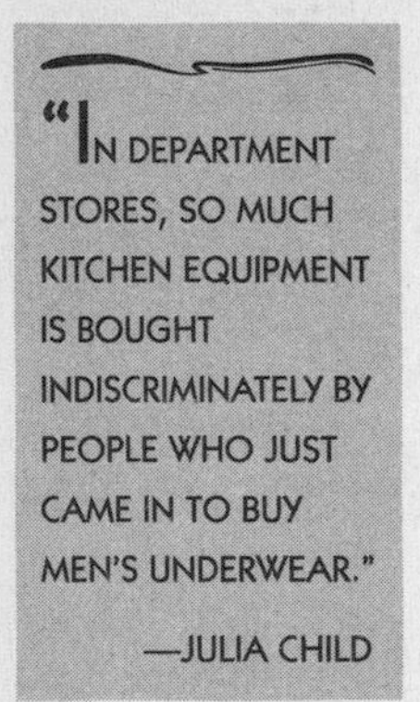

"IN DEPARTMENT STORES, SO MUCH KITCHEN EQUIPMENT IS BOUGHT INDISCRIMINATELY BY PEOPLE WHO JUST CAME IN TO BUY MEN'S UNDERWEAR."
—JULIA CHILD

- Kitchen shears. Any pair will do as long as they're sharp and large enough to cut a pizza, slice through dried fruits, and snip chives into confetti.
- Vegetable peeler. Perfect for transforming a chocolate bar into dessert curls or a lemon into drink-brightening spirals. It's also good for its original purpose of skinning a carrot or stripping a potato.
- Apple wedger. A handy tool for sculpting the fruit into symmetrical, coreless wedges to serve with cheese and nuts.
- Butter slicer. A rectangular frame strung with horizontal wires that makes perfect pats in one quick stroke. It's also handy for slicing hard-cooked eggs into neat little disks.
- Coffee grinder. Even if you don't like the taste of coffee, this baby makes the kitchen smell like Sunday at Starbucks. Priced under $20, it's cheap enough to have an extra one for grinding nuts and spices.

- Lid opener. A flat, textured, rubber disk that gets a grip on cemented-tight jars of olives, artichokes, and other necessary provisions.
- Garlic press. Smashing and squeezing are more gratifying than slicing and dicing the little stinkers. The tool also releases more of the garlic flavor, and keeps hands from smelling like a pizzeria.
- Pyrex cups. Handy measuring pitchers that can go from fridge to microwave. Look for the ones with snap-on caps and grater tops.
- Tongs. Have at least a couple: one for turning meats, poultry, fish, and vegetables on the grill without piercing their skins, the other for adding ice, without fingerprints, to drinks.
- Serving tray. An underutilized item when it comes to entertaining. Before the advent of aisle-blocking airplane carts, trays were used to deliver drinks, snacks, and meals to passengers. As a former flight attendant, I still use trays to serve food and drink, as well as gather up debris after the party is over. Keep one near the good glasses, another close to the dining table, and have plenty of extras for recruited help.

POTS AND PANS

- Buy the right pan for the job. A nonstick skillet with flared sides is perfect for flipping omelets and sautéing vegetables. A heavy cast-iron pan is good for browning chicken and blackening Cajun-style catfish. Decorative ceramic glass is ideal for baking, serving, and storing everything from a vanilla custard to a vegetable casserole.
- Use plastic utensils on nonstick surfaces. Even the thicker "new generation" coatings are subject to scratching from metal utensils.
- Look for a "porcelain"-finish pot exterior It's not just another pretty face, it cleans easily, and keeps its good looks.
- Shop for pancake-flat bottoms. Ridges and bumps prevent pots and pans from heating uniformly, especially on an electric cooktop.
- Make sure lids fit tightly for quick and efficient cooking.
- Avoid pots and pans made from matte-gray anodized aluminum since it stains easily.
- Hang it, show it off, or arrange flowers in that copper cookware you got for Christmas. Just don't cook in it, since it's a killer to keep clean.
- Check out commercial-style cookware. It's pricey, but its heft, durability, and open stock options may be worth the extra bucks.

KNIVES

- Go for quality, not quantity. Professional chefs may own scores of knives, but an efficient kitchen only needs a few well-balanced, feels-good-in-the-hand models. A four-inch parer, an eight-inch chef's knife (also known as a French or cook's knife), and a long, serrated-edged bread slicer can handle just about any meal.
- Stay sharp. A good sharp knife makes fast work out of anything that needs slicing, while a dull knife slows the operation. As most emergency room personnel can attest, the greater pressure required by a dull blade, the greater the chance it will julienne the fingers.
- To sharpen a dull knife, the J. A. Henckels knife company recommends drawing the blade over a whetstone in a circular movement. To maintain the edge, the company suggests holding the knife at a 20-degree angle and drawing the blade toward you about a half dozen times on each side.
- Avoid "no need to sharpen" knives. According to Consumers Union, the coating of hard metal particles not only dulls the blade, it makes it impossible to hone.
- Serrated knives seldom need sharpening. But if they do, take them to a pro since amateur attempts may damage them.
- Save the blade by only slicing on wooden or plastic cutting boards, and using a pair of scissors or a letter opener to tear into packages.
- Store knifes in a knife block to keep blades sharp and safe.

KEEP IT ORGANIZED

- Collect clutter somewhere outside the kitchen, since every out-of-place item is a magnet for more stuff. Having to move things every time we need to whip up a dish or accommodate kitchen company is tedious and time-consuming.
- Keep flatware and utensils sorted and easy to grab in molded drawer organizers.
- Stash it where you use it. Kitchen designers recommend keeping pots and pans near the stove, baking pans near the oven, and knives near the chopping block.
- Store a set of measuring spoons near the dried herbs and spices, and measuring cups inside canisters of rice, flour, and sugar.
- Attach clip-on wire bins to pantry shelves for onions, potatoes, and other produce that requires air circulation.
- Replace that cheesy plastic ring that is *supposed* to hold together a nest of measuring cups with a metal binder ring found at an office-supply store.

- Check out auxiliary bins, racks, carousel trays, and can dispensers to get the most out of refrigerator, pantry, and cabinet space.

"There's no space for clutter in an efficient kitchen."

—Mary Gilliatt, interior designer

MAKE IT EFFICIENT

- If remodeling, consider installing an extra sink separate from the main one so a helper or two can easily team up in preparation and cleanup.
- Avoid decorating with too much feminine froufrou if you want male cooks and bottle washers to feel at home in the kitchen.
- Tighten up a work triangle with a large utility cart or worktable. Make sure the top is about three inches below elbow level for easy chopping, rolling, and other pressure-related tasks.
- Tape spice charts, equivalent measures, roasting times, and other frequently referred-to information on the insides of cabinet doors.
- Position a pad and paper close to the fridge or pantry, and train family members to write down whatever they use up.
- Keep favorite recipes on individual cards in three-by-five boxes, mounted in notebooks, or anywhere other than that bulging drawer of "will-trys."
- Place frequently used foods like lunch-making supplies on the refrigerator and freezer doors so they're quick and easy to find.
- Keep the freezer fairly full so it cools more efficiently. If you're low on food, fill the gaps with bags of ice.
- Label and date all bound-for-the-freezer soups, sauces, and stocks to know exactly what's on hand and how long it's been there.

"There is nothing more attractive than a man who knows his way around the kitchen without making a huge production out of it."

—Laurie Colwin, **More Home Cooking**

EXTEND SPACE

One of the best kitchens I've ever had was so small I could cook with one hand and reach all my supplies with the other. As I stirred a pot of spaghetti sauce, I'd grab the oregano in the pantry, pull an onion from the fridge, and retrieve the serving dish from the dishwasher simply by pivoting. The only drawback was a lack of counter and storage space, but I learned it's possible to manage fine with just a few changes:

- Free counter space by putting away little-used small appliances.
- Create temporary counters by topping pulled-out drawers with large baking sheets or cutting boards.
- Buy an over-the-sink cutting board with a small wire basket for rinsing fruits and vegetables.
- Lengthen a butcher-block island with a hinged top. A large island would have blocked traffic and refrigerator access in my present kitchen, so I simply extended the top with a hinged, drop-down extension. A counter can be extended much the same way.
- If a built-in island is not in the picture, buy a portable one. A sturdy unit with bins on the bottom and a cutting board on top adds storage as well as work space.
- Clean out the refrigerator before shopping for company so there's more space and less waste.
- When cooking for a party, move jobs not dependent on the stove or oven elsewhere. Slicing veggies, tossing a salad, or dividing a pie can be done on any stable, easy-to-clean surface like a counter in the breakfast room or a plastic-covered ironing board in the laundry room.
- Free up refrigerator space for a big event by cooling drinks in an ice-filled bathtub, on a cold patio, or in a nearby snowdrift.
- If there's a freezer in the basement, garage, or utility room, stock it with larger, less used items like roasts. Use the more accessible unit in the kitchen for batches of chopped onions, shelled nuts, juice concentrates, and other convenience items.
- If the oven is too full to warm the dinner rolls, heat them in a plug-in slow cooker or place them in the dishwasher set on the heat cycle.
- Rent a plug-in burner or two to extend cooking capacity.

BRIGHTEN UP

A kitchen that's easy and safe to work in has ample lighting and little glare. Some options:

- Paint the walls and ceiling white, ivory, or another light-reflective tone if there is little natural light.
- Consider a skylight. I recently had a new type installed called Solatube, a factory-made, mirrored cylinder that creates a twelve-inch disk of light in the ceiling. It looks like a recessed fixture, cost us $350, and took only a couple of hours of installation in our tile roof.
- Mount compact fluorescent lamps under the front lip of overhead cabinets to light the counter work spaces. Aim them at a 45-degree angle to avoid glare on a shiny countertop.

- Hang track lights on the ceiling about two to three feet from the walls, aiming each bulb at workstations.
- Bring in a simple floor, counter, or wall lamp to the work area if built-in lighting is inadequate. A kitchen doesn't have to look like a laboratory.

PLAY IT SAFE

- Prevent fires by keeping curtains, dish towels, and long, flowing sleeves away from the cooktop.
- Install a smoke detector just outside the kitchen. Check its batteries in the spring and fall, and replace it when the warrantee is up.
- Put a lid on it. According to the Fire Safety Institute, placing a lid on a stovetop fire is the safest and quickest way to douse it. The force of a fire extinguisher can flare flames up into the curtains or cabinets, while water and baking soda can splash grease out of the pan onto our clothes.
- Keep electrical plugs well away from water.
- Always turn handles inward, so they're out of spilling distance; and get in the habit of favoring back burners.
- Buy a step stool with nonskid rungs to reach high shelves.
- Lose the scatter rugs. If tired legs need a soft surface, lay a nonskid cushioned mat instead.
- Free the counter of dangling extension cords with a plug-in power strip. It's available at most hardware and home centers for under $20. Look for one that has its own circuit breaker.
- Equip electrical outlets, especially those near the sink, with ground fault circuit interrupters. They cut the flow of electricity when plugs get wet or wiring goes berserk.
- Rinse and wipe knives individually. Soaking them in the dishpan is risky, since suds can conceal a razor-edged blade.

DIMINISH DISHWASHING

- Use self-sealing plastic bags instead of dishes and bowls for marinating. Flip the bag every so often so the contents get a penetrating soak.
- Line cookie sheets, bread, and cake pans with foil, waxed paper, or parchment paper to cut down on scrubbing.
- Chop all the dry ingredients in the food processor first, then blend the liquids so the bowl and blade don't need scrubbing after every step.

- Add ingredients to drained pasta in the cooking pot to reduce the number of dirty pots and pans.
- Squeeze double duty out of a container. Mix salad dressings and pasta salads in their serving bowls, wiping residue off the rims before they hit the table.
- Measure dry ingredients before liquids, so measuring equipment doesn't need rinsing after each use.
- Instead of dragging out a new mixing bowl or saucepan, rinse and dry what's already been used.
- Use only one pan when sautéing meats and vegetables separately. It seldom even needs wiping.
- Wipe the rims of muffin tins and other baking pans before they go into the oven so drips don't bake into cement.
- Rinse eggy pots, pans, and bowls with cold water before washing in hot, since heat turns eggs into glue.
- Marinate scorched pots and pans in a foam of spray-on oven cleaner.
- Face the crustiest pots toward the water spray in the dishwasher.
- Roasted turkey leaves a roasted mess. Cook that big bird in a disposable pan. If he's humongous, line one pan with another for stability.

A CLEANER KITCHEN

No matter how hard we may try to divert them, guests always end up in the kitchen. So it's a good idea to develop a few habits and strategies for keeping the place from shaming us.

- Clear the sink of all dishes and pans before starting a meal.
- Clean as you cook, putting away ingredients as used, wiping up spills, and rinsing bowls and utensils.
- Fill the food processor only to the bottom of the white-capped head of the blade to prevent messy spillovers.
- Contain splatters by using a large-enough bowl and placing it in the sink when whipping cream, tossing salads, or beating batter.
- Cook in generously sized pots so they don't bubble over and crud up the burners.
- Keep dishwashing detergent always at hand by pouring it into a pump dispenser that's pretty enough to hang out by the sink.
- Contain leaky garbage in plastic bags, or line the bottoms of brown paper bags with Styrofoam meat trays.

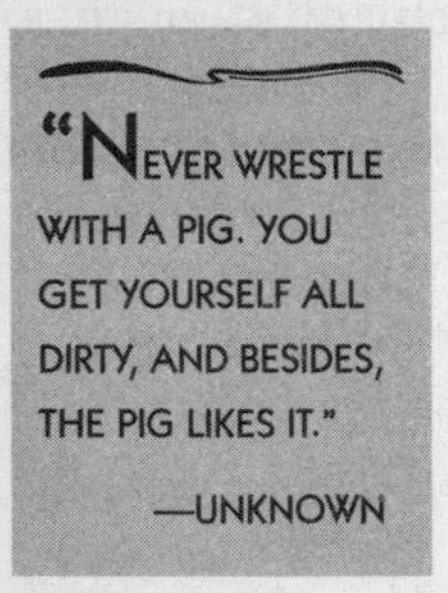

"NEVER WRESTLE WITH A PIG. YOU GET YOURSELF ALL DIRTY, AND BESIDES, THE PIG LIKES IT."
—UNKNOWN

- Line the bottom of refrigerator drawers with paper towels. Towels not only absorb spills and moisture, they make cleanup easy as well.
- Keep a platter next to the cooktop to rest a coated spoon, or for food-to-pan or pan-to-food transfers.

APPLIANCE ACTUARIAL TABLE

If the fridge shimmies and the oven groans, they could give up the ghost in the middle of a big bash. Just to give us fair warning, *Appliance* magazine, a publication that serves the kitchen industry, offers the estimated life-expectancy rates of the following appliances:

Dishwashers, gas water heaters, and garbage disposals—nine years
Freestanding freezers—twelve years
Microwave ovens, electric water heaters—ten years
Electric cooktops and refrigerators—fifteen years
Gas ranges—eighteen years

ROVER ON A ROLL

There's little that can compare with the taste of a succulent chicken or marbled roast slowly rotating over an open flame, as evidenced by the popularity of rotisserie restaurants popping up everywhere. But spit cooking has been around for aeons.

The tedious turning was done by hand until the fifteenth century, when an Englishman figured his hyperactive dog could do the trick. He rigged up a pulley from the spit to a wheel-shaped cage above the hearth, where a small, specially trained terrier ran gerbil-style, rotating the cage, which in turn cranked the spit.

The dog-powered appliance was a hit in European kitchens for a few decades until a heat-powered model, and finally electricity, gave paws a rest.

The rotisserie run may have been rough on Rover, but he got his choice of leftovers, a bed by the fire, and an esteemed place in the household. Plus, no one ever had to walk him after dinner.

CHAPTER 6

FLOWERS AND FLOURISHES

Flowers are never *necessary,* but they do perk up the place, especially when they're worked into those big, knock-your-socks-off arrangements designers concoct. But when thumbs are brown and funds are tight, there are plenty of additional ways blooms and other flourishes can add warmth and festivity to a setting.

> "BREAD FEEDS THE BODY INDEED, BUT FLOWERS FEED ALSO THE SOUL."
>
> —THE KORAN

KEEP THEM AFFORDABLE

- Buy flowers in season. Lily of the valley, violets, and calla lilies are relatively cheap and sturdy in spring, while mums and delphiniums are at their best and least expensive in the fall. "Out-of-season flowers are typically grown in hothouses thousands of miles away," explained floral designer Vicky Van Arsdale of Feather Acres Farms and Nursery in Del Mar, California, "so they're more expensive and shorter lived."
- Keep options open. Better to buy what looks best from the flower seller than to haul home something we've set our hearts on that is not quite up to snuff.
- Check out the local farmer's market as a source. Since they're usually one- or two-day-a-week affairs, with no middleman, flowers are often fresh, cheap, and plentiful. Just make sure they haven't been frying in the sun all day.

- Cut off their heads. Investment adviser Garrie Gorby says her mother always buys pruned geranium heads for pennies at a northern Michigan nursery in winter when other flowers are priced sky-high. She also buys potted mums at the supermarket when they're on sale, decapitates and floats them in a glass bowl, then plants what's left of them in her garden come spring.
- Bargain for a few spent roses at the nursery, pull them apart, then sprinkle their petals amid floating candles in a brandy snifter or a wide and shallow glass bowl.
- Grace a breakfast table with a $2 special: a single rose, a stem of iris, or a single spray of orchids in a favorite bud vase.
- Cut a few multiblossomed, long-stemmed flowers like asters, mums, or day lilies, and arrange them in a small container like a creamer or coffee mug.
- Place inexpensive filler flowers in fun containers: baby's breath in a silver baby cup, Queen Anne's lace in a watering can, and heather or alstroemeria in a cluster of canning jars.

FROM BOGUS TO BOUNDLESS

Flowers have long been popular in the home, but, surprisingly, not always the garden variety. In seventeenth- and eighteenth-century France, real blooms were thought to be too rustic and uncultured indoors, so feather, beaded, and even skillfully cut vegetable imitations were favored on tables, sideboards, and consoles.

It wasn't until the nineteenth century that the real McCoy became fashionable again. However, like many excesses of the Victorian era, flowers became so profuse and elaborate on dinner tables they often blocked vision, overpowered the nose, and upstaged the food.

Some hosts went well beyond flowers when it came to bedecking their tables. French count Robert de Montesquiou had small, jewel-encrusted turtles crawl among his diners, while nineteenth-century heiress Caroline Astor once mounded sand down the center of her long board in which she buried tiny but real emeralds, rubies, and sapphires. Each place setting held a small silver beach bucket and shovel so guests could dig for treasure while waiting for dessert.

FREE FOR THE TAKING

- Cultivate a few blooming plants in the garden, on the patio, or in the house, so there's always a ready supply of color. Daisies, statice, and geraniums are easy to grow outdoors, while kalanchoe, gloxinia, and bromeliads do well in.
- Greenery is especially easy to grow. Asparagus fern and evergreens round out skimpy bouquets, and are practically idiotproof when grown in the garden or in pots on the patio.
- Keep a bowl of greens in the house when they're available, whether they're graceful branches from a tree, or cuttings from a hedge, bush, or ground cover. Add seasonal flowers, berries, and seed heads when you can get them.
- Bare can be beautiful. Graceful branches like corkscrew willow, birch, and kiwi vine stand alone splendidly. They can also be threaded with tiny white Christmas lights to cast a glow.
- Prune forsythia, dogwood, apple blossom, and other early bloomers in late winter, and arrange them in a deep container. Place them on a sideboard or on the floor by the front door. The warmth of the house forces their buds open long before spring arrives.
- If there's no room for a garden or even pots, explore the surrounding countryside for wildflowers, grasses, and interesting foliage that can be made into informal, though usually short-lived, bouquets.

EASY ARRANGEMENTS

Unlike the teased and tortured arrangements of the past, today's style is relaxed and natural. "It's an English country garden look," says floral designer and special event coordinator Vincent Carletti of Surroundings in Manhattan. "Flowers don't look arranged, and they don't need a lot of propping."

- Choose "cluster flowers" that practically arrange themselves. Lilacs, peonies, sweet peas, and hydrangeas, for example, are so voluptuous they require no help from extra foliage and flowers. "The key is to use good-quality flowers that are beautiful on their own," says Carletti.
- Work with nature, not against it. A glass globe of naturally drooping tulips, or anemones spilling from a silver gravy boat, is prettier and preferable to wiring them stiff and forcing them into a contrived arrangement.
- Strive for understated elegance: a single tiger lily on a sideboard, individual freesias on a mantel, or a flotilla of gardenias on a side table.

- Choose flowers that animate a color scheme or a favorite painting. A predominantly yellow room, for instance, takes on new life with yellow roses mixed with coral snapdragons and blue bachelor buttons. Soft pink, blue, and lavender blooms enhance a poster of Monet's water lilies. Full-blown, jewel-tone flowers look spectacular next to an Old World still life.
- Set up a flower station in the laundry room, kitchen, or bathroom. I have a sink and counter in my laundry room, so I store vases, cutters, and other supplies within easy reach.
- Get in the habit of always having fresh flowers in the house, so arranging them becomes second nature.

"THERE'S SOMETHING A LITTLE BIT SCARY ABOUT MAKING AN 'ARRANGEMENT.' YOU HAVE A FEELING IT HAS TO BE PERFECT AND ARTISTIC. BUT NATURE IN ITSELF IS ARTISTIC."

—GEORGEANNE BRENNAN, **LES IMMORTELLES**

CONTAINERS AND THINGS

Baccarat and Wedgwood vases are beautiful, but fine crystal and porcelain aren't necessary if we keep our eyes open for fun and interesting containers like soup tureens, teapots, and cordial glasses. Other possibilities:

- teacups
- ice buckets
- spice jars
- cologne bottles
- cheese crocks
- gravy boats
- whiskey shot glasses
- goblets
- steins
- toy trucks, wheelbarrows, and beach pails
- goldfish bowls
- carafes
- eggcups
- casserole dishes
- salad bowls
- punch bowls
- sugar bowls
- water pitchers
- baskets
- wooden wine boxes

- apothecary jars
- screw-top salt and pepper shakers

- Choose the right-sized container. "People often make the mistake of picking too large a container for the amount of material they have," says Vincent Carletti. "If you pick a vase with a wide neck, for instance, you need enough branches and stems to control the arrangement."
- Keep proportion in mind. "The old rule of thumb that an arrangement should measure at least one and one half times the height of the container is a good one," says Vincent Carletti. "But rules can be broken. You just have to look at the flowers and think about where they're going to be placed."
- Be wary of tall blooms in tall and slender containers. They can look overly formal and be less than stable.
- Place a smaller jar inside a favorite cracked container to waterproof it.
- Waterproof a basket by lining it with a few layers of plastic cut from a heavyweight trash bag. Plop in a lightweight plastic pot liner for extra insurance.

TRICKS OF THE TRADE

- Start with the greenery to get the overall shape of the bouquet, the largest flowers first, and the fillers last.
- Crisscross the stems of greens to give support to the flowers.
- Ensure maximum impact by placing arrangements in high-visibility areas like the entry, the dining area, and the powder room.
- Place fragrant flowers in the entry so the first thing guests notice is the enticing scent.
- Add aromatic herbs to flowers with little scent. Mint, dill, sage, and basil combine well with many blooms. Pinch their leaves as you pass to perfume the air.
- Give a vase stability and flowers support by filling the container with pebbles or florist marbles.
- Long-stemmed flowers are difficult to arrange. Don't be afraid to cut them down to a manageable length.
- Open tight flowers and buds by standing them in a bucket of warm water. Certain flowers respond to the warm-water wake-up call better than others, explains Vicky Van Arsdale. Lilies, roses, and gladiolas are particularly responsive.
- Use a standing tray to frame an arrangement, or place the flowers in front of a mirror to double the impact.

KEEP THEM GOING

- Pick flowers with staying power: alstroemeria, daisies, mums, gladiolus, statice, carnations, and lisianthus can last for well over a week.
- Make sure the container is clean, since a residue of bacteria breaks down blooms. Soaking a glass or ceramic container with a little diluted chlorine bleach or full-strength distilled vinegar takes care of the crustiest deposits.
- Pick flowers from the garden early in the day for greater longevity. "They're moist and full of nutrients in the morning," says Vicky Van Arsdale. "But they're under stress in the heat of day."
- Select blooms with firm stems, leaves, and petals. Throw in a few buds for interest and long life.
- Carry a bucket of water while gathering from the garden. Flowers, like fish, won't hack it long without water.
- Cut stems on a slant so more of their surface absorbs water.
- Pull off leaves that sit beneath the waterline, otherwise they turn slimy, pollute the water, and hasten wilting.
- Set flowers away from direct sunlight, heating vents, and cold drafts. Flowers, like people, prefer cool, airy rooms to hot, stuffy ones.
- Change the water and cut the stems every day or so. Clean water and open stems are the keys to longevity.
- If the arrangement is too unwieldy to monkey with, place it under the tap and let the fresh water flood out the old. Or give it a drink from a long-spouted watering can.

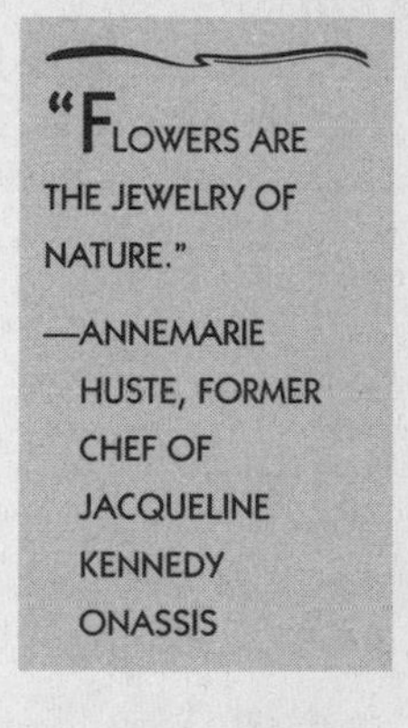

"FLOWERS ARE THE JEWELRY OF NATURE."

—ANNEMARIE HUSTE, FORMER CHEF OF JACQUELINE KENNEDY ONASSIS

- Florist pebbles displace water, so keep an eye on the water level.
- Make blooms happy with a swig of citrus soda like 7-Up, Sprite, or Slice. Or mix two tablespoons of white vinegar with two tablespoons granulated sugar in a quart of water. The sugar feeds the flowers, and the vinegar or citrus inhibits bacteria.
- Keep flowers away from overripe fruits, vegetables, and decaying blooms. They emit a gas that speeds up the wilting process.
- Revive wilted roses by trimming their stems and submerging them up to their heads for about thirty minutes in warm water. "Baby-bottle warm is about the right temperature," says Vicky Van Arsdale.
- When some of the blossoms in an arrangement die, replace them with fresh recruits. Or rescue the survivors, recut their stems, and make a smaller bouquet in a petite container.

- Gladiolas age from the bottom up, so cut still-fresh tips from wilting stalks and arrange them in a pint-sized vase.
- Toss flowers as they wither. There's little sadder than a bowl full of dead and decayed blooms.

BULBS AND PLANTS

- Bulbs make a spectacular display, providing we have a few weeks to force them into bloom. Daffodils, crocuses, anemones, and other spring bloomers are cheap and available at nurseries and florists from fall through early winter. They're easy to grow, especially if purchased preplanted in their own baskets or pots. Place a utilitarian pot into a larger, prettier container.
- Pair bulbs with houseplants. Baskets of maidenhair fern surrounding crimson amaryllis, needlepoint ivy entwining paper-white narcissus, and baby tears teamed with blue hyacinths are captivating and easy to arrange.
- Use large potted plants as a backdrop to smaller flowering varieties of houseplants. A choice poinsettia or pepper plant takes center stage when backdropped by the green leaves of a large and lush houseplant.
- Consider decorating with yard-bound trees. Instead of bothering with cut flowers, one homeowner lined her living room with a half-dozen five-gallon flowering peach trees she bought in the morning for a housewarming party that night. The next day, she simply planted them around her patio.
- Hang pots of ivy geraniums, fuchsia, or other cascading blooms from the branches of trees for an outdoor party.
- Feed and water houseplants with discarded vase water. It may look and smell yucky, but it's full of body-building nutrients.

> "NOW IS THE SEASON FOR SPLENDOR IN THE VASE."
>
> —SARAH BAN BREATHNACH, **SIMPLE ABUNDANCE**

TABLE TALK

- Keep the dining arrangement low and compact so it doesn't entangle the cutlery and block the view. No one should have to peek around the petunias or part a jungle of foliage to talk to a tablemate.
- Dunk the blooms of freshly cut garden flowers in soap suds before arranging them to make sure nothing crawls from the arrangement into the salad.

- Choose subtly scented blooms so their fragrance doesn't compete with the bouillabaisse or the chocolate mousse.
- Stick with the genuine article under the close scrutiny of diners. Silk and dried arrangements can fake it elsewhere.
- Arrange blooms in florist's foam rather than water, so if the container spills, laps and linen stay dry.
- Submerge florist's foam for at least an hour before working with it so it's fully saturated.
- Keep a trivet, tile, or tray under the arrangement so it doesn't wet the linen and stain the table. A mirrored surface works beautifully, since it also reflects the flowers.
- Purchase a few plastic vials from a florist, fill with water, poke in small blossoms, and push into the soil of a pot of trailing ivy.
- Keep large arrangements off the coffee table. The space is too valuable as a landing pad for drinks and snacks.
- Look beyond cut flowers. Pony packs of bedding plants like impatiens, pansies, and fairy primroses are attractive when clustered in a low basket. Cover the plastic pot rims and gaps with sphagnum or Spanish moss for a finished surface. When the party is over, either plant them in the garden or present the individual pots to departing guests.

TABLE FLOURISHES

- Make it edible. One host draped big bunches of red grapes over a bed of ferns down the middle of long, rectangular tables at one party she hosted. "Food is interactive," says host Kathi Mallick. "Guests nibbled on the centerpiece all evening."
- Consider an arrangement of glossy eggplants, ripe tomatoes, and green and yellow zucchini. They can be the centerpiece one night and ratatouille the next.
- A show of fruits and vegetables is also effective, even when guests aren't inclined to munch them. Floral designer José Santamaria combined white and brown eggs, cauliflower, mushrooms, onions, and birch branches in pale straw baskets for a Beverly Hills spring luncheon. "Sometimes texture is more important than color," he explains. "Especially when you want an understated, elegant look."
- Turn fruits and vegetables into vases. Scoop out a large cabbage, melon, or small pumpkin just wide enough to hold a plastic tube or tub, and fill with flowers and/or candles.

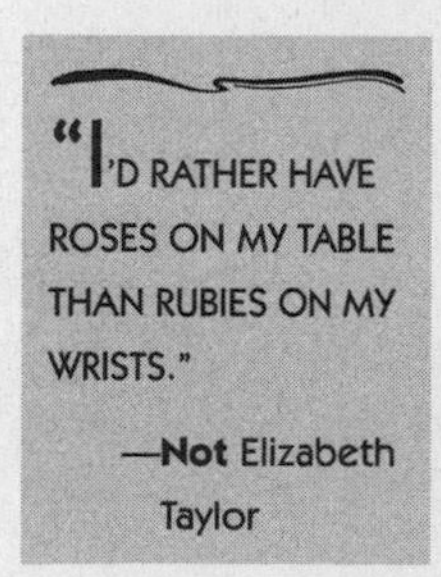

"I'D RATHER HAVE ROSES ON MY TABLE THAN RUBIES ON MY WRISTS."
—Not Elizabeth Taylor

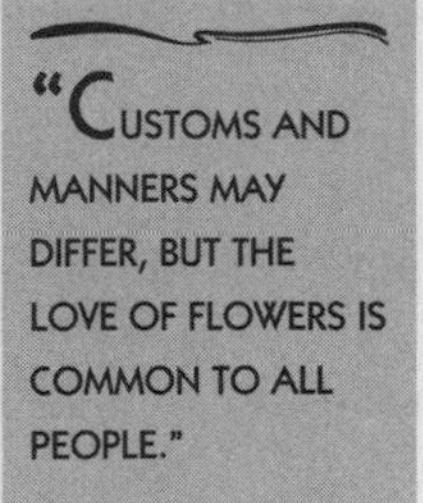

- Use other natural elements like autumn leaves, minerals, or shells. One of the prettiest tables I've seen was simply strewn with river rocks, seashells, and beach grasses.
- Encircle a punch bowl or a clear shallow container of floating candles within a blooming or evergreen wreath.
- Cut a block of florist's foam into a cylinder, soak it, and poke in sprigs of evergreen to make a tiny Christmas tree.
- Pile tiny pinecones in a shallow basket, tucking in a few berries or evergreens among them.
- An arrangement can be *above* a table instead of *on* it. I like to hang shiny Christmas balls at different lengths from the chandelier with transparent fishing line to catch the flicker of candlelight. Hollow Easter eggs, curling ribbon, and other lightweight elements can also be suspended when there's no room for an arrangement.
- Sprinkle confetti, sparkles, or strew streamers down the center of the table for birthdays, showers, and other festive dinners.
- Tie multicolor streamers to helium balloons and let them drift to the ceiling. Balloons add color and fun without a big investment.

PART II

EVENTS

CHAPTER 7

SHARING THE FUSS AND THE FUN

Picture the dining table laden with fragrant loaves of rosemary bread, baby greens dressed with goat cheese and toasted pine nuts, a subtly spiced Tuscan bean salad, and a platter of garlic-sautéed prawns nestled among angel hair pasta. Over on the sideboard sits a silky tiramisù that will accompany freshly brewed cappuccino.

In the flickering candlelight sit your friends, glasses of Soave raised to the chef. *"Moi?"* you ask. Not exactly. Everyone has had a hand in this fabulous feast. And they will again next month, when the menu and venue change.

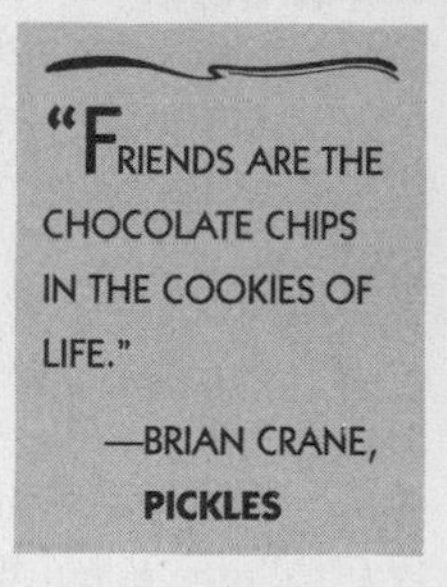

"FRIENDS ARE THE CHOCOLATE CHIPS IN THE COOKIES OF LIFE."

—BRIAN CRANE, **PICKLES**

Co-op dining groups are increasingly popular these days when time is short, budgets tight, and neighbors are the faceless people next door. In addition to the time, work, and money saved, there's a psychological benefit; by taking part in the preparation of the meal, each guest plays an active role in the outcome of the evening—an experience more satisfying than passively taking in whatever is being dished out.

It's not difficult to organize a group. All that's needed are a few reliable souls who have a sense of adventure, possess some basic cooking skills, or at least have a willingness to learn them.

Even if we don't have enough friends to fill the dinette set, organizing a group is a good way to make them. New to Boston, Helen Chan knew only a handful of people at her insurance agency. But she invited each of them to bring a dish and a friend to a potluck at her place. There, over a meal of what she described as a weird conglomeration of spring rolls, enchiladas, empanadas, Caesar salad, and baklava, they found they all shared a love of ethnic meals, but a lack of time and audience to justify making them. Thus was born a co-operative dinner group that has met fairly regularly for the past couple of years.

The group takes on new life with every dinner, since each rotating host invites a guest or two.

"It's a perfect way to set up your friends in a nonthreatening atmosphere," says Chan. "You get a better sense of someone at a dinner party than you do in a bar. But even without the guy thing, I've gotten to make close friends, and have learned a lot about food. It's also nice to be able to devote yourself heart and soul to one dish, without worrying about the rest of the meal."

THE RESURGENCE OF THE COMMUNITY FEAST

Rural life has a long history of community cooking and dining with church suppers, harvest festivals, and block parties. But television, computers, and the automobile have taken their toll on such gatherings.

In southwest France, however, neighborhood bean banquets, or moungetades, *are making a comeback and revitalizing the sense of community.*

Nearly everyone in town contributes to the annual affair with food, cooking, or entertainment, writes Professor Margaret Visser in The Rituals of Dinner. *On the town's patron saint's day, trestle tables are set out in the main square, and designated cooks tend huge vats of simmering white beans laced with pork and sausage. Writes Visser, "All pay an equal fee for the dinner, and all participate in the lusty singing and the raucous jokes as course after course is served under strings of fairy lights in the open air; dancing goes on in the square to deafening amplified music till dawn."*

Villages compete for the best feast given. The feeling is, writes Visser, that "any village that cannot get it together to mount one every year scarcely counts as a living community at all."

HOW IT'S DONE

- Dinner groups can range from six to sixteen people, and often meet four to ten times a year. In smaller parties, the host often prepares the main dish and provides the wine. In larger groups, the host only provides the setting, and if they meet monthly, only half the group cooks every other time.
- Shari Shields, author of *The Gourmet Grub Club,* finds that eight people, a core set of three couples plus a guest couple, works best for her Seattle group. "It's a manageable size, with just enough people to share the cooking and the expenses," says Shields. "Eight feels like a party, but not like a crowd."
- One San Diego monthly group finds ten the ideal number, since each member hosts only once in the course of a year. There are other perks to a large team as well. "Cooks seem braver in numbers," says member Theresa Ruiz. "When the work is shared, anything seems possible. We've tackled everything from eight-course Chinese banquets to Indonesian rijsttafels to Middle Eastern feasts. The food isn't *always* great, but the camaraderie is."

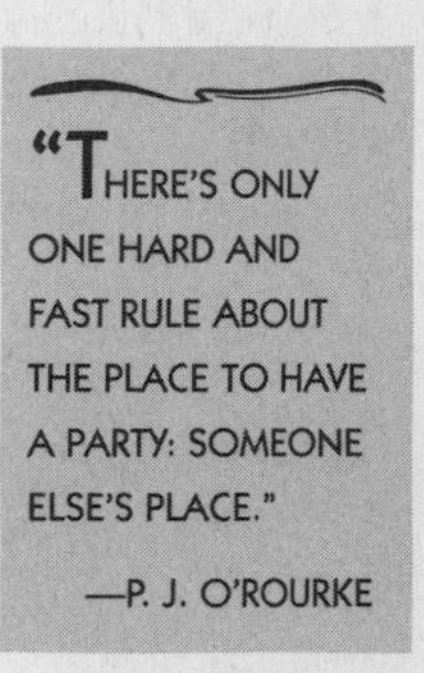

"THERE'S ONLY ONE HARD AND FAST RULE ABOUT THE PLACE TO HAVE A PARTY: SOMEONE ELSE'S PLACE."
—P. J. O'ROURKE

- The group works out the space crunch by scattering card tables throughout members' homes. They also make use of parks and other outdoor locations. They break for the summer, but their ranks swell to about thirty friends and family each Labor Day, when they host a bash on the beach. Last year, it was a luau, complete with roast suckling pig, poi, and hula lessons. This year it will be a New England clambake.
- My husband and I found ourselves part of a group of thirty-two wannabe cooks and diners at the Newcomer's Club in Deerfield, Illinois. We simply split into four groups that reshuffled periodically. We got to know a large number of like-minded people and a good deal about food.

MAKING IT WORK

- Stick to a consistent date each month for better attendance.
- Plan on a weekend evening, since it's when people are most relaxed.
- Set a theme: a lot of mileage comes out of regional American and international cooking. Celebrating the seasons or holidays works well, too.

- Elect a chairperson to assign a host or cohosts for each month so they can plan the menu and distribute recipes for the upcoming dinner. Depending on the size of the group, the host is usually responsible for preparing the setting, providing predinner drinks, while the cohost prepares the main dish.
- Plan the menu at least two weeks before the dinner. Photocopy the recipes and distribute them to the appropriate cooks.
- Have dishes as complete as possible in their own serving containers with the appropriate utensils.
- Keep an extra cooler or two on hand in case refrigerator space is scarce. An ice-filled child's wading pool can be pressed into service.
- Assign posts. Shari Shields suggests someone be posted as kitchen chief overseeing the delivery and disposition of dishes, and to keep an eye on simmering sauces and baking breads. Her group also assigns a cohost who is responsible for refilling drinks, keeping track of the music, and passing the hors d'oeuvres. No one, however, should get stuck in the kitchen or behind the bar, stresses Shields. "Floating," she says, "is encouraged for hosts and guests alike."

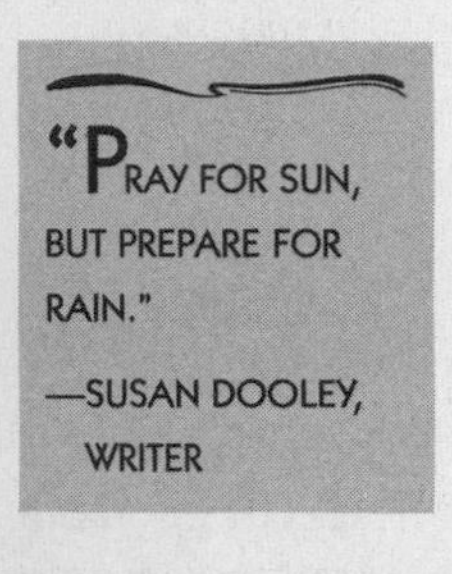

"PRAY FOR SUN,
BUT PREPARE FOR
RAIN."
—SUSAN DOOLEY,
WRITER

- Appoint a cleanup committee in advance. Two or three works out well in most kitchens; any more and they're crashing into each other.
- Decide how to deal with cancellations and no-shows. Substitutes are fine as long as they come bearing the required offerings.

LOGISTICS

- Any shape, size, and configuration of tables is fine, as long as each place setting is at least twenty-four inches wide and eighteen inches deep.
- Consider topping folding square card tables with one-half-inch-thick, forty-eight-inch round plywood tops cut at the local lumberyard. A standard thirty-inch square card table only fits four. With a plywood round, it seats six. Cut and hinge the plywood rounds in the middle for easy storage.
- Seat a crowd by forming a T with an existing rectangular dining table and a folding table or tables perpendicular to it.
- Consider seating a large group in the family room or living room if the dining room is small. If the place is impossibly tiny, serve a Japanese, Persian, or Arabian feast on the floor.
- Borrow extra tableware, linens, and other necessities from members. One large group chipped in for a set of folding chairs that rotates among homes.

- Provide hot plates and warming dishes to keep food at serving temperature.

SPICING IT UP

- Dress for the occasion. A Western barbecue calls for cowboy gear. Togas (compliments of the bedsheets) are fun on Greek night, and leis and luaus are a natural. Just be sensitive to ethnicity: dressing as coolies, slaves, or any downtrodden group can be offensive.
- Grub Club founder Shari Shields suggests awarding prizes to the most creative getup. A bottle of wine, designer vinegar, or fancy preserves are perennial prize favorites.
- Consider playing out themes with decorations, music, and professional entertainment. Belly dancers are fun at Middle Eastern feasts; a fortune-teller is a hit at a New Year's party.
- Replicate the sounds of the surf, a mountain meadow, or other theme with an environmental tape. I have a tropical-rainforest recording with the sound of birds, waterfalls, and soft rain that's the perfect background for a Caribbean or South American dinner.
- Have the creator of a particular course explain its origins, unusual ingredients, how it's prepared, and anything else that makes it interesting. A group of oenophiles could enlighten the group by researching the wine that's offered with each course.

DETAILS

- Check to see if reservations or permits are needed if a park or beach is the designated party spot. Make sure there are rest room facilities, and plan a bad-weather alternative location.
- Stabilize a dish in a car trunk by placing it in a cardboard box or, better yet, in a handled basket with a couple of brick "bookends." Keep it warm or cold with layers of insulating newspaper.
- Decide what to do with leftovers. Are they left with the host, divided among the group, or do they go home with their makers?
- Keep on hand plastic tubs, extra foil, and self-sealing plastic bags for take-home or stay-home leftovers.
- Have cooks tape their names to the bottom of their serving dishes so the host doesn't have to search for the owners of forgotten plates, platters, and bowls.
- Discourage the use of large glass containers. I once brought a salad in a huge glass bowl that was so unwieldy, it shattered and broke as the host rinsed it, cutting her hands. I've used big Plexiglas bowls ever since.

- Provide recipes to share. Decide whether to photocopy them to fit on three-by-five-inch index cards or on eight-and-a-half-by-eleven-inch sheets for a three-ring binder.
- Share the wealth. The easiest way to handle expenses is having each member absorb the cost of the dish they contribute. It usually all works out in the end and there's no awkward divvying up after dessert. If the group wants everything even-steven, save receipts and split the bill over brandy.

SECRETS OF SUCCESS

- Find inspiration for recipes, menus, and cooking techniques at the local library, bookstore, on TV cooking programs, in magazines, and the food section of the newspaper.
- Befriend the butcher, an ally in the search for special orders, cuts, and service.

"AMONG FRIENDS ALL THINGS ARE COMMON."
—IRISH PROVERB

- Most supermarkets offer a wide range of exotic ingredients today, but don't give up the opportunity to explore the offerings of local specialty stores. An Asian market in my area offers the riches of the Orient with hard-to-find spices, herbs, and produce.
- Be open to serendipity. Our group changed course from Russian to Cajun when a member called to say she'd be flying from New Orleans the afternoon of the party with fresh beignets. A menu of gumbo, cornbread, and black-eyed peas quickly replaced the planned borscht and blintzes.

VARIATIONS ON SHARING THE WEALTH

It isn't necessary to commit to a dinner-of-the-month club. Potlucks can come together annually, or just about anytime we have the energy to dust off the table and organize a group.

- A story in *Sunset* magazine tells of a Washington State couple who host an annual black-tie chili party for two dozen friends who arrive with assorted salads, desserts, and "presents with presence." The hosts provide the chili, accompanied by grated cheese, sour cream, tortillas, and salsa. The evening's entertainment involves judging the most creative interpretation of black tie, as well as an absurd white elephant gift exchange.
- Another couple is on the four-year plan. Poll watchers Jim Smothers

and Merle Henderson host a presidential potluck every election year. "Everyone is a delegate with a delegated dish," says Merle. The last "Come to the Aid of Your Party" menu consisted of political punch, assorted nuts, lame-duck salad with democratic peas and independent beans, republican stew, tax rolls, and campaign peaches. Televised election results, along with wagers, provided the entertainment.

"I NEVER SEE ANY HOME COOKING. ALL I GET IS FANCY STUFF."
—PRINCE PHILIP

- Others go against the grain. When everyone else in Palm Springs dresses up and swills down champagne on New Year's Eve, Barbara and George von Rosen take the down-home, early-to-bed approach. Each of the four invited couples brings a plug-in pot of soup and a loaf of homemade bread. Barbara simply makes a big salad, plugs in the Crockpots, and guests serve themselves. "We've had some of the best meals and most relaxed New Year's this way," says Barbara. "There's no forced gaiety and they all leave at a decent hour so they're safe on the road that night."
- When Kathi Mallick wanted to get to know her neighbors better, she went to the homeowner's association for a plot plan of the neighborhood. She and a couple of friends then went to thirty-four houses and either personally delivered or left an invitation to a 7:00-to-9:00 P.M. "Bring an Hors d'Oeuvre and Bottle of Wine Party" in her backyard. "Forty people showed up and it was the easiest party I ever hosted," says Mallick. "We set up the hors d'oeuvres on a couple of picnic tables, kept the wine cool in an ice-filled garbage can, and guests took home their leftovers when it was over. Best of all, there were no dishes to clean. We all had such a good time we're making it an annual event at rotating houses."
- A Springfield, Massachusetts, theater-going group launches their summer theater season with an after-the-play pie festival. Everyone brings a pie to the host's home, and the host provides coffee and ice cream. There are always leftovers, so each person gets to bring home a sampling of pies.

OTHER POSSIBILITIES

- Keep 'em movin' with a progressive party. Each host or host couple prepares a course and serves it at home, and the party moves from one course and location to the next. My husband and I enjoyed a movable feast with our neighbors last summer. We started out with sangria and hummus at our house, migrated next door for iced gazpacho, moved on down the road for chicken scaloppine, and finished up at the end of the street with strawberry tarts. The change of locations kept it interesting, the stroll was good for digestion, and no one got stuck with too much preparation and cleanup. Progressive dinners work best in mild weather months, with three to four locations, preferably but not necessarily, within walking distance of each other.

- Make cooking the entertainment. The host shops for the ingredients and sets up cooking stations with instructions. The guests bring a particular ingredient for, say, a stew, shish kebab, or bouillabaisse party. There's more advance work for the host than a "bring your own prepared dish" evening, but it's great fun for the guests and less work for the host than the traditional dinner party. Variations include: bread or cookie baking, torpedo-sandwich building, artistic pizzas, ice-cream sundae making, or an old-fashioned taffy pull. Everyone eventually gravitates to the kitchen, so we might as well put them to work.
- Sometimes just initiating the thing is all it takes. We have seaside friends who organize a very loose, very open potluck beach party every so often to which people bring their own dinner or the ingredients to grill it, as well as a side dish or a dessert to pass around. Since it's held on the beach, all the hosts do is launch a phone network, yet everyone is so grateful they took the initiative.

GET REAL

- Even if you enjoy hosting traditional dinner parties, brunches, and such, never pass up a good offer. "Can I bring dessert? I make a mean cheesecake," "Let me get drinks for everyone while you're doing that," "I love loading the dishwasher" are music to the ears of any realistic host. When we learn to dance to that music, we're more relaxed, our guests feel more at home, and everyone has more fun.

CHAPTER 8

COOL COCKTAIL PARTIES

Despite its reputation for warm drinks, cold food, and inane banter, the cocktail party remains popular. Guests sip, sup, and schmooze, while the host entertains a multitude without having to stuff and seat them.

The party is best when it's brief, has a focus like welcoming a new neighbor, or when it precedes another event elsewhere. It's beastly when it lasts too long, is too big for the premises, and has too many unconnected people.

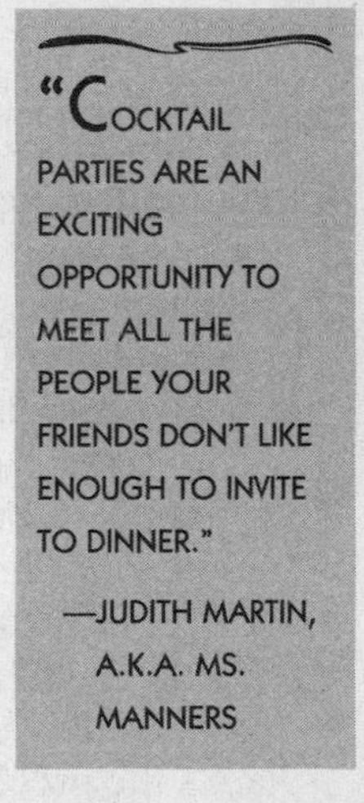

"COCKTAIL PARTIES ARE AN EXCITING OPPORTUNITY TO MEET ALL THE PEOPLE YOUR FRIENDS DON'T LIKE ENOUGH TO INVITE TO DINNER."
—JUDITH MARTIN, A.K.A. MS. MANNERS

THE GUESTS

- Make sure there's sufficient room for bodies to circulate. It's no fun to balance drink and dip while being crushed from all sides by the masses.
- Since this is not the event for forging meaningful relationships, don't invite too many unconnected people. One of the biggest flops I've witnessed was a cocktail party hosted by a magazine for "Fifty People to Watch." The magazine spent a fortune on the food, the drink, and the band, but made no introductions or attempts to mix guests, who were mostly unknown to each other. So 250 strangers milled about aimlessly, with nothing to connect them.

- Invite fresh faces to inject new blood, but make sure they're introduced and taken in by the group.
- Pepper the guest list with plenty of extroverts and have a close friend or two keep an eye out for wallflowers. Otherwise, you'll work like a cruise director all evening.

THE BIRTH OF THE COCKTAIL PARTY

The Prohibition Act of 1919 is mainly responsible for driving American men out of the bars and into the living rooms with the women. And the newly liberated, postwar woman was more than happy to accommodate with a new kind of party.

According to Stephen Birmingham, in his book The Right People: *"Cocktail parties were a gesture of defiance against those who had inflicted Prohibition on the country. They were the bold, the daring, the naughty thing to do. There was an air of excitement about these primordial parties, the kind of excitement that is generated by breaking the law. Each cocktail was an adventure, too. Depending upon the bootlegger, a few swallows might make one pleasantly tiddly or violently ill."*

THE INVITATION

- Extend invitations by phone for a party of a dozen or fewer guests. "Can you come for drinks around five, before Sunday's concert?" The phone gives immediate results, provided we catch the intended in the flesh. One telemarketer confides she's more apt to find her prey at home between 5:00 and 9:00 on weekday nights, and 10:00 A.M. to 2:00 P.M. on weekends.
- Try to make all the calls on the same day, so if word gets out, no one feels like an afterthought.
- A clever postcard invitation is good for setting the mood and solidifying the facts, provided there's time to follow it up. Issue them one to three weeks ahead. Any sooner, the invitees may forget. Any later, there's the problem of baby-sitters and previous plans.
- Be sure to include the four W's: Who, What, Where, and When on the invitation. Including the dress code and other pertinent information is also a nice touch. One of the cleverest invitations I've seen included an alphabetized list of everyone invited. It alleviated the fear

of not knowing a soul, and cut the risk of spilling the beans to those left out.

- Include a map. I once searched for a party in a new development where every unit was identical and every street number a mystery. I had no luck finding the place in my car, so I parked and scouted in the freezing rain. I was not a happy camper by the time I located the party, which, not surprisingly, turned out to be smaller than intended.

PLANNING

- Make a "to do" list. Pam Barnett, fund development associate at the San Diego Blood Bank, keeps a party-planning list in her computer. "It's a compilation of all I have to do before company comes, so I don't have to worry about it each time I entertain," she says. Pam prints and divides jobs on her calendar. The Tuesday before, for instance, she'll set the table with linens and platters. On Wednesday, she'll buy the food and drink, and on Thursday, she'll prepare it. "There's always last-minute stuff," says Barnett, "so I might as well do as much as I can ahead."

A supply checklist might include:

- linens
- glasses
- small plates
- candles
- matches
- ice
- flowers
- pitchers
- trays and platters
- food and drink
- garnishes

A job list might include:

- clean the house
- provide coat-hanging space
- clear the driveway and walkway
- move the car
- turn off the sprinklers
- make sure the house number is visible
- tie a balloon, banner, or bouquet to the front door or mailbox

THE WELCOME

- Review the guest list to avoid blanking out on names. In the fluster of the moment, we can forget the names of people we've known for years.
- Assign a topic to a name. Social graces didn't come naturally to Richard Nixon, so he'd study the White House guest list for at least a half hour before each event so he could say something like "I'm so glad to see you again. I remember we met years ago at a campaign rally." "It was not because of any gift," he said later in life, "I worked at it. People were my business."
- Provide a big welcome at the door. Insecurity melts with a warm hug or two-handed handshake.
- Have a coatrack near the door so guests don't have to stand awkwardly while the greeter runs down the hall with the wraps. An old-fashioned bentwood rack is a space-savvy solution to a bulging closet.
- Designate a spot for purses. One host I know neatly corrals her guests' bags on a long wooden bench in the front entry. Boots are parked on a mat under the bench in bad weather.
- Handle gifts discreetly. "Look what Betty brought me!" makes the empty-handed *feel* empty-handed.
- Offer new arrivals drinks from a tray. It's a welcome gesture that also reduces the crush at the bar.
- Once a few guests have arrived, position a partner at the door so you're free to carry out introductions and make everyone feel like a VIP. "During the first hour of the party," wrote TV journalist Barbara Walters, "you are what it takes to make the person glad he came."
- Keep everything on a first-name basis. It's hard for host and guest alike to remember a litany of names.
- Cruise and schmooze. Literary agent Sandra Dijkstra has a knack for making everyone feel like the guest of honor at her soirees, where she flits from group to group making introductions, and massaging egos. "Bob you must meet Amy," Sandra bubbles. "She has just finished the most delicious book on backpacking through Eastern Europe." "Amy, Bob is a dynamite publicist who lived in Czechoslovakia." Dijkstra makes it a point to know and share something about everyone she invites.
- Focus on making people comfortable, rather than trying to impress them. Thirty to 40 percent of the population possess some degree of shyness, reports a Stanford University study. The best way to quell our own insecurities is to alleviate our guests'.

HELP

- Consider co-hosting with a friend to share the responsibilities and the glory.
- Send anyone in the household who's too young to be certifiably helpful off to the sitters. Send anyone too ornery off to the movies.
- If it's a big to-do, and there's no caterer, hire a student or favorite waiter from a local restaurant to pass drinks and hors d'oeuvres, and to keep the table presentable. When the host takes on too many duties, the party suffers.
- Ask helpers to arrive at least an hour before partytime, so they're familiar with the layout and their duties.
- Write a task description for each of the help so they're steadily occupied but not totally frenzied.
- Set the dress code. A student one host hired wore a flowered sundress at the interview, but showed up for a pre-opera party in ripped jeans, halter, and high-tops, saying she was "dressed for action."

DRINKS

Once upon a time, a good host was expected to keep a fully stocked bar and hold a degree in mixology. With today's trend toward lighter fare and away from complicated concoctions of ice and spice, many guests prefer simpler drinks like wine, beer, and bottled waters.

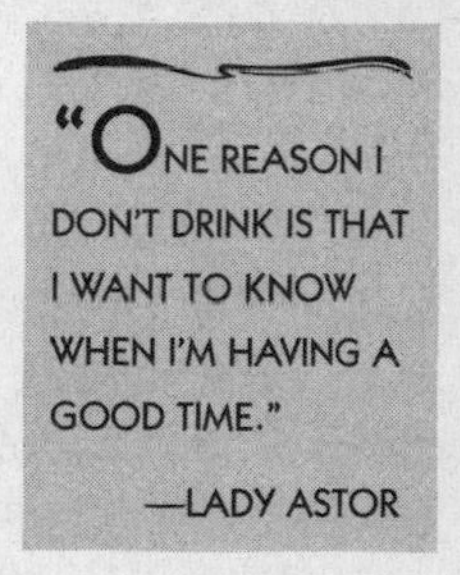

"ONE REASON I DON'T DRINK IS THAT I WANT TO KNOW WHEN I'M HAVING A GOOD TIME."
—LADY ASTOR

- If you like variety, consider a "white bar." Champagne, white wine, vodka, gin, vermouth, club soda, tonic, mineral water, and ginger ale accommodate a wide range of tastes, and if anything dribbles, it won't stain the goods.
- Set up at least one tray of filled glasses before guests arrive.
- Line drink trays with paper doilies for a finished look and to give glasses stability.
- Cover the bar space with a floor-length cloth so there's plenty of hiding space for the reserves and empties.
- Tie a cotton napkin or bandanna around the handle of a pitcher of drinks. It adds color and style, and makes a sweaty handle easier to grip.
- Keep a large tray at the bar for runs to the kitchen.
- Position the bar well away from the food and seating areas to avoid congestion.

- Keep extra bottles and cans cold in an ice-filled bathtub, washing machine, or child's wading pool.
- Avoid cheesy plastic glasses, and rent the real thing. Renting glassware for a large affair doesn't cost much more than buying plastic, and is environmentally sound. It also avoids post-party washing and broken-glass regrets.
  - People mislay drinks easily, so rent three glasses for every guest expected.
  - Figure at least three drinks and one pound of ice per person for a two-hour party. A standard bottle of wine pours about five drinks, depending on the glass size and the skill of the server.
  - Always have more drink than you think you need. Buy it from a source that takes back unopened bottles.

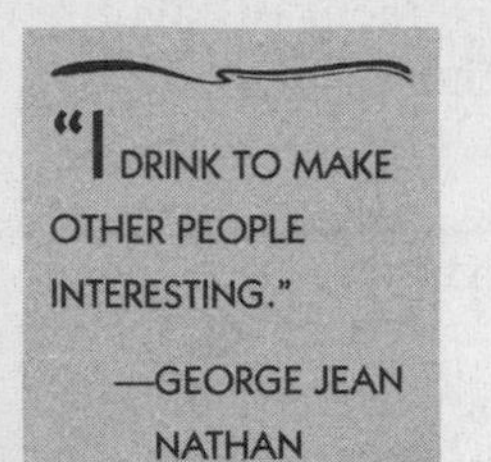

"I DRINK TO MAKE OTHER PEOPLE INTERESTING."
—GEORGE JEAN NATHAN

- Drink the opened wine the next day, or use it throughout the week as a marinade or to enhance the flavor of soups, stews, and sauces.
- If it's a big catered event, look into hiring a freelance bartender. A freelancer is almost always cheaper than catering help. Just make sure to check out his or her references.

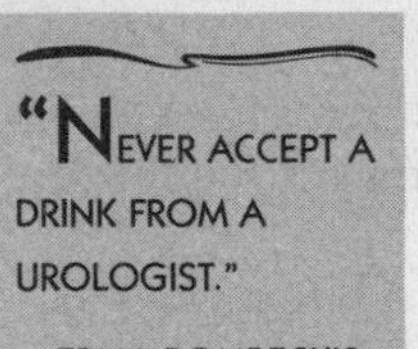

"NEVER ACCEPT A DRINK FROM A UROLOGIST."
—ERMA BOMBECK'S FATHER

LOWER THE RISK OF OVERINDULGENCE

- Offer an assortment of nonalcoholic beer and wine, and sparkling apple juice. Or make a pitcher of something festive and easy like virgin piña coladas. Upscale watering holes from San Francisco to Boston are offering fruit-based "mocktails" to an appreciative crowd.
- Give nonalcoholic drinks prominence by embellishing them with fruit or flower garnishes. Just don't get too carried away with looped straws, eye-poking parasols, and flaming pineapples.
- Make wine spritzers by mixing white wine with equal amounts of carbonated water, or mimosas with equal parts orange juice and champagne.
- Provide plenty of alcohol-absorbing food.
- Send a drunk home with a sober friend or keep the number of the local cab company close by.

SOBERING THOUGHTS

There was a time when a party wasn't a party unless most of the guests got drunk or close to it. Today, with health concerns and a crackdown on driving laws, heavy drinking is no longer safe or even fashionable. However, since there's always the possibility of overindulgence, it's good to keep the following in mind:

- *Nearly half of all driving accidents involve alcohol.*
- *Someone dies in an alcohol-related accident every twenty-five minutes.*
- *It only takes a 12-ounce beer, a 4-ounce glass of wine, or a 1¼-ounce shot of 80-proof liquor in one hour for a 129-pound person to risk a DUI arrest.*
- *The host is responsible, in many states, if a guest kills someone in a car accident.*

THE FOOD

Cocktail fare is more than a belly filler. It provides conversational material as well as an excuse to circulate.

- Make it interesting by contrasting color, taste, and texture: creamy cheeses, crisp breads, and brilliantly colored vegetables. We taste with our eyes before we taste with our tongues.
- Line platters with curly endive, grape leaves, Swiss chard, and other interesting greens for a pretty base and to absorb oil.
- Brighten a platter with a single nonpoisonous flower like a red hibiscus, a yellow rose, or a bright geranium.
- Avoid oozing, sticky, and greasy hors d'oeuvres that threaten furnishings, wardrobes, and dignity.

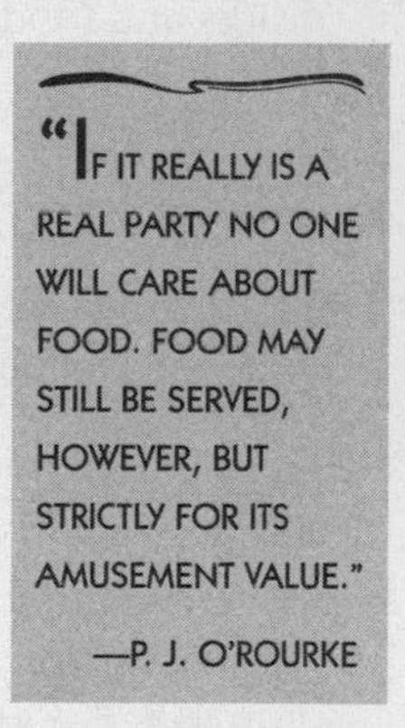

"IF IT REALLY IS A REAL PARTY NO ONE WILL CARE ABOUT FOOD. FOOD MAY STILL BE SERVED, HOWEVER, BUT STRICTLY FOR ITS AMUSEMENT VALUE."
—P. J. O'ROURKE

- Stick to neat "one-biters" on circulating trays. Dips and spreads are best left on the table.
- Dodge potential projectiles. I once bit into a cherry tomato that squirted seeds into the face of someone I was trying to impress. I achieved my goal.
- Arrange each hors d'oeuvre on its own plate so it's quickly identified without interrupting a conversation.

- Serve one lavish item like chilled jumbo shrimp or domestic caviar, and economize on other platters of seasonable vegetables, fruits, and interesting spreads.
- Avoid labor-intensive hors d'oeuvres. Let Mother Nature do the work by serving oysters on the half shell, whole roasted nuts, generous bricks of cheese, and big bunches of seedless grapes. Food should never look as if it's been handled too much.
- Stick mainly with foods best served cold or at room temperature. Plan no more than one dish that needs last-minute cooking or heating.
- Remove cheese from the refrigerator about one hour ahead, so it warms to its peak flavor and consistency.
- Avoid using toothpicks, skewers, and other nonedible implements. Guests never know how to dispose of them, so the devices end up cluttering tables and impaling bottoms.
- Plan on about five bites per person, but always have more than you think you'll need on hand. Leftovers are good eaten the next day, made into soup, frozen, or sent home with departing guests.
- Figure using about five cocktail napkins per person to be used with drinks and food. A party for twenty needs at least one hundred cocktail napkins.

> "YOU PUT YOUR LEFT INDEX FINGER ON YOUR EYE AND YOUR RIGHT INDEX FINGER ON THE CAMEMBERT . . . IF THEY SORT OF FEEL THE SAME, THE CHEESE IS READY."
>
> —M. TATTINGER

THE PARTY BATHROOM

The bathroom gets a workout at a cocktail party, so it's important to keep it well stocked and in good condition.

- Hang an identifying sign on the door so no one has to play traffic director all night. One of my favorite restaurants simply says "Yes" on the restroom door.
- Keep a big box of tissues on the counter, and stock a cabinet with aspirin, Band-Aids, and tampons.
- Provide a dispenser of paper cups. No one wants to gargle with the family glass.
- Place a big basket of toilet paper within sight. Running out can have dire consequences.
- Keep a pump dispenser of soap by the sink. Bar soaps get germy and slimy.

- Hang a roll of paper towels. Few want to sully those cute little guest towels or wipe their hands on the family terry.
- Have a toilet brush unobtrusively available.
- Light a fat, scented candle for ambience and air freshening.
- Assign a helper to check the condition of the room every so often. Sinks and mirrors get messy with a crowd, and forgetful types neglect to flush.
- Keep a container of premoistened towels under the sink for quick cleanups.

GIVE 'EM SOMETHING TO TALK ABOUT

The Quilted Northern Bathroom Tissue Report found 39 percent of adults admit to snooping in other people's medicine cabinets. The same report asked those queried, "What is the most unusual thing you've seen there?" Among the responses:

- *a rattrap*
- *an ice pick*
- *a hairpiece*
- *a can of beer*
- *a glass eye*
- *a bagel*

CALMING PARTY NERVES

Almost everyone feels edgy just before guests arrive. We worry if people will show, if the place looks decent and the food is acceptable. This also seems to be the time when the kids act up, our partners get cranky, and all hell breaks loose.

There are those who have things so under control they can schedule a leisurely bath and a catnap to soothe frayed nerves. But for the rest of us, no matter how much we plan, we're likely to be combing cocktail sauce out of our hair, snapping at housemates, and trying to clean up the chaos in the kitchen as guests arrive.

We just have to remember that pre-party tension is a given and we can manage well if we:

- Keep things simple. Elaborate preparations make for elaborate jitters.

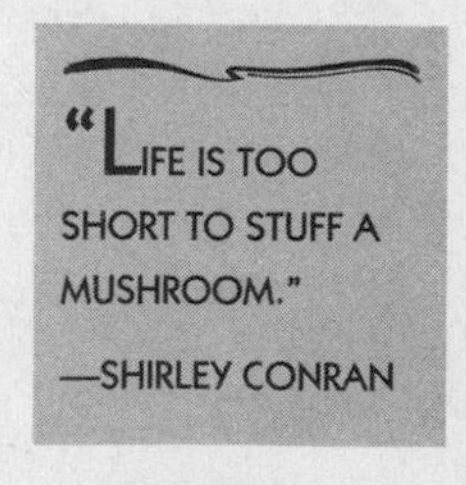

"LIFE IS TOO SHORT TO STUFF A MUSHROOM."
—SHIRLEY CONRAN

- Turn nervousness into enthusiasm. Seasoned public speakers use this trick to ignite their talks with energy. A host can spark a party much the same way.
- Give every one in the household a job. A busy person has no time for tantrums.
- Request emotional help from normally nervous housemates. "I get so flustered before a party, would you help keep me calm?" Appointed bomb defusers seldom set off explosives.
- Eat a little something. A level head needs a full stomach.
- Ask a good friend to arrive a little early to lend a hand, share a drink, and alleviate no-show worries.
- Don't feel the ball can't roll along without you. Introduce and involve guests, then relax and let it happen.

CHAPTER 9

*B*ODACIOUS BUFFETS

A buffet is a great way to serve scads of people without the fuss and formality of a conventional sit-down dinner. The setup is similar to a cocktail party, but since the fare is more substantial, finding easy and graceful ways to serve it, balance it, and consume it are important.

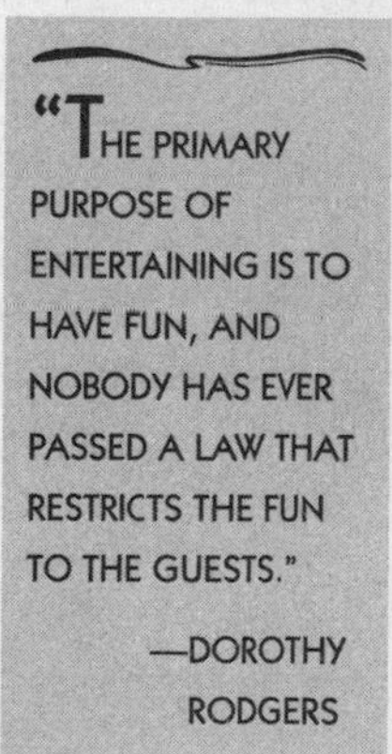

"THE PRIMARY PURPOSE OF ENTERTAINING IS TO HAVE FUN, AND NOBODY HAS EVER PASSED A LAW THAT RESTRICTS THE FUN TO THE GUESTS."

—DOROTHY RODGERS

WHAT TO SERVE

- Fit the food with the hour. Tea sandwiches, tiny canapés, and pastries arc fine before 5:00 and after 9:00 P.M., but anything in between should be more substantial. I once arrived famished at a 7:00 P.M. party to face a buffet table laden with nothing but pies, cakes, and other sweets. Chocolate mousse and strawberry crepes make a tasty dinner only if guests are willing to risk the night in the bathroom and the morning on the Stairmaster.
- Rely on foods that are appetizing at room temperature, so there's no worry about keeping dishes hot, cold, or running out of oven or cooling space. An Italian buffet of bruschetta, marinated vegetables, pasta salad, fresh fruit, and lemon tarts, for example, means there are no electrical cords, leaping flames, or melting puddles of ice to deal with.

- Don't serve anything that requires last-minute attention. Omelets, perfectly seared steaks, and flaming desserts can make the mellowest host a harried one.
- Balance the exotic with thc familiar. Ostrich meat, haggis, and Rocky Mountain oysters may be fun for some, but less adventurous types appreciate more familiar fare.

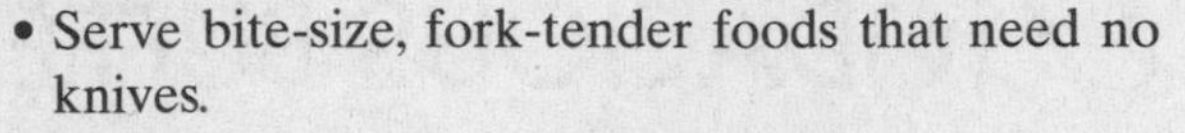

- Serve bite-size, fork-tender foods that need no knives.
- Replace rolls and loaves that need buttering and slicing with crispy breadsticks.
- Offer substantial quantities of a few things rather than lots of little plates of this and that.

"LIFE IS A BANQUET AND MOST SUCKERS ARE STARVING TO DEATH."

—MAE WEST

HOW TO SERVE IT

- Keep hot food hot in a chafing dish or Crockpot, and cold food cold on a mound of ice. Chilled shrimp, for example, stays cold and looks impressive when its container is nestled in a larger crystal or silver bowl of ice.
- Alleviate mystery and add a little pizzazz by labeling foods. Accomplished cook and host Deidre Little makes beautifully scripted folding place cards with her computer and places them in front of various dishes on her buffet table. "I cook Creole-style," says Little, "so I need to identify certain dishes for guests who may not be able to recognize them."
- Balance the complex with the simple. Hot and spicy meatballs are better over a plain bed of pasta than a mound of Spanish rice. A rich beef bourguignon teams well with a simple green salad.
- Get creative with containers: a hollowed-out watermelon for fruit salad, a pumpkin for cooked vegetables, and seashells for seafood sauces.
- Contrast dark foods on light platters, and pale foods on deep-colored platters.
- Serve in abundance. When there are at least three major food groups, caterers figure on approximately a quarter pound of boneless meat, fish, or poultry per person (or three-quarters pound bone-in). They also provide at least a quarter pound of vegetables, and about one-third pound rice, potatoes, or pasta per person.

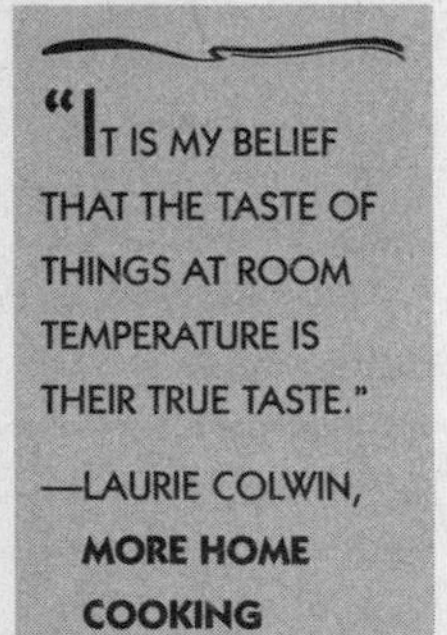

"IT IS MY BELIEF THAT THE TASTE OF THINGS AT ROOM TEMPERATURE IS THEIR TRUE TASTE."
—LAURIE COLWIN,
MORE HOME COOKING

- Pre-slice meats and casseroles. It's hard to juggle a plate while trying to tear at a turkey or divide a pan of lasagna.
- Allow roasts to settle a bit, after they come out of the oven, for easier carving.
- Identify a variety of sandwiches by cutting them in code. One picnic

A FRENCH-AMERICAN-BRITISH BUFFET

What does a British-born U.S. ambassador to France serve on the Fourth of July? Strictly finger foods. According to food writer Maureen Clancy, Ambassador Pamela Harriman no longer wastes her staff's time rummaging for lost tableware under two acres of shrubbery at the embassy picnics in Paris. So "napkins only" is now the rule.

With a mountain of paper napkins at the ready, diplomats, dignitaries, and expatriates dined on the following at the 1995 Independence Day fete, orchestrated by Le Cordon Bleu:

Escargots in Puff Pastry Shells
Roquefort Walnut Tarts
Wisconsin Cheese
Coleslaw in Pastry Cups
Alaska Salmon
Fried Chicken Legs and Wings
Miniature Maryland Crab Cakes
New England Lobster Rolls
Lightly Sauced Baby Back Ribs
Baked Virginia Ham
Corn Bread
Parker House Rolls
Southern Biscuits
California Grapes
Tiny Ice Cream Cones

TINY TARTS OF:
New York Cheesecake
Pecan Pie
Apple Pie
Banana Cream Pie
Key Lime Pie

specialist diagonally cuts sandwiches spread with mustard, those made with mayonnaise get a square cut, and those cut into rectangles have the works.

- Consider serving hand-held desserts like tiny tarts, brownies, and giant chocolate chip cookies. Plates aren't necessary, guests don't have to leave their seats, and there's no last-minute space jam in the kitchen.
- If pies or cakes are part of the fare, set them up on a separate table and cut them ahead of time so they handle easily and stay tidy.
- Remove the first piece and place it on a plate. No one wants to deflower a virgin pie or a towering torte.
- Consider dessert as a centerpiece. A cake or pie on an elevated platter makes a delectable substitute for flowers at each table.

CONTROL COSTS

- Serve generous portions of vegetables, fruits, and grains, and use meat, fish, and other budget busters as condiments.
- Use smaller serving utensils. Michel Malecot, owner of the French Gourmet, a catering service and restaurant in La Jolla, California, uses silver-plated iced-tea spoons in most dishes. "Everyone likes a taste of everything on a buffet table, and these are the perfect size," he says. "Plus, their long handles prevent them from getting lost in the sauce."
- Use the old restaurant trick of placing the most expensive item, a dish of smoked salmon, for instance, at the end of the table, so plates fill with the starches and vegetables first.
- Divide foods into individual servings. Otherwise, guests load up with more than they can chow down. Popovers, pastry shells, hollow vegetables, and ramekins are pretty vehicles for portion control.
- Provide your own liquor. Most caterers substantially mark up wine and other spirits.

GIVE IT FLAIR

- Go for a bountiful look with baskets brimming with bread, greens piled high in a crystal bowl, huge clusters of grapes cascading from a tiered stand. Food is more enticing when it seems to burst and spill from its container, rather than looking lost on an enormous platter.
- Add the visual excitement of height. Food stylists pile fruits on epergnes, stuff long breadsticks into flowerpots, elevate quiches and alads on overturned bowls, and decorate with tall candles and vertial flower arrangements. "Flat buffets are visually boring," says

WHEN YOU WANT TO BE CATERED TO

Having a good caterer means we relinquish the fuss and enjoy the fun of the party. But "good" is the operative word. Finding and enjoying the best takes a little spadework.

1. *Ask friends and co-workers. Like tracking down a good doctor, dentist, or hair stylist, word of mouth from those we trust is always the best bet.*
2. *Check with florists, party rental suppliers, and bridal shops. They've seen the good, the bad, and the ugly in catering.*
3. *Keep your eyes open. Any time you attend a successful event with a well-served spread, request the caterer's business card.*
4. *Peruse the Yellow Pages. A well-designed ad is a good indication of style and taste. An ad also tells the extent of services offered, including: furnishings, tableware, flowers, and entertainment. One ad in my local Yellow Pages emphasizes theme parties: Out of Africa, Arabian Nights, and Medieval Feasts. Another features corporate events and weddings. Still another states they're "radio dispatched and specialists to construction sites," which may not be the best bet for that little black tie affair.*
5. *Look for a track record. A new caterer may be cheap and snazzy, but could be a fly-by-night. When it comes to our money, stomachs, and peace of mind, it's best to deal with the tried and true.*
6. *Tell the candidates what you have in mind and what you need in the way of goods and services, then ask for a cost-per-person estimate.*
7. *After narrowing the selection to two or three candidates, request references. Ask the references about the food quality, quantity, and presentation, as well as the punctuality, efficiency, and attitude of the staff. Also ask whether they would hire the caterer again.*
8. *Request a copy of the license and health certificate with the written proposal. "Without a licensee you risk safety and tax legality," says Michael Roman of the International Food Service Executives. "If a worker falls and is not covered by workmen's compensation, or a guest gets sick from improper food handling, a simple dinner party can turn into a nightmare of legal problems."*
9. *Get everything, including the menu and the number of servers, in writing.*
10. *Relax. Once you've found the right caterer, the chances of having a good time at your own party are practically guaranteed.*

Chicago food stylist Kelly Tokay. "You want foods to build gradually, keeping taller items at the back for drama, and to minimize toppling from reaching hands."

- Use empty boxes, sturdy bowls, overturned flowerpots, to elevate foods. Cover them with matching or coordinating cloths.
- Stage a dress rehearsal. Caterer and chef Michel Malecot arranges empty serving platters and bowls on the table to make sure everything fits. "It's always a good idea to visualize where everything goes and how it's going to work," he says.
- Instead of flowers, decorate the serving table with whole fruits, vegetables, and nuts. They may or may not be eaten during the party, but the effect is lavish.
- Hide utilitarian baking pans in napkin-lined baskets, or in nests of ferns and/or other foliage.
- Line or decorate platters, plates, and bowls with sturdy, wiltproof garnishes like kale, parsley, radicchio, rosemary, Belgian endive, pepper slices, lemon and lime wedges. "A garnish that droops and dries out before the coffee is served is hardly a garnish," says one food stylist.
- Tableware doesn't have to match. Houston caterer Jamie Sanders uses a hodgepodge of pottery, china, copper, and pewter on many of her buffet tables. "I find a mix is often more interesting than a perfectly matched set," she says. "You just have to keep the mood and the food in mind."
- Keep a meat-carving operation presentable with a little camouflage. Michel Malecot places roasts on a carving board just above greenery-covered trays so juices drip into a cover of leaves. "It's important the table looks as pretty for guests at the end of the buffet line," he says, "as it does for those at the beginning."

THE SERVING TABLE

- A long, rectangular top is good for a buffet, whether it's a sideboard, desk, or dining table. Improvise with three card tables or a hollow-core door propped up on a couple of sawhorses. Drape it to the floor with fabric.
- Set up a separate table for dessert and coffee. If space near the main course is tight, serve the last course in another room. Interior designer Marie Kinnaman frequently sets up a dessert buffet on the desk in her den, while artist Denise Hunter serves hers on a gold-lamé-draped dresser in her bedroom. "It's the biggest room in my apartment," says Hunter. "If it didn't seem so weird, I'd serve the whole meal there." Early twentieth-century style setter Elsie de

Wolfe had no qualms about perceived weirdness. She often served dessert in her favorite Paris setting: her enormous silver-and-white bathroom.

- If the table is too small for the dessert service, arrange plates and silver on an auxiliary table, cart, or sideboard.
- Set out a colorful variety of napkins to stretch the linen supply. Solid-color napkins complement coordinating prints, and a primary, pastel, or jewel-toned assortment makes any table festive.
- Make the fork and napkin easier to handle by tying them together with a colorful satin streamer or a short twist of wired ribbon. Stack them in a narrow basket so they take up little room.
- Fill a child's red wagon or a new wheelbarrow with iced-down soft drinks, beer, and wine. Both look festive and can be wheeled where needed.

KEEP 'EM MOVIN'

- Ask a friend, ahead of time, to start the buffet line. No one ever wants to be the first to dig in.
- Place plates at the beginning of the buffet, and napkins and forks at the end, so one hand stays free to scoop and serve.
- Give guests only one plate to carry, since extras require the balance of a juggler. Drinks, rolls, and other goodies are best when they're placed on dining tables, or served from trays once guests settle.
- Arrange the food logically: mustard next to the ham, parmesan next to the pasta, whipped cream next to the bread pudding.
- If the group is larger than fourteen, place duplicate platters on either side of the table so two lines can serve themselves at once. Divide the two sides with a long arrangement of flowers, fruits, or vegetables, and make sure there are no trailing electrical cords.
- If the group is larger than twenty, arrange separate serving tables around the room or garden: one for the salad, one for the main course, and one for the dessert. Separate food stations alleviate traffic jams and give guests more opportunity to mingle.

SEATING

- Forget place cards with a large group, and let seating happen naturally. There's little worse for eager eaters than waiting at an empty table while assigned tablemates are still at the bar or the back of the food line.
- If there's no room for standard table and chair arrangements, pro-

vide a perch for every plate. Coffee tables, raised hearths, benches, and even stairs can support plates and glasses.

"I DON'T CARE
WHERE I SIT AS
LONG AS I GET FED."
—CALVIN TRILLIN

- Make sure less agile guests have a comfortable place to sit. Stairs and floor cushions arc fine for the young, but old bones need more support.
- Use extensions or plywood tops to accommodate everyone at one table, if numbers allow. Otherwise, there's always the suspicion that a better time is happening at the other table.
- If more than one table *is* necessary, split yourself and your partner between them. If there are more tables than hosts, assign a "parent" to make sure introductions are made, seconds are offered, and dishes are cleared.
- Seating guests is always best, but if that's not possible, look into "belly bars" or "kiosk tables" at rental stores. These are tall twenty-four-inch, thirty-inch, and thirty-six-inch round tables that accommodate a crowd of standing diners. A thirty-inch table, for example, easily serves seven standing guests. If guests were to be seated around it, it could only accommodate four of them.

THIS 'N' THAT

- Conserve refrigerator space by covering garnishes with damp towels, and stacking them on the counter.
- Keep an eye peeled for messy and nearly depleted platters. Have ready-to-go reserves in the wings, or refill dishes in the kitchen, behind closed doors.

HOSPITALITY GONE HAYWIRE

The problem with buffets is that they're so easy to serve, many hosts have been known to invite more guests than they can realistically handle. Take the case of Andrew Jackson, our gregarious, though rough-hewn president who opened the White House to all at his 1829 inauguration. The mob of thousands not only wolfed down the spread in minutes, they broke the china, overturned the furniture, and spit gobs of tobacco on the rugs. The party got so wild, Jackson had to flee through a window to a nearby hotel. The guests were induced to leave the mansion only after the staff set vats of punch out on the lawns.

- Always have plenty of backups in case there's a hungry horde or the party runs late: canned pâtés, olives, cheese, nuts, and frozen something-or-others are always good bets.
- The possibility of stains increases when people serve themselves from a buffet, so top pale carpeting around the table with an easily cleaned rug.
- Use nonbreakable tableware around a pool. A broken glass or plate in the water means a costly draining.

"YOU KNOW YOU'RE GETTING OLDER WHEN YOU TELL YOUR BEST FRIEND YOU'RE HAVING AN AFFAIR AND SHE ASKS YOU WHO'S CATERING IT."

—UNKNOWN

CHAPTER 10

SECRETS OF SUCCESSFUL SIT-DOWN DINNERS

It's not surprising that the traditional dinner party has become an endangered species, considering the work involved. Personally, I prefer hosting the potluck kind, but there are times when we have to honor tradition, and asking guests to "BYOF" just won't cut it.

So here are some thoughts on making the event easier to choreograph, whether it's a family-reunion barbecue or a black-tie bash.

> "IT'S NOT SO MUCH WHAT'S ON THE TABLE THAT MATTERS AS WHAT'S ON THE CHAIRS."
>
> —W. S. GILBERT

THE GUESTS

- Limit the number. A party of six to eight is not only manageable, it can carry on a general conversation as well. Any more and things get complicated.
- Make sure that most of the guests are either acquainted or have a common thread. It takes a highly skilled host to pull together a table of strangers.
- Mix listeners with talkers, with the emphasis on the latter. Extroverts add life to the table.
- Never feel you have to have an equal balance of men and women. A few extra of one sex can make the evening more interesting for the other.

THE CHURCHILL WIT

British statesman, soldier, and Nobel Prize–winner Winston Churchill was a popular dinner guest throughout his long life, but not always with the desired results for the host.

On a trip to the United States in the 1940s, he was the guest of a pompous Baltimore socialite. When seconds of chicken were offered, Churchill asked, "May I have some breast?"

The host corrected, "Mr. Churchill, we do not *refer to parts of the body in this country. We ask for white meat or dark meat."*

The next day, the host received a large corsage from her guest of honor. The enclosed card read, "I would be most obliged if you would pin this flower on your white meat."

THE PLAN

- Call the key guests first to see if they're available or if the date or time needs adjusting. Fill in with supporting players.
- Spread the preparation over a few days. The more you work before the party, the less you'll have to labor *during* it.
- Toss the green cottage cheese, the gray corn, and the half-eaten taco out of the fridge to make way for the party food.
- Shop for groceries, marinate meats, slice vegetables, and measure the rice or pasta a couple of days ahead.
- Organize the refrigerator so that separate shelves hold separate courses. Store the ice water and other drinks on the door.
- Set the table down to the candles and matches at least a day ahead, checking to see if platters fit and linens need attention.
- Lay the sideboard with dessert plates and the coffee service for a smooth transition between courses.
- Select the radio station or stack the CDs. Low-volume instrumentals are good choices since they're soothing and nonintrusive to table talk.
- Hang the menu and a checklist on the fridge to ensure there are no forgotten side dishes in the fridge or lost buns in the oven.
- Use a kitchen timer as a reminder to stir a sauce, remove a pot, or turn off a burner.
- Empty the sink, dishwasher, and garbage can just before guests arrive so after-dinner cleanup is easier.

KIDS AND PETS

- Send young children off to the sitter's. I once made the mistake of setting up the family room with toys, videos, and every other possible diversion, and brought in a sitter for our own and our guests' children. It was a disaster. If the kids weren't wailing, or clobbering each other, they were escaping into the dining room with "He hit me!" "She smells funny!" "I want to go home!"
- Put older children to work, taking coats and putting in a polite appearance. Then vamoose. Children and dinner parties mix like oil and water.
- Whatever you do, don't have kids perform. We once attended a dinner party where guests had to watch the offspring struggle through long and painful renditions of Chopin and Mozart on the piano and violin. It was dismal and embarrassing.
- Feed, comfort, and confine pets before the party. Your guests may be animal lovers, but many people are allergic to cats, and dogs have the most embarrassing way of checking people out.

DRINKS AND APPEKILLERS

- Hors d'ouevres are not only unnecessary before dinner, they're also unnatural. Do we normally sit and snack before a meal? Cheese, dips, and kabobs dull the appetite and interfere with the pleasant buzz of the wine. If it's necessary to stave off hunger pangs, serve something light like a fan of precut vegetable sticks.
- Stick to dry white wines before dinner.
- Offer something special to nondrinkers like sparkling apple juice served in a wineglass.
- Have drinks poured and ready to pass. "It's flattering to guests to look as if we're anticipating them," says former restaurateur Linda Ellis, who always has wine chilled, uncorked, and waiting for her first arrivals.
- Limit the cocktail hour to just that. Any longer makes for restless and sometimes boozy guests. Famed early twentieth-century host Elsie de Wolfe always specified and stuck to "Cocktails at 7:45. Dinner at 8:00." A bit extreme, but even though she entertained a notoriously tardy set, her guests knew she meant business, and invariably arrived at the appointed time.
- If the weather cooperates, consider having drinks on the deck or in the garden before dinner in the dining room. The change of scenery adds another dimension to the evening.

SEATING

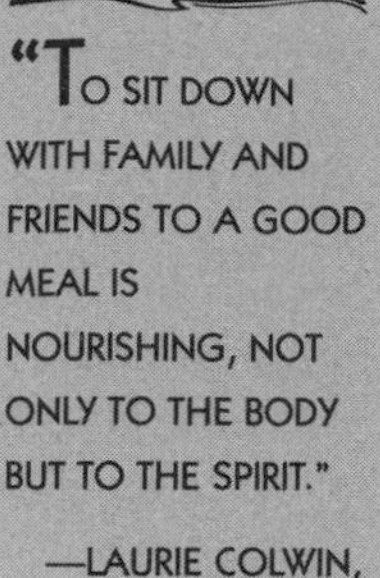

"TO SIT DOWN
WITH FAMILY AND
FRIENDS TO A GOOD
MEAL IS
NOURISHING, NOT
ONLY TO THE BODY
BUT TO THE SPIRIT."
—LAURIE COLWIN,
MORE HOME
COOKING

- Remove the chairs of no-shows. No one wants to sit next to an empty seat.
- Use place cards. They take the last-minute uncertainty out of who sits where, and show forethought and care. A card can be anything from a child-made masterpiece to a maple leaf inscribed in golden ink.
- If using a traditional folding place card, write guests' names on both sides for the benefit of those sitting across the table.
- It's not necessary for the host to sit at the head or the foot of the table. Sit closest to the kitchen in order to exit unobtrusively.

TABLE TALK

- Pair talkers with listeners, and keep spouses, best buddies, and conversation hoggers at opposite ends of the table.
- Get 'em gabbin'. We don't have to be profound or witty to get the conversational ball rolling. Just toss up questions about the latest movie, play, or restaurant, and see where they fall.
- Don't be afraid of so-called taboo subjects. Sex, religion, and politics make for fascinating conversation as long as it doesn't get personal, and guests are open-minded, big-picture people.
- Keep it upbeat. Dinner is not the time to be discussing the latest disease, disaster, or diaper. If the conversation gets gloomy or tedious, guide it to a higher level.
- Listen intently. As hosts, we need to subdue our own egos and concentrate on making our guests shine. When we find ourselves in anything more than a three-minute monologue, we're taking advantage of our roles.
- Prompt the introvert. "If you explore beneath the shyness or party chit-chat, you can sometimes turn a dull exchange into an intriguing one," wrote Joyce Carol Oates. "I've found this to be particularly true in the case of professors or intellectuals who are full of fascinating information, but need encouragement before they'll divulge it."
- Spread the wealth. My friend and neighbor Dorothy Mann asks the men at her parties to move two seats down when dessert is served. "No one should be stuck with the same two conversational partners all evening," says Dorothy. "This mixes things up nicely."

THE QUIET CONVERSATIONALIST

Legend has it that when the always reticent Calvin Coolidge was seated next to a vivacious woman at a dinner party, she turned to him and said with a smile, "Someone bet me ten dollars that you wouldn't say three words to me all evening." To which Coolidge dryly replied, "You lose."

WHAT TO SERVE

- Plan on easily made dishes that need no last-minute fussing. Dinner doesn't have to be a culinary extravaganza. Simple food served with a little flair is always well received.
- Collect recipes for do-ahead dishes. The flavors of coq au vin, lasagna, curry, and most sauced dishes develop fully after a day or two in the fridge. "The secret of stress-free entertaining is to make as much ahead of time as possible," advises food writer Marcia Adams.
- Perfect the dishes you do well and don't be afraid of repeating them. No one will complain about a repeat performance of an exquisite boeuf bourguignon, duck satay, or lemon mousse.
- Don't serve unusual food unless you're sure your guests will love it. Organ meats, wild game, and raw fish may be adventurous, but the adventure could be at the expense of the guests. If you want to serve something exotic, offer a universal favorite like roast chicken as an alternative.
- Try out new recipes beforehand. Families make better guinea pigs than guests.
- Develop sources for quality prepared dishes to complement homemade specialties. Who made it isn't as important as who serves it. "If a prepared dish is good, take the credit," says one culinary cheater. "If not, you can always blame it on the source."
- Serve in-season vegetables that require minimal preparation. Sliced cucumbers and tomatoes, for instance, require no cooking, and little, if any, seasoning.
- Go for a balance of color, texture, and flavor with every meal: crunchy breadsticks complement a creamy soup, a simple green salad sets off a complex stew.
- Contrast temperatures: warm rolls with cold pasta salad, vanilla ice cream with hot fudge sauce.

- Save the corn on the cob, fried chicken, steamed artichokes, ribs, and tacos for picnics. Most people are self-conscious about hand-held food and greasy chins at a sit-down dinner.
- Serve rolls or breadsticks instead of having to slice a loaf of bread at the last minute.
- Share your recipes with anyone who asks. It's good karma.

THE ROMAN DINNER PARTY

Pity the poor host of old who was expected to throw a banquet at every dinner party. In Weird History 101, *writer John Richard Stevens recounts the following suggested menu from an ancient cookbook:*

APPETIZERS

jellyfish and eggs • sow's udders stuffed with salted sea urchins • patina of brains cooked with milk and eggs • boiled tree fungi with peppered fish-fat sauce • sea urchins with spices, honey, oil, and egg sauce

MAIN COURSE

roast parrot • turtle dove boiled in its feathers • ham boiled with figs and bay leaves, rubbed with honey and baked in pastry crust • fallow deer roasted with onion sauce, rue, Jericho dates, raisins and honey • dormice stuffed with pork and pine kernels • boiled ostrich with sea sauce • flamingo boiled with dates

DESSERT

hot African sweet wine cakes with honey • stoned dates stuffed with nuts and pine kernels, fried in honey • fricassee of roses with pastry

HOW TO SERVE IT

- Avoid jumping in and out of your seat by either eliminating the first course, or serving it in the living room.
- Place the salad on the table before seating the guests.
- Decide whether you want to arrange the meal on each plate or let guests serve themselves from the sideboard. Self-service is easier on the host, and guests can take as much or as little as they want. However, portion and appearance are better controlled in the kitchen, there are fewer platters to wash, and there's more space on the table for flowers and other flourishes.

"THE LESS FRAZZLED YOU ARE AS A COOK, THE MORE AVAILABLE AND RELAXED YOU'LL BE AS A HOST OR HOSTESS."
—MARTHA ROSE SHULMAN, COOKBOOK AUTHOR

- If you go the self-service route, use an oversized platter to hold the main course and several vegetables. Just make sure the platter isn't too large and heavy to pass.
- Encourage second helpings by putting a bit of food on your own plate when platters make the rounds.
- Offer seconds, but don't force-feed. Remarks like "You eat like a bird, Zelda, have some gravy" won't win anyone the host-of-the-year award.
- Unless you're a master carver, perform surgery behind closed doors. Many a roast has slid from platter to floor under the knife; a situation easily salvaged in the privacy of the kitchen, but impossible in front of a dining room audience. Some have turned this mishap into high drama, however. According to an account by Alexander Dumas, one nineteenth-century host had his servants stage dropping a rare 170-pound Caspian sturgeon in front of his guests. As they gasped in shock and disappointment, he ordered an even larger sturgeon immediately brought to the table.
- Don't fret if a dish isn't up to snuff. "Marvelous food never saved a bad evening," said Letitia Baldrige, "and a burned roast never ruined a good evening."

"THE COUNTESS WILL SIT ON YOUR LEFT HAND, AND THE DUCHESS WILL SIT ON YOUR RIGHT," SAID THE HOSTESS. "THEN HOW WILL I EAT?" ASKED GROUCHO MARX

DEALING WITH GLITCHES

- Set the tone. If you laugh about a mishap, whether it's an overflowing toilet, burned bread, or a malfunctioning freezer, your guests will laugh, too. However, when we become upset, we make everyone uncomfortable. With a cool head, a sense of humor, and a little ingenuity, most situations can be salvaged.

HELP

- Capitalize on a partner's barbecue prowess, and have him or her grill the main course and vegetables.

- Train family members to be sous chefs. Spouses, older children, and bribed roommates can set the table, clean and chop vegetables, and load the dishwasher.
- Write out instructions for helpers so no one gets rattled at the eleventh hour.
- Be ready with specific chores for helpful guests. They can fill the water glasses, set out food platters, light the candles, clear the plates, pour the coffee, and cut the cake without inflicting too much damage.

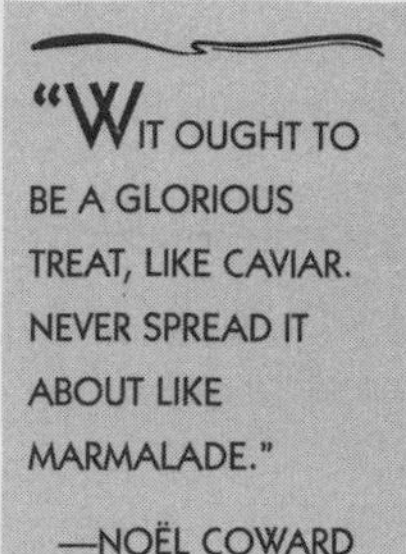

"WIT OUGHT TO
BE A GLORIOUS
TREAT, LIKE CAVIAR.
NEVER SPREAD IT
ABOUT LIKE
MARMALADE."
—NOËL COWARD

- Limit help to one or two guests between dinner and dessert to avoid clearing the table of diners.

WINE SIMPLIFIED

- Don't be intimidated. "It's just a bottle of fermented grape juice," says master of wine, International Wine Center director, and *Wine for Dummies* co-author Mary Ewing-Mulligan.
- Take the mystery out of food-and-wine combinations by color-coding them. Red wine generally goes best with red meats and dark sauces. White wine goes well with white-meat poultry, fish, and white sauces. Anything in between, like ham and duck, goes with blush wines.
- Ask a wine merchant, either at a specialty or grocery store, for advice about particular food pairings. Set a price range and shop early in the week, before he or she gets busy with other brain pickers.
- Patronize a merchant whose suggestions are always on the mark. Discounters may be cheaper, but good advice is worth it in the long run.

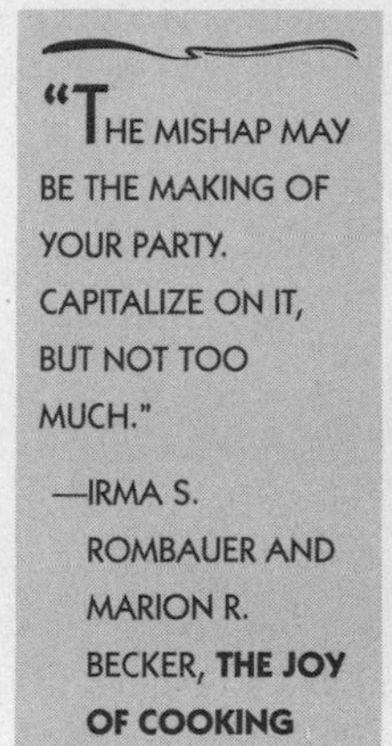

"THE MISHAP MAY
BE THE MAKING OF
YOUR PARTY.
CAPITALIZE ON IT,
BUT NOT TOO
MUCH."
—IRMA S.
ROMBAUER AND
MARION R.
BECKER, THE JOY
OF COOKING

- Keep it simple. *Entertaining Light* author Martha Rose Shulman says she usually serves only one wine that works with all courses throughout the meal.
- If you've taken the time to find the perfect wine, serve a gift bottle a guest brings *before* dinner, or tell the donor you'd like to save it for another special occasion.
- Figure at least two glasses of wine per person with dinner. A 750-milliliter bottle holds four to six servings, depending on the glass

size, so a dinner for eight requires at least four bottles of wine; more if courses are many and dinner is long.

- Fill a glass only two-thirds full for breathing and swirling room.

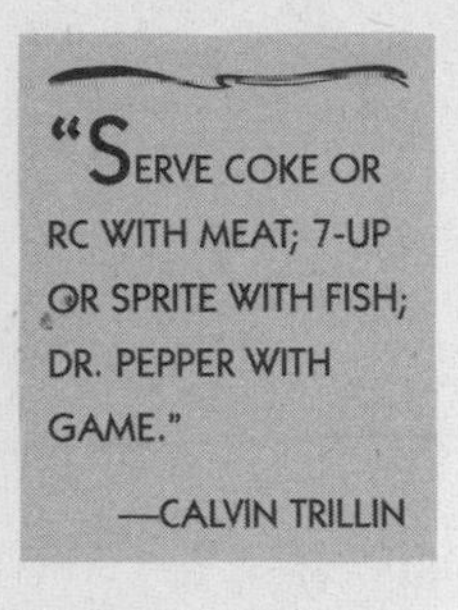

- Avoid drips and display flair by giving the bottle a slight turn of the wrist as you finish pouring.
- Serve white and blush wines cold, and red wine at room temperature.
- Thoroughly chill champagne. The warmer the bottle, the greater the chance the cork will ricochet off someone's noggin.
- Chill white wine no longer than a few hours before it's served. Too long in the fridge may affect the flavor.
- Uncork red wine an hour before dinner so its flavor fully develops.
- Keep water glasses filled so no one has to rely on alcohol to wet their whistle.

TOASTS

Toasting is an old custom that gives meaning to the occasion, connects guests, and gets the conversational ball rolling. The best toasts allude to the event, and are short, simple, and to the point: "To friendship." "To days of ease and nights of pleasure." "To our best friends, who know the worst about us but refuse to believe it."

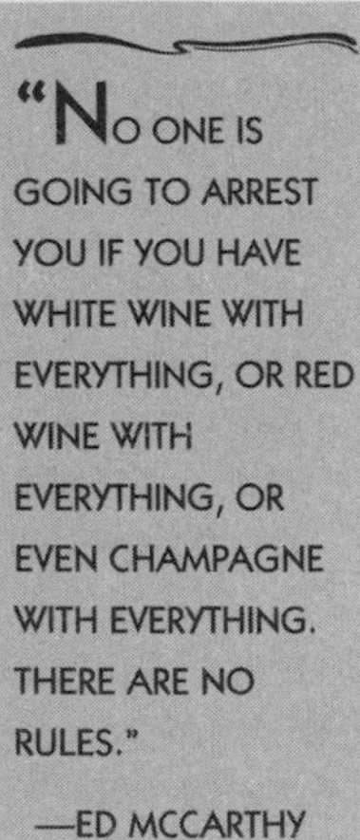

- To build up a toast repertoire, check out Paul Dickson's book *Toasts,* a collection of fifteen hundred zingers for every occasion. It's also full of quirky legends like "the original intention of the clink was to produce a bell like noise so as to banish the devil, who is repelled by bells."

THE FINALE

- Brew after-dinner coffee before guests arrive and keep it hot in a thermos. Coffee turns bitter when it sits on a burner. Pour it into a pretty pot just before serving.
- Serve dessert and coffee at the table if the party is going strong. Moving everyone to the living room changes the dynamics.

- Let nature take its course. When fatigue sets in and conversation peters out, move the party to the living room or patio.
- Clear the table, if you must, but save the dish-washing until later.
- If the vibes are good, offer after-dinner liqueurs, more coffee, and stoke the fire. If you're ready to call it a night, subtly dim the lights, close the bar, and shut down the kitchen.

"MAY THE ROOF ABOVE US NEVER FALL IN, AND MAY WE FRIENDS GATHERED BELOW NEVER FALL OUT."

—IRISH TOAST

CHAPTER 11

A GRAB BAG OF ENTERTAINING IDEAS FOR ALL AGES

SIMPLIFIED CELEBRATIONS

A party doesn't have to be a major event with a multitude of preparations. Inviting someone in for a drink before the movies, or everybody over for chili after the final soccer game, is a good way to strengthen the bonds of friendship. However, when you want to get a little more festive, but still keep the sweat factor to a minimum, consider the following excuses to party. Each has the recipe for success: focus, guest involvement, and ease of operation.

> "PARTYING IS SUCH SWEET SORROW."
>
> —ROBERT BYRNE

- New Year's Day. Have a few people over to watch the Rose Bowl game on the tube. Go for a hike if the weather permits. Serve soup, bread, and apple tarts for dinner.
- "Welcome to the Neighborhood." Invite longtime neighbors and friends to bring the names and numbers of service people, doctors, and favorite restaurants to share with the new neighbors. Make it a "drinks and hors d'oeuvres" or a "coffee and dessert" event.

- Valentine's Day. Get together for a fireside game of Pictionary or a romantic old movie like *Casablanca* or *Doctor Zhivago* on the VCR. Shape thawed pizza dough into heart shapes, provide bowls of sauce, cheese, and a smorgasbord of toppings. Divide guests into teams for a do-it-yourself "Most Creative Pizza Contest."
- "Stroke an Ego." I eased the trauma of my husband's fortieth birthday by inviting only women to a tea just for him. One woman read him a poem, another belted out a song, and the rest of us just made him feel like God's gift to the world.
- "Stock a Freezer." Ask guests to bring casseroles, spaghetti sauce, lasagna, or anything else that can be frozen for a new mother, surgery patient, or recent widow or widower. (The recipient doesn't have to be present.) "Party Lines" syndicated columnist Susan Manlin Katzman suggests asking guests to bring two batches of the same dish: the larger one wrapped for the freezer, the smaller as a sample to be shared among guests.
- "Surprise Yourself." The first year I lived in Illinois, I invited the few friends I had made to a Sunday midwinter lunch during a glut of televised football games. What I didn't tell anyone until I popped the champagne was that it was my birthday. It was the perfect situation: no one had to worry about presents, they escaped the tube, and I was surrounded by people I enjoyed.
- Thanksgiving. Include an outsider or two along with the usual brood, so normally squabbling family members are on their best behavior. Make meal preparation easy by delegating dishes, picking up an already-smoked turkey, and serving pie-shop pies. Set up the TV in the kitchen after dessert so the football fans can do the dishes. Take everyone else on a walk in a nearby woods, park, or beach before they go into an "I-wish-I hadn't-eaten-so-much" stupor.

MORE AMBITIOUS BUT DOABLE

The following may sound work-intensive, but since the entertainment is generated more by the guests than the host, they're easier than they may seem.

- Orchestrate a "This Is Your Life" party. Decorate with old photos blown up into posters, and intersperse framed snapshots with ribbons or flowers on the buffet table. When realtor Jane Carlin sent out invitations to her mother's eightieth birthday, she requested, in lieu of a gift, that guests send her a photo, letter, or other piece of memorabilia for a guest-of-honor scrapbook. The night of the party, guests told stories, recited poetry, and sang songs in homage to the birthday girl. Plus, she got to take home, treasure, and show off her unique book of memories.

- Throw a "Retro Anniversary." Two Southern California couples celebrated their twentieth anniversary by asking guests to come to dinner in their original wedding finery. Most women came dressed in traditional white gowns, and men in tuxedos, but there was everything from full dress military regalia to black leather jackets. "The women took this *very* seriously, dieting and letting out seams," said co-host Gretchen Simpson, whose feet, at least, went casual in tennis shoes. The evening's entertainment included sharing the wedding albums everyone was requested to bring.
- Plan an "Historic Family Reunion." Make the food a group effort,

A REUNION TO FORGET

My twentieth high school reunion was a textbook case of how not *to throw a party. First of all, the registration table was positioned in a tiny vestibule below the Elks Club hall, so guests had to wait in a long line outside on a chilly November night. Not a good start.*

When we finally picked up our name tags, we noticed they not only lacked the requisite yearbook picture, they did not have our maiden names. Also, spouses of classmates were not identified, making it difficult for the class of five hundred to try to figure who was who.

The first half hour was *fun as we greeted each other with shrieks, squeals, and you-have-not-changed-a-bits. But then the lights darkened and the rock band cranked up, so not only were we left in the dark, we couldn't talk over the din.*

After the dinner of what seemed to be a salute to cafeteria cuisine, our class vice-president–thug got our attention by bellowing into the microphone, "Shut your damned mouths, it's time for the awards!" The awards, however, were not for the classmate who traveled the farthest, had the most kids, or even the most divorces. Nope. Names were simply drawn from a hat for the two, if not imaginative, perhaps fitting prizes for the representatives of the class with no class: an Elvis Presley album and a six-pack of beer.

It was, to say the least, an unsatisfying event. However, we had the reunion picture to look forward to. What arrived in the mail a month later was a stunner: an eleven-by-fourteen blur of three hundred pinhead-sized people.

and use the event as an opportunity to appreciate and record family history. One good way is to assign the younger generation the job of interviewing each member of the senior generation, posing questions like: What did you do for fun as a child? What was your childhood house and neighborhood like? Who was your first friend? What did you want to be when you grew up? And the old Barbara Walters zinger: What would you most like to be remembered for? Give reporters about an hour to interview, then videotape them as they share their stories with all.

- Host a "Come as You Were." Everyone dresses as they did on a former job and demonstrates a skill from the past. I attended one where a buckskin-clad camp counselor had us all make funny hats, a former dance instructor moved us in the mambo, and a forty-two-year-old pep-squad leader led everyone in a series of cheers. We dined on sentimental favorites: pigs-in-blankets, giant submarine sandwiches made with four-foot loaves of French bread . . . and for dessert? Popsicles.

> "HOSTING IS SPENDING A LOT OF MONEY ON A PARTY YOU WEREN'T EVEN INVITED TO."
>
> —JERRY SEINFELD

- Have a "Come as Your Favorite Ad." Instead of the usual blood-and-guts Halloween theme, one Lincolnshire, Illinois, couple asked guests to come as an advertisement. The ads were loosely interpreted, so there was everything and everybody from Mr. Clean to a six-pack of Bud. The winners? A twosome dressed as a big box of Preparation H and a papier-mâché hemorrhoid.

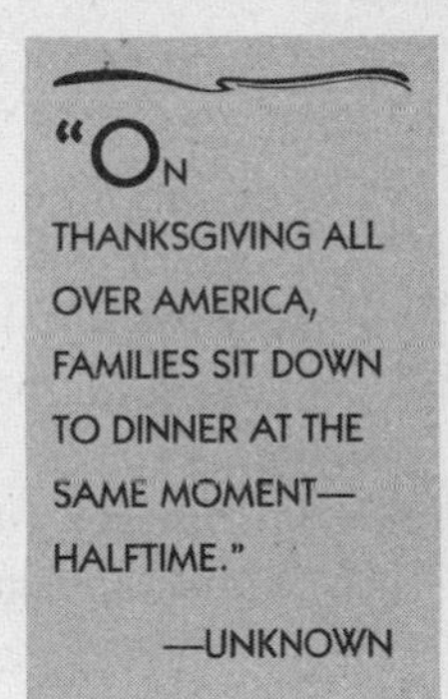

"ON THANKSGIVING ALL OVER AMERICA, FAMILIES SIT DOWN TO DINNER AT THE SAME MOMENT—HALFTIME."
—UNKNOWN

- Celebrate a "Christmas Take." Instead of the usual cocktail party, host an early-in-the-month tree trimming, cookie exchange, or a "gift taking." With the latter, everyone brings, say, a $10 wrapped gift. After the presents are arranged under the tree, each guest is given a number. Number-one ticket holder has first pick of any gift. However, guests with higher numbers can either take a gift from under the tree, or take one from someone holding a lower number, who in turn selects another gift. The rules are: (1) a gift can only be traded three times; (2) a gift cannot be taken back till three more people have selected theirs; (3) number-one guest has the last laugh and gets to choose any gift he or she wants.

CHILDREN'S PARTIES

Kid's birthday parties are often hard on the host as well as the home. Rather than the traditional in-house cake, clown, and chaos, consider staging the party some place other than the living room. The backyard, local park, or playground are practical choices. Other good locations might include the following:

- children's museum
- "hands-on" aquarium
- ice-skating or roller rink
- orchard for fruit picking
- slot car racetrack
- local zoo
- amusement park
- miniature-golf course
- bowling alley

Keep the location fairly close to home to minimize transportation hassles. If the children are preschoolers, have the parents stay on the premises. You'll not only share the responsibility, you'll have "big people" to talk to.
Also:

- Let children help design their own invitations with drawings, glitter, and stickers.
- Unless the whole class is invited, send invitations rather than hand-delivering them at school. Small hearts break easily when left out in the cold.
- Keep it short. One and one-half to two hours is about all young children and their handlers can take.

If the party is at home:

- Keep it simple. Small children don't need circus characters, magicians, and pony rides to enjoy themselves. "If you provide a balloon, a colored napkin, and a few friends, it's a party," says nursery-school director Carol Doughty. "When we start throwing elaborate parties when children are small, there'll be nothing left for them to experience by the time they're into their teens."
- Plan more activities than you think you'll need. I spent weeks poring over books of party games for my daughter Kelley's fourth birthday.

After a half hour into it, I had run out of ideas and energy. All the kids wanted to do was run wild. All I wanted to do was run.

- Concentrate on involving children more than entertaining them. Carol Doughty says that a cookie-baking party for one of her daughters was one of the most successful she ever threw. She made a personalized apron for each child, and everyone mixed, rolled, and baked. "It was a treat for all of us," she says. "And it gave each little guest a sense of 'can do.'"
- Give arrivals something to do as they're waiting for the party to begin. Have the birthday child show off his or her room or collection, or lay out a simple project for them to start. One mom requested a refrigerator carton from the local appliance store, and had arrivals decorate the "birthday house" with markers.
- Balance quiet and energetic games to keep a lid on energy levels. Gunnysack races and balloon relays need to be interspersed with quieter pursuits like storytelling, or simply going for a walk to see what treasures can be found, coming back, and gluing them to a piece of poster board.
- Keep games noncompetitive by removing goal lines and such. "If there are going to be winners, there are going to be losers," says Carol Doughty. "And no one wants to feel like a loser."
- Stick to finger foods and serve them in small portions. Little party guests are often too excited to eat much.
- Serve healthy and fun fare like peanut-butter sandwiches in cookie-cutter shapes. Cheese, popcorn, pretzels, and grapes are also good choices. Kids get so strung out with the excitement of the party, they don't need a sugar high.
- Have children stay seated while eating to avoid choking and other injuries.
- Instead of the traditional decorated cake, let kids decorate individual, unfrosted cupcakes with icing, candy sprinkles, nuts, raisins, gumdrops, coconut, and candles.
- If there is a mountain of gifts to open, consider having the birthday child present each giver a small token gift, in place of the grab bag, to open simultaneously. Children get squirrelly watching someone else get all the goodies.
- Consider forgoing the gift giving altogether. Putting an emphasis on fun and friendship rather than acquiring loot is an enlightened approach some parents are taking.
- As children get older, let them plan their own parties, only giving guidance where it's warranted. "When parents get overly involved," says Carol Doughty, "parties often become spectacles to impress other parents."

- Once children get into double-digit birthdays, double the amount of food you think you'll need. Teenage boys, in particular, can go through a spread like locusts on saplings.
- Consider an intergenerational party. One La Jolla, California, couple has celebrated their fourteen-year-old's Fourth of July birthday on the beach since she was a baby. Since the beach is usually mobbed by noon on the holiday, Pat and Charleen Boyl stake out their spot at sunrise, and serve a Mexican brunch from 8:00 A.M. to noon. "Our daughter and our thirteen-year-old son invite their friends and their families, and we invite all of our friends as well," says Charleen. "We usually have between seventy and eighty people, but we've been doing it so long it's easy."

KEEP IT MANAGEABLE

It's fun to celebrate birthdays, holidays, and other events when we can do so without knocking ourselves for a loop. A few tips for making them fun for all, *including* ourselves:

- Focus on what you like to do. If it's cooking, recruit someone else to do the cleaning. If it's decorating, use those skills to embellish prepared foods. If it's just having a good time, delegate as much as possible.
- Stick to hors d'oeuvres and/or dessert parties for groups over ten. Full meals are expensive and the hardest to produce.
- Investigate locations other than home. Boats, billiard parlors, as well as private dining rooms in theaters and stadiums can add a fun dimension to a party. As a bonus, we don't have to worry about the condition of our home before or after the event.
- Share the work, the expenses, and the cleanup with a buddy. Since our extended families live far away, a friend and I alternated our Thanksgiving and Christmas dinners with our immediate broods at each other's homes for years.

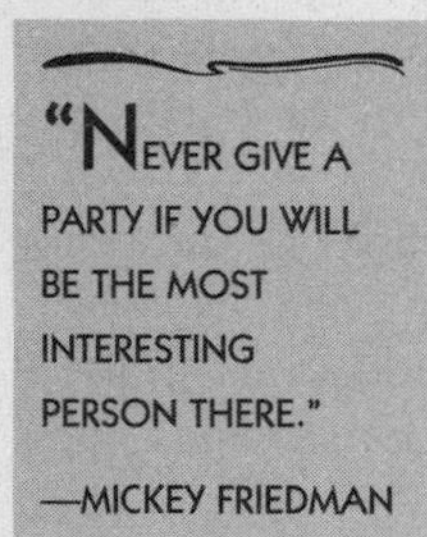

"NEVER GIVE A PARTY IF YOU WILL BE THE MOST INTERESTING PERSON THERE."
—MICKEY FRIEDMAN

SECRETS OF SUCCESS

- Plan parties with a purpose, whether it's a theme, holiday, or milestone, so it's easy to get everyone in the mood.
- Find a way to involve guests. Eating and small talk are fine, but peo-

ple are happiest when they're part of the action. Drinking is also less apt to be a problem when there are fun things to do.

- Plan a group participation party like a softball game at a local park or a murder-mystery game at home. Murder mystery kits can be found in game stores and come equipped with clever invitations, scripts, and even menu suggestions.

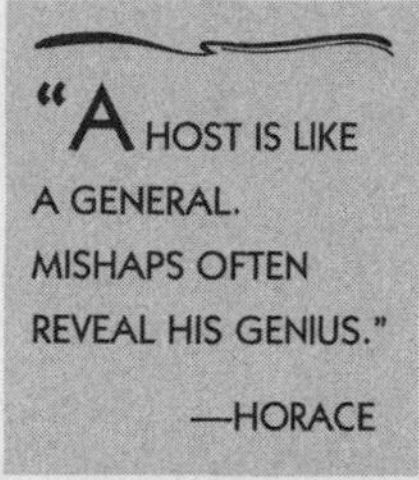

"A HOST IS LIKE
A GENERAL.
MISHAPS OFTEN
REVEAL HIS GENIUS."
—HORACE

- Consider hiring a karaoke DJ to get guests singing. A good one not only comes equipped with a sound system, but also has hats, props, and the ability to turn reluctant guests into hams.
- Look into booking a fortune-teller, caricaturist, handwriting analyst, or anyone who can turn a passive guest into an active participant.
- Provide inexpensive disposable cameras for all and ask for copies of the best pictures. A camera not only involves a guest, it gives the busy host a party to remember as well.
- If it's a multigenerational party at home, consider setting up a spare room or the garage for the kids. One couple hosts an annual "after the school play party" for parents and their children. While the adults schmooze in the big country kitchen, the children play Ping-Pong and other games in the empty garage downstairs. "Other than a few cookie raids, we've hardly known the kids were there," said one grateful guest.
- Be adaptable. Weather changes, food fails, and people flake. Flexibility and a sense of humor have saved the day for many a host.
- If it's an outdoor party, have a pavilion, tent, or alternate site in case of bad weather. Sometimes a sudden change in weather can *make* a party. I once co-hosted a tea for new church members in our minister's garden. It was all very pretty but staid, with guests primly nibbling, nodding, and sipping, when a sudden downpour drenched us all. Everyone grabbed a tray, a table, and whatever else they could, and reassembled on the porch. Then a funny thing happened; once guests noticed what a mess everyone else was, they loosened up and *enjoyed* the event.
- If only a handful of people show, hide your disappointment and make the best of the situation. Sally Stoughten planned a big birthday bash for her stockbroker husband on a night when Philadelphia came to a standstill from an early spring blizzard. "Only six of the twenty guests showed," said Sally. "I was pretty upset at first, but had to pretend everything was just ducky. We hauled out a game of Gender Gap and, surprisingly, it turned out to be a really fun evening."

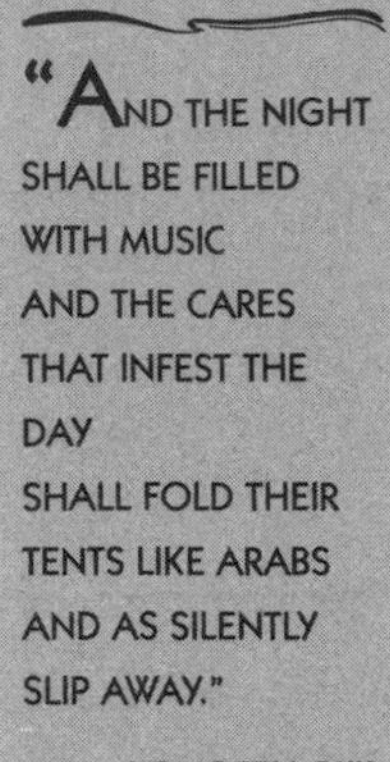

CAVEATS

- Don't take on more than you can handle. An elaborate soiree with scads of guests may make you so strung out you'll be biting people's heads off before it's over.
- Avoid hosting a New Year's Eve party. Not only are expectations high, but people typically drink too much, try too hard, and then end up turning on the tube at midnight to watch *others* having a good time.
- Avoid springing a surprise party on anyone unless you're sure the recipient will love it. I've seen too many guests of honor (including my husband, and a good friend) look as if they wanted to murder the perpetrator.
- Give up the pursuit of perfection. There is no such thing as a perfect party.

HOW TO INCREASE YOUR SOCIAL LIFE

When we are new in town, want to widen our horizons, or simply give up the monastic life, there are plenty of good ways to make new friends.

- *Start a play group for preschoolers in which parents meet at alternating homes and network while children play under watchful eyes.*
- *Join a church or temple. Look for one that not only reflects and strengthens your beliefs, but also offers opportunities to meet others.*
- *Seek out like-minded individuals. There's a club or organization for almost every interest, whether it's gardening, investing, or stamp collecting. Some unlikely candidates have hidden social benefits. I joined Toastmasters, for example, to develop public-speaking skills. In the process, I discovered a group of party animals who throw at least a couple of big bashes a year.*
- *Join a philanthropic organization like Big Brothers, the Cancer Society, or Junior League. There's not only the satisfaction of helping those in need, there's also the opportunity to connect with good people.*
- *Take a class. Whether it's art, astronomy, or acting, learning more about a pet subject can be intellectually as well as socially stimulating.*

- *Get physical. Joining a gym, walking group, or running club has health, as well as communal, benefits.*
- *Start a book club. Ask a few friends to bring people who have a sense of commitment and are willing to share new ideas. Then appoint a discussion leader for each month, read an agreed-upon book, and discuss it over snacks, dessert, or a simple meal. Twelve to fifteen members work best, according to* The Reading Group Handbook, *by Rachel W. Jacobsohn.*

PART III

TRICKY TIMES

CHAPTER 12

DEALING WITH DROP-INS

Dishes overflow the sink, toys carpet the floor, and the cupboard is nearly bare, when we hear the dreaded "Honey, guess who I brought home?"

Unless we live in a cave, it's not easy to avoid the friends our partner surprises us with, the relatives who just happen to be driving through, or the neighbor who needs a warm ear and a cold drink.

While that impromptu appearance may strike terror in our hearts, we need to keep in mind that the best thing about unexpected guests is that there are no expectations of us. The house doesn't have to sparkle and the refreshments don't have to look commissioned. In short, there's no need to make excuses. This is how we live.

What is impressive is how we rise to the occasion and pull it off with style and grace.

THE READY ROOM

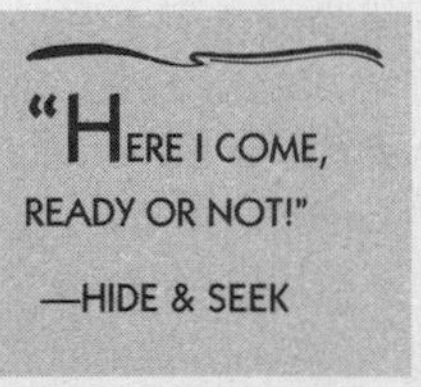

- Keep one spot in the house in reserve as a retreat. It's not that it *can't* be used, it's *how* it's used that counts. Make it off-limits to family snacking, shedding pets, messy projects, and anything else that has pigpen potential.
- If there's a family room, save the living room for good clean fun like reading, playing board games, and listening to

music. A comfortable dining room, provided it can be closed off to the rest of the house, is another possible retreat.
- Designate the area a junk-free zone, and furnish it with easy-to-maintain fabrics, flooring, and accessories. Company or no company, it's nice to have a spruced and serene refuge when the rest of the house is in shambles.

DRINK OFFERINGS

- Be specific. Rather than asking, "What can I get you to drink?" when the larder is dry, say, "How about a tall glass of ice water?" Then serve it in a good glass garnished, if you have it, with a slim slice of lemon or lime.
- Keep a few cartons of bottled water on hand. MiniBar North America, a company that stocks hotel in-room bars, reports that bottled water is the preferred drink of hotel guests. It outsells the company's alcoholic drinks by more than six to one.
- Keep clear sodas around as well, especially for little visitors who tend to dribble and spill.
- Stash away a few bottles of decent wine and/or imported beer. Save the generic brands for yourself if drop-ins turn into long-term houseguests.

A PROPER POT OF TEA

From Boston to Bombay, tea is a hospitable and easy way to welcome guests, whether they're the invited variety or not. Make a decent pot by following these steps:

- *Reserve a pot exclusively for tea, since coffee can alter its flavor.*
- *Fill the kettle with cold water and set it to boil.*
- *When the water is nearly boiling, swirl some of it in the pot to take off the chill.*
- *Empty the pot.*
- *Toss in a teaspoon of fresh leaves for each cup.*
- *Bring the kettle to another boil, but don't let it boil long or the water will lose oxygen and taste flat.*
- *Fill the teapot with boiling water.*
- *Let green and oolong teas steep for two to three minutes, and herbal, black, and white teas for five to seven minutes.*
- *Serve the pot of tea alongside a smaller pot of hot water so guests can dilute it to taste.*

- Don't feel you *have* to stock and serve alcohol if you don't imbibe. It's your turf, after all.

SPONTANEOUS SNACKS

It pays to lay in a few offerings that we can whip out of the freezer, fridge, or pantry on short notice. The trick is to have stuff that won't tempt the rest of the household. There's no way I can keep chips, pretzels, or salted nuts in the house without me or my family swilling them. On the other hand, raw nuts, olives, and popping corn are relatively safe from my brood. We just have to be realistic about what we can and cannot keep lying around.

- Hide a can of pâté or bean dip in the back of the pantry or, better yet, with the cleaning supplies. No one will ever find them there.
- Try a jar of caponata, a tasty eggplant, olive, and herb spread. It's festive enough to serve guests, yet looks weird enough to scare the kids.
- A bowl of Mediterranean olives makes a tasty, no-work offering, and once opened will last for months in the fridge. Try Kalamata olives from Greece, Manzanilla from Spain, or niçoise from France. Simply drain, dump, and serve them cold or at room temperature in a pretty glass bowl, and provide a second bowl for the pits.
- Keep a box of miniature egg rolls, pizzas, or quiches in the freezer. Lead no one into temptation by wrapping it in an opaque plastic bag.
- Crisp limp chips, pretzels, or crackers under the broiler for a few moments, watching carefully. Or nuke them in the microwave by lining a basket or bowl with a paper napkin, and zapping two cups at a time on high for one minute.

A POET'S CUP OF TEA

The brewing and the serving of tea have long been an art form in some cultures, as evidenced by the advice of one eleventh-century Chinese poet: "Take water from a running stream and boil it over a lively fire. Water from the springs in the hills is best, river water is next best, while well water is the worst. . . . When making an infusion, do not boil the water too hastily. At first it begins to sparkle like crab's eyes, then somewhat like fishes' eyes, and lastly it boils up like pearls innumerable, springing and waving about."

- A tub of salsa can save the day. It's spicy and lean, and makes a colorful dip, salad dressing, or baked potato topper. Plus, it lasts for weeks in the fridge. Serve it au naturel in an earthenware bowl, or spoon it over a block of cream cheese, and surround it with raw veggies, crackers, or chips.
- Serve precut carrot, celery, or other veggie sticks with a favorite creamy salad dressing.
- Offer a big wooden bowl of nuts in the shell along with a nutcracker or two. Drop-in guests should have to work for their food.
- Shelled raw nuts keep three to four months in the pantry or up to a year in the freezer. Toast them in a 350-degree oven for five to ten minutes.
- Store popping corn up to a year in the freezer and pop it in an air popper. Air-popped corn is a quick and easy guilt-free snack. Give it personality by spraying it with butter, cooking spray, or water and tossing it with garlic or chili powder and grated parmesan. Serve it in a big wooden bowl or wicker basket.
- Break out the cheese. If there's a long-lost wedge of Brie, Gouda, or almost anything besides processed cheese in the fridge, slice off any dry parts, and present it with a cheese plane or cocktail knife on a serving platter. Surround it with crackers and fresh fruit, if you have them.
- If there's only a bit of cheese on hand, make crispy chips by cutting cheddar, jack, or any semisoft cheese into half-inch cubes and nuking them for a minute or so on a dinner plate.

"BE NOT FORGETFUL TO ENTERTAIN STRANGERS, FOR SOME HAVE ENTERTAINED ANGELS UNAWARES."

—PAUL OF TARSUS

THE TOP TEN NIBBLES

We don't have to knock ourselves out to keep guests happy. America's favorite snacks, according to the USDA, in descending order of preference are:

1. *potato chips*
2. *fresh fruit*
3. *popcorn*
4. *cookies*
5. *crackers*
6. *ice cream*
7. *pretzels*
8. *candy bars*
9. *other candies*
10. *nuts*

OH YES, DARLINK, WE ALWAYS LIVE THIS WAY

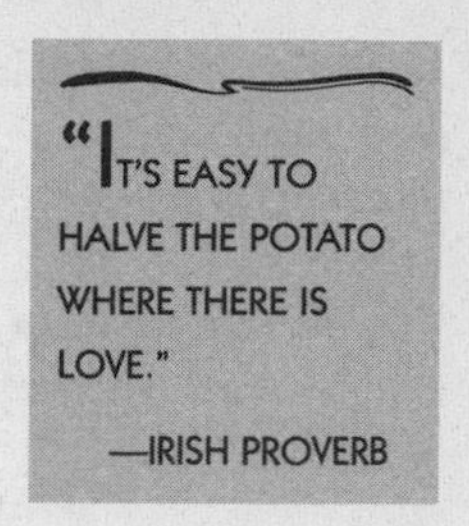

"IT'S EASY TO HALVE THE POTATO WHERE THERE IS LOVE."
—IRISH PROVERB

- Stock up on candles and pretty napkins when they're on sale, and store them where they're accessible. They're a form of social security.
- Keep a large serving tray or two on hand. Serving drinks and snacks from a tray is not only elegant, it's efficient. Trays make cleanup easier as well.
- Line trays with paper leaves or doilies for a finishing touch, and to hide those spots that never got polished.
- Reserve a shelf in the kitchen for a set of unspotted and matched glasses so there's no rummaging around the dining room for something other than a Ronald McDonald mug.

IMPROMPTU MEALS

Keep a phone file on hand of a few good take-out restaurants, especially ones that deliver. If you're a Mother Teresa type, and you really *want* to have drop-ins stay for dinner, consider stocking a few of the following convenience foods and meal stretchers.

Frozen lasagna. Buy the jumbo size from a warehouse grocer, and save leftovers for a family meal later in the week.
Boneless chicken breasts. Slice a few into slivers and freeze for a quick stir-fry with a bag of veggies.
Frozen stir-fry vegetables. Buy the kind with its own pack of sauce, sauté with the above chicken, cook up a pot of rice, and you've got dinner.
Rice. The instant varieties may be fast, but for an extra fifteen minutes, the long-grained versions yield better taste and texture. Rice is not only a good side dish and bed for sauced entrées, it's also a soup and stew stretcher.
Pasta. Freeze the fresh stuff, or stock a package or two of the quick-cooking variety like cappellini. Instead of the usual meat sauce, sauté a chopped onion in a little butter and olive oil, toss in a can of drained tuna, a dollop of Dijon mustard, a splash of balsamic vinegar, and a sprinkling of chopped parsley. Or use the pasta plain to add bulk to a soup or salad.
Tuna. Stock up on the fancy white albacore kind packed in spring water. Toss it with a small head of shredded red cabbage, a cup of thinly

sliced celery, a little chopped onion, capers, and vinaigrette made with red-wine vinegar.

Baking mix. Crown a stew with dumplings or stretch any meal with biscuits.

Ramen dried soup mixes. Add fresh or frozen veggies, meat, poultry, or fish to turn these tasty seasoned noodles into a hearty, exotic, and speedy meal.

RELYING ON BACKUPS

When you have your own version of the perfect quick meal, but are out of one key ingredient, the following understudies can come to the rescue:

Fresh milk ½ cup evaporated milk plus ½ cup water, or 1 cup water and 1 cup dry milk powder.

Buttermilk 1 cup yogurt or 1 cup milk plus 1 tablespoon lemon juice or white vinegar.

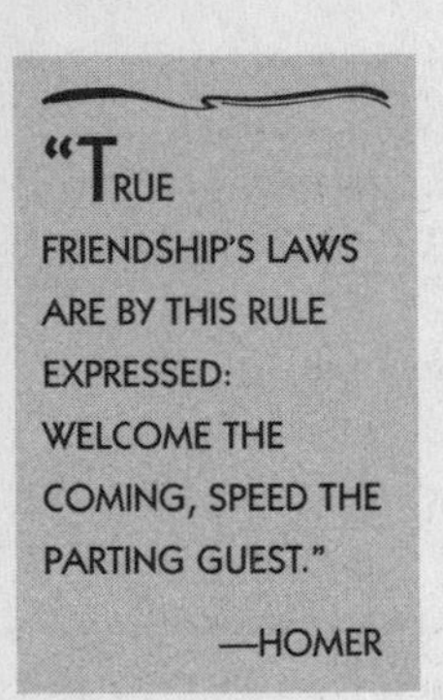

"TRUE
FRIENDSHIP'S LAWS
ARE BY THIS RULE
EXPRESSED:
WELCOME THE
COMING, SPEED THE
PARTING GUEST."
—HOMER

Cream for cooking and baking; ¾ cup milk and ½ cup butter substitute for heavy cream, while ⅞ cup milk plus 3 tablespoons butter stand in for light cream.

Fresh mushrooms 4 ounces canned or 2 ounces dried equals ½ pound fresh.

Lemon juice half the amount white vinegar.

Prepared mustard ½ teaspoon dry mustard plus 2 teaspoons vinegar equals 1 tablespoon prepared.

Dried herbs 1 tablespoon fresh equals 1½ teaspoons dried.

Bread crumbs packaged bread stuffing, croutons, or crackers buzzed in a blender or food processor.

Tabasco equal amounts of cayenne.

Beef, vegetable, or chicken broth 1 cube or teaspoon instant bouillon plus 1 cup boiling water equals 1 cup canned. (NOTE: Beef, vegetable, and chicken broths are interchangeable in most recipes. Many cooks simplify things by only stocking chicken broth.)

Cornstarch twice as much all-purpose flour.

Honey equal amounts molasses or 1¼ cups granulated sugar for each cup honey. (NOTE: when substituting dry for liquid ingredients, increase ¼ cup of whatever liquid needed.)

1 cup brown sugar 1 cup white granulated sugar plus 2 tablespoons molasses.

Granulated sugar 2 cups powdered, or 1 cup brown sugar.
Superfine sugar Blend granulated sugar in the food processor or blender.

NECESSITY IS THE MOTHER OF INVENTION

Improvisation has saved the day for many a cook. In fact, some of the best dishes in history have come out of situations in which the cook was caught short.

When Napoleon defeated the Austrian army at Marengo, for example, he invited his top officers for a celebratory dinner in his tent the following evening. The trouble was, according to legend, his chef had only a flask of cognac, a bottle of wine, some olive oil, and a few herbs. The rest of his supplies were far to the rear of the column.

In a frantic search of the area, the chef rounded up a few chickens at a deserted farm, as well as tomatoes, wild onions, mushrooms, and garlic. He rapidly threw together a dish that brought accolades from the general and his men. Chicken Marengo is, to this day, a culinary classic.

Innovation also saved the day for Ruth Wakefield back in the Depression. With a full house expected at the Toll House Inn in Whitman, Massachusetts, she discovered she was out of raisins for the big batch of cookies she was about to bake for her guests. Instead, she diced a Nestlé's semisweet chocolate bar, folded it into the batter, and created what became America's favorite cookie.

DESSERT THE TABLE

- Instead of stocking up on tasty little tidbits meant to impress the guests but that end up thickening the thighs, take 'em out for frozen yogurt. Suggest taking two cars, "So you won't have to come all the way back here." That way guests can be sent home diplomatically and at a reasonable hour.

GETTING THEM TO LEAVE

Who wants to leave when they've been coddled, cozied, and fed all evening? Hosts have been facing this dilemma since the first cave dwellers dropped in on their neighbors. Ancient Roman hosts simply went to bed and let the slaves deal with the stragglers. However, more drastic measures were taken in Elizabethan England. Prankster hosts

presented long-lingering guests with damp towels to "freshen up." The towels, however, were impregnated with a sulfur-based dye that stained anything and everything it touched.

Before resorting to more contemporary shenanigans, like slipping melatonin into the decaf, try these subtle and not-so-subtle ways of sending guests home in a timely manner:

- Avoid overfeeding. Even active types can take root on the couch after a big meal.
- Keep a large chiming clock, set slightly ahead, on the mantel as a reminder of the late hour.
- Don't make a fuss when guests make a move to break camp. Politely protesting "It's so early" may convince them it is.
- Ask, "Shall I start another pot of coffee?" Nine times out of ten, they'll say, "Oh no, we really should be going."
- If that fails, try, "We must show you Junior's birth video. The labor took hours, but the delivery was dramatic."
- Recite poetry. Executive recruiter Marla Winitz says she used to read poetry to college dates who overstayed their welcomes. "Shakespeare, Chaucer, and P. G. Wodehouse were particularly effective," says Winitz. "It only took about twenty minutes before they'd hightail it home."
- Play annoying music. "I really didn't want everyone to leave so early at my last party," says Garrie Gorby. "But the harpsichord tape seemed to put everyone on edge. Next time, I'll play it when I need it."
- Simply say good night. Mike Dorano takes the seldom-used honest approach. He gets up from his seat, extends his hand, and says, "We've all got to get up in the morning, so let's call it a night. It's been great seeing you." Another candid host turns to his wife and says, "Well, Elvira, let's go to bed so these nice people can go home."

CHAPTER 13

ENTERTAINING IN A RESTAURANT

Hosting in a restaurant may be the easiest and most enjoyable way to entertain since there's no worry about cooking, cleaning, and kicking out stragglers. And because the host is less territorial, everyone is more relaxed about manners and mores.

The drawbacks are its anonymity and expense. Some ideas on overcoming both, as well as making the affair a rousing success:

KEEPING COSTS IN LINE

- Meet with the manager ahead of time to arrange the menu, sample the wine, and work out the details, including the price. Kevin Mabbutt, manager of Delicias, an elegant restaurant in Rancho Santa Fe, California, says that the initial meeting is the key to avoiding surprises and enjoying a successful dinner. By taking control in advance, no one will get carried away by ordering caviar, lobster, and French champagne.

"YOU ARE WHERE YOU EAT."
—PAMELA FIORI

- Negotiate the price in the planning stage. My husband and I organized an annual dinner for the community's youth-soccer coaches for years, and discovered prices were open to bargaining with every restaurant we dealt with. We'd ask, "What kind of a price can you give us for a choice of your

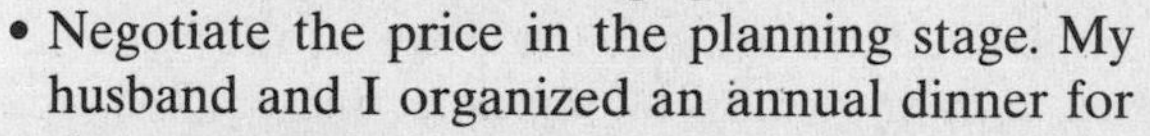

best chicken or fish dinner?" They'd say something like "Eighteen dollars a head." We'd counter with "We only have a budget for twelve dollars a head, can you do it?" They always did. "Few people realize that the meal, the drinks, and everything else can be negotiated in advance," says restaurant critic Eleanor Widmer.

- Avoid sushi bars. "They may be fun, but it's five dollars for this little bit and seven dollars for that little morsel," says Eleanor Widmer. "Before you know it, you've spent a fortune."
- Consider hosting a lunch or a brunch rather than a dinner. A midday menu is usually cheaper, and chances are good that budget-busting drinking will be minimal. A Saturday or Sunday brunch is a nice way to celebrate almost any event, especially since there are usually no workweek deadlines and schedules to worry about.

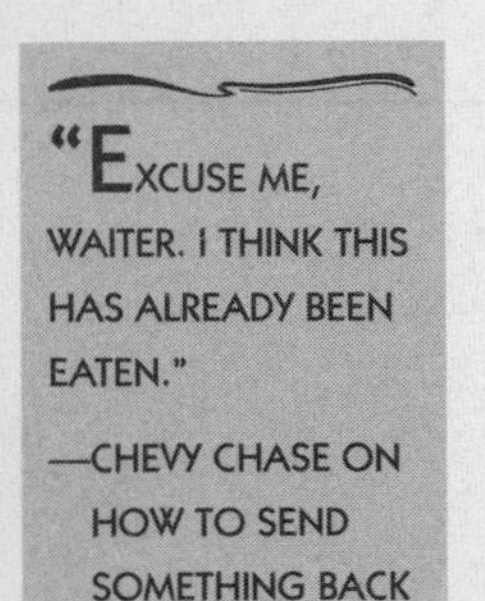

"Excuse me, waiter. I think this has already been eaten."
—Chevy Chase on how to send something back to the kitchen

- Investigate "sunset specials." Many restaurants slash the price of entrées before 6:30 or 7:00 P.M.
- Check out "prix fixe" dinners. Often served on weekday nights, these multicourse meals are often a good value.
- Find a restaurant that doesn't serve alcohol so you can either bring your own or forgo it altogether, since a restaurant's markup on liquor is enormous. New restaurants that haven't yet received their liquor licenses are often good bets, providing they've gotten their service and food up to par.
- If more than two people are having wine, consider ordering a bottle instead of buying it by the glass. A $15 bottle yields around five glasses—the better deal if a glass costs $4 or more.
- Ask if you can bring your own wine to a restaurant that serves spirits. There's a corkage fee, but it's usually cheaper than ordering from the wine list.
- Occasionally, a restaurant will have a free-corkage night early in the week. Check around.
- If your wine of choice is on the restaurant's list, they may not allow you to bring in your own supply. Check ahead.
- Order the house wine for a good value. But make sure to sample it in the planning stage to ensure its quality.
- If the meal isn't preplanned, always ask the price of the "special." One Palm Springs restaurant gouges the unsuspecting with its "specialty of the evening": a $58 lobster tail. "At one time, the cheapest item on the menu was the 'blue plate special,'" says restaurant critic Eleanor Widmer. "Today, it's almost always the opposite."

- Check into package deals. Some restaurants offer group dining and limousine packages that are fun for all, yet may cost little more than the meal itself. I once surprised my husband with a "Johnny Rockets Birthday Package": a limousine whisked eight of us to the fifties restaurant for hamburgers, Cokes, apple pie, and party favors for only $149.95. He may never forgive me for surprising him, but the evening was great for the rest of us, and the price was right.
- Consider ordering the dessert sampler platter. It's usually cheaper and everyone gets a taste of the menu offerings without the accompanying guilt of a full dessert. A $5.25 platter of tiny portions of crème brûlée, raspberry tart, and mocha brownies easily serves six at one upscale California eatery, whereas individual desserts average $4 apiece. If the restaurant doesn't normally offer a sampler, ask for it in the planning stage.
- Use a frequent diner's card. Some offer as much as 20 percent off the total bill. Set it up with the manager ahead of time so guests don't view you as a penny-pincher.

CHOOSING THE PERFECT RESTAURANT

- Go for the ambience. The local "eat it and beat it" may serve the best food in town, but a party needs atmosphere. We always take out-of-town guests to an outdoor oceanfront restaurant so close to the breakers you can feel the sea spray. The food is average, but the ambience, especially for the landlocked, is spectacular.
- Take out-of-towners to a regional restaurant. We may become blasé about our own native fare, but visitors are itchin' to sample the lobster in Boston, the gumbo in New Orleans, and the salmon in the Northwest, especially when the restaurant's decor reflects the locale.
- Avoid bringing foreign visitors to their own ethnic restaurants. Since the food has to appeal to the locals, it's apt to be a watered-down version of what they're used to at home. When my husband and I visited Budapest years ago, our host couldn't wait to take us to "the most elegant restaurant in the city." The place was only open on the weekends, so we dined on goulash and schnitzel in gypsy cellars throughout the week. When we were finally ushered into this fabled spot, we were greeted by sputnik decor, tough "Amerikan style steak," and an orchestra playing "I Left My Heart in San Francisco." We couldn't wait to get back to the real Budapest.

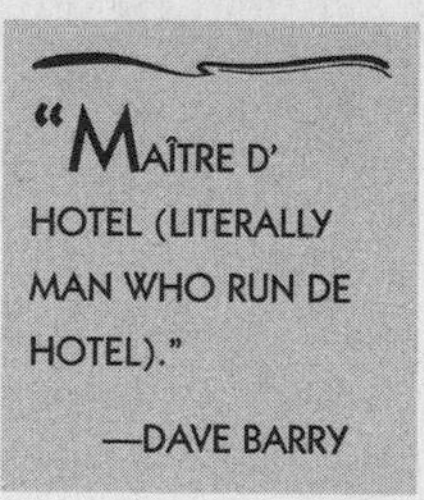

"MAÎTRE D' HOTEL (LITERALLY MAN WHO RUN DE HOTEL)."

—DAVE BARRY

- Be sensitive to the noise factor. The trend in new restaurant design is sound-reverberating hard surfaces and wide-open spaces. They create a bustling, high-energy, "happening" effect, but are not conducive to conversation.
- Look for a place with a private dining room for a party of eight or more. There's seldom an extra charge, the event will be more intimate, and the guests can get as boisterous as they want without bothering, or being bothered by, other diners.
- Ask to have your area screened off with panels or plants for a feeling of privacy if a separate room isn't available.
- Look into booking a restaurant when it's not normally open. A place that serves only dinner may be willing to host a lunch or breakfast, or open on the night it's usually closed, if the party is large enough.
- Consider using your or a friend's private business, university, or country club. It's fun to capitalize on the exclusivity element and the highly personalized service.

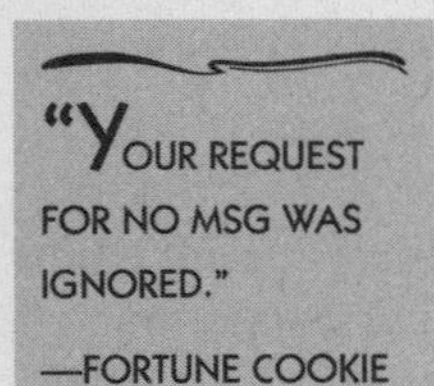

"YOUR REQUEST
FOR NO MSG WAS
IGNORED."
—FORTUNE COOKIE

- Check out a new spot. The discovery factor is always intriguing for guests, and since the restaurant is hungry for business, the staff is anxious to please. Just make sure it's gone through its shakedown phase.
- Always try the place first to scope out the menu, the quality of the food, and the professionalism of the staff.
- Request a particular table or at least one where you're not viewing the rest room or are within earshot of the kitchen or bar. If there are no guarantees, book elsewhere.
- Check out the rest room. Its sanitation is a good indication of the cleanliness of the kitchen and the overall attention to detail.
- Visit the place at the time of the party. A restaurant with a spectacular view by day may have icy sheets of glass by night. A place dramatically lit in the evening may look a little frowsy in the morning. I once made the mistake of choosing a quiet little place I liked for lunch, only to find the bar scene so deafening at dinner, we had to shout over the din.
- Select a central spot that's easy for most of the guests to get to. A waterside restaurant may be romantic, but not after a thirty-mile rush-hour drive.
- Make sure the parking is easy and accessible. Anyone who has seen *Ferris Bueller's Day Off* is no fan of valet parking.
- Be realistic if there are young children in the party. Everyone will feel more relaxed in a casual atmosphere, when there are fidgeters and squealers along, than they will at Le Snob Elegante.

THE NO-HOSTER

It's not always necessary or even appropriate to play the bill-paying benefactor. I recently organized a farewell lunch in a restaurant for a mentor who was moving out of state, for example. I knew few of her friends, so I asked her to choose the restaurant and fax me the names and phone numbers of everyone she wanted invited. I called the two dozen women, said I was "organizing a no-host lunch for Diane at Cafe Pacifica a week from Sunday." I then phoned in the final count to the restaurant two days before the event. The party was fun, easy, and other than the phoning, work-free.

- Consider following up the phone invitation with a fax or postcard so there's no question as to time, place, and who pays. Not everyone understands the "no-host" concept.
- If someone suggests going in on a group gift, appoint him or her buyer and cash collector.
- Be the first to arrive, especially if there are guests who are unknown to each other. "No-host" means sharing the bill, not letting guests fend for themselves.
- When the bill comes, ask the honored guest to take a hike to the rest room while everything is divided up. Avoid the tedious "You had the iced tea and you had the salad" business. An even split is not always equitable, but is far more graceful.

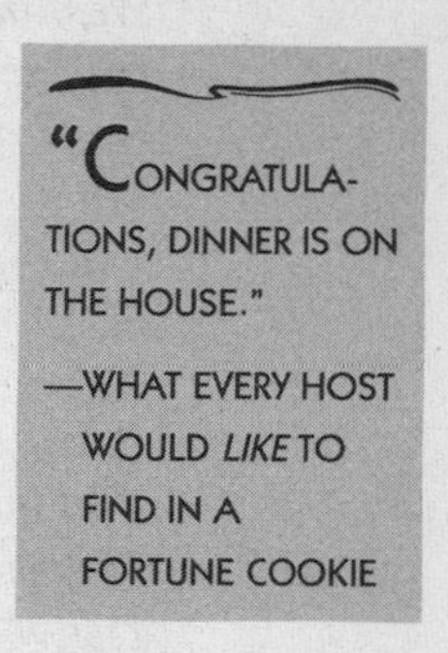

"CONGRATULATIONS, DINNER IS ON THE HOUSE."
—WHAT EVERY HOST WOULD *LIKE* TO FIND IN A FORTUNE COOKIE

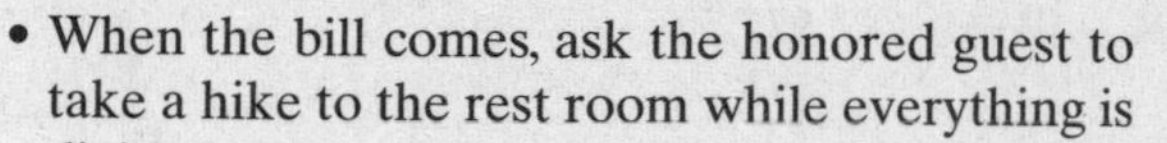

GETTING THE MOST FROM A GOOD RESTAURANT

- Patronize a favorite place regularly, and get to know the staff.
- Ask the server the station number of a well-situated table, to ensure securing it, and to simplify the phone reservation. Requesting "table number 10" gets better results than asking, "May we have that window table that's kinda close to that strange painting of the ugly nude?"—especially when the owner is the artist and the nude is his wife.
- Get in the habit of requesting a favorite server. Service can make or break a meal.
- Dress well. "It's human nature to give more attentive service to better-dressed patrons," confided one Manhattan restaurateur, "than to the ones who look a little shabby around the edges."
- Tip generously at a favorite spot for the assurance of attentive service whether it's for two or for twenty.

THE TRAVELING HOST'S GUIDE TO AVOIDING STICKER SHOCK

According to a recent Zagat Survey, *the average price for a restaurant dinner in cities across the country is as follows:*

New York	*$29.81*
Philadelphia	*$25.17*
San Francisco	*$24.78*
Los Angeles	*$23.90*
Washington, D.C.	*$23.88*
Chicago	*$21.87*
Boston	*$21.83*
Miami	*$21.80*
Honolulu	*$20.86*
Seattle	*$18.62*
Atlanta	*$18.49*
Portland	*$18.11*
Phoenix/Scottsdale	*$17.58*
Dallas/Fort Worth	*$17.51*
Denver	*$17.06*
San Diego	*$16.72*
Salt Lake City	*$16.28*
Kansas City	*$12.15*

- Pose questions. If you don't know what tomato coulis or tapenade is, ask. An admission of culinary ignorance often benefits everyone at the table.
- Notify the waiter or manager if something is amiss *during* rather than after the meal, so the situation can be rectified when it matters.

DETAILS

- If the party is large, discuss the size, shape, and the arrangement of the tables with the manager.
- The average restaurant table is a lot more versatile than the one at home. Squares can be made into circles, circles into ellipses, ellipses into whatever with a few flips of a commercial topper, extension, or leaf.

- Let it be known if there are special needs ahead of time: high chairs, wheelchair access, larger-than-life tables, and other requests.
- Call ahead if you're going to be late. I nearly lost a table for eight when our group showed up twenty minutes late at a popular San Francisco restaurant. When there's a long wait for a table, a frantic maître d' won't wait long to swoop up yours.
- Make place cards for a large party, and check to see if you can bring along decorations and/or flowers (if they're not provided) to personalize the table. It doesn't have to be home to look homey. Ever original, society host Elsie de Wolfe once laid her best china and silver at New York's self-service Automat.
- Always offer guests the better view when seating.
- If the party is going to the theater or some other event after dinner, notify the reservation taker when booking the meal. Remind the waiter of the time restriction when ordering as well, and allow at least an hour and a half for dining.
- Arrange ahead to have a candlelit cake delivered to the table with the appropriate fanfare if you're celebrating a birthday or anniversary. Ethnic restaurants are especially fun for this when servers sing in their native tongue.
- Give the maître d' your credit card number in advance so there won't be any embarrassing check wrestling from fellow guests. Either sign the bill at the end of the dinner when you quietly slip away from the table, or have the restaurant mail it to you the next day.
- Make sure you're not near your monthly limit before you hand over that credit card. "Hey, guys, I've got a bit of a problem here" is not the best way to cap off a party.

CHAPTER 14

HOUSEGUESTS— THE ULTIMATE TEST

When there were big houses, scads of servants, and plenty of leisure time, having a house full of guests was a treat. Today, having houseguests is like having children. They may be lovable, but they create work, discombobulate the routine, and are the ultimate test of our good graces. However, there *are* ways to make their presence, if not pleasant, at least tolerable.

"PEOPLE UNDERFOOT, MESSING UP MY HOUSE AND ROBBING ME OF MY PRIVACY ARE VERY STRESSFUL TO ME. I HAVE GOTTEN PHYSICALLY SICK KNOWING I HAD TO DEAL WITH HOUSE GUESTS."

—FED UP IN OHIO TO "DEAR ABBY"

EVERY GUEST A WANTED GUEST

- To avoid an unplanned visit from an unloved acquaintance, head 'em off at the pass. When you hear, "Billy-Joe, the twins, and I are going to be driving through the week of the Fourth, and we're hankerin' to spend some time with you." Counter with: "Oh, that's too bad, we're planning a trip ourselves" or "My parents may be staying with us that weekend." A little white lie is always better than a full-blown hassle.
- Know your limit. That old maxim about guests and fish smelling after three days is usually true. So unless the guest is that rare individual who is more help than a hindrance, limit the length of the stay.

- Pin down the departure date *before* guests arrive. Diplomatically asking, "How long can you stay?" ahead of time is easier than whimpering, "When are you leaving?" *after* guests have driven you bonkers.
- When the stated visit seems too long, be ready with something like "I'm sorry I'll be tied up most of that weekend, but I'd love to have you here Friday night." As Ann Landers says, "No one can impose on you unless you let them."

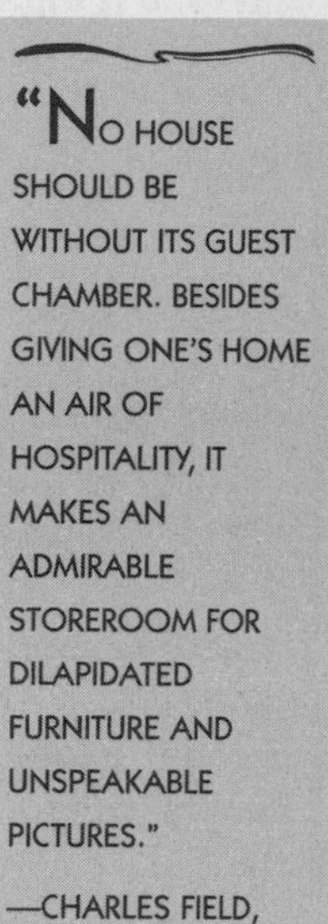

"NO HOUSE SHOULD BE WITHOUT ITS GUEST CHAMBER. BESIDES GIVING ONE'S HOME AN AIR OF HOSPITALITY, IT MAKES AN ADMIRABLE STOREROOM FOR DILAPIDATED FURNITURE AND UNSPEAKABLE PICTURES."
—CHARLES FIELD, JR., TURN-OF-THE-CENTURY WRITER

THE PINCH-HIT GUEST ROOM

Few homes today have the space for a room dedicated to the occasional visitor, so the key is to outfit a switch-hit space for easy flexibility.

- If the room doubles as an office, playroom, or hobby area, provide plenty of closed and organized storage, so papers and other paraphernalia are quickly and neatly stashed when guests invade.
- Hang an over-the-door-hook rack if the closet's already bulging. Sturdy plastic-coated steel racks can hold up to a dozen or so garments without interfering with the door closing. Find them in closet shops and mail order catalogs for under $20.
- Turn a twin bed by night into a sofa by day by pushing the long end against the wall, propping the pillows into back cushions, and covering it all with a tailored bedspread and pillow shams.
- Shop for a good sofa bed. According to the La-Z-Boy Chair Company, a quality sofa sleeper should open and fold smoothly and quietly, and have a firm innerspring mattress that's at least five inches thick.
- Air out a fold-up mattress every so often, since it can easily mildew in its dark and cramped position. When our sofa-sleeper came out of storage, I didn't notice the little green spots as I quickly made it up for my neatnick brother-in-law. I couldn't understand why he cut his planned visit so short till I changed the sheets. Yuck! Mold and mildew had permeated the whole bed.
- Check out pull-down beds. They're "now you see 'em, now you don't" arrangements that take about eight inches of wall space by day and fold down into a full-sized bed by night.

- Look into air mattresses. The Hold Everything chain carries a self-inflating model that accommodates standard sheets and folds up into its own duffel bag.
- Consider a hammock. One Seattle apartment dweller keeps a self-framed model in his home office for naps and the occasional guest. "It has the beauty of being comfortable enough for a short visit," says Joe Montani, "but not comfortable enough for a long one."
- Build a window seat/bed. One couple framed the wide windows in their Chicago town house with deep bookcases. They then nailed stock kitchen cabinets between them, and topped the cabinets with a slab of plywood, and a seventy-two-by-twenty-four-by-four-inch piece of upholstered foam. Filled with bolsters and pillows, it easily transforms from daytime seating to a nighttime bunk.

"ALL GUESTS MAKE US HAPPY . . . SOME BY COMING, SOME BY GOING."
—FRAMED SAMPLER AT A VERMONT INN

- Cover an inactive file cabinet with color-coordinated fabric and top it with a piece of cut-to-fit glass. I recently covered a bedside cabinet with a Wedgwood-blue tablecloth, a short white lace topper, and glass. The blue cloth was much too long for the piece, but instead of cutting and hemming, I simply gathered and hid the excess fabric behind the cabinet, next to the wall.

THE SUSPECTED ORIGIN OF THE WOMEN'S MOVEMENT

Emily Post may have discouraged more than a few would-be hosts in 1930, when she advised: "The hostess should get up early enough to precede her guests to the kitchen. She makes coffee, prepares fruit or juice, and cooks bacon and sausage enough for everyone. This can be kept warm on a hot plate or in a very low oven. She may put butter, eggs, and frying pan, or pancake batter and griddle by the stove, bread by the toaster, and an assortment of cereals and milk and cream on the table, which she sets with places for everyone. She may wait for her guests or she may eat her own breakfast and be ready to help the latecomers as they arrive."

- If the closet is the vault for the family's out-of-season clothes, make the most of rod space with multiple skirt, shirt, and trouser hangers, to make room for a visiting wardrobe.
- Provide a clothes tree, or consider lining the room with a band of Shaker-style pegs if the closet is hopelessly stuffed. Professional gardener Mary Culver dries flowers and herbs from some of the wooden pegs that encompass her country-style guest room. The rest of the pegs leave room for a hat, jacket, or robe.

WHEEL IT IN

- The best setup is having a guesthouse complete with kitchen and bath so guests and hosts have both privacy and autonomy. But some find renting an RV is nearly as good. Matthew and Marie Quinn of Orlando, Florida, rent one every January when their snowbird relatives descend from frozen New Hampshire. The motor home sleeps six, comes with a shower and kitchen, and hooks up to the main house with an extension cord. "Our tolerance level is much higher with 'Big Bertha' in the driveway," says Marie. "We're no longer tripping over suitcases in the living room and dealing with damp towels on the furniture."

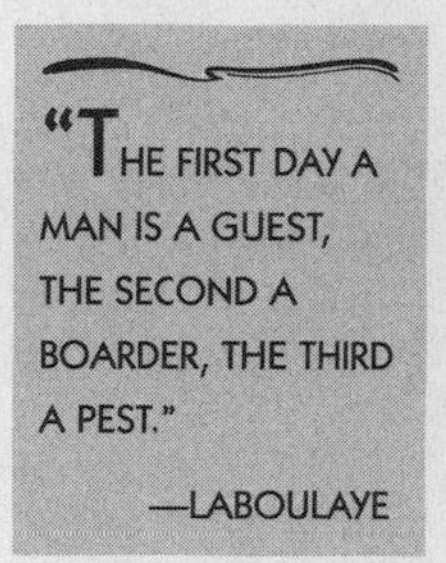
"THE FIRST DAY A
MAN IS A GUEST,
THE SECOND A
BOARDER, THE THIRD
A PEST."
—LABOULAYE

- Check the rules of the homeowners' association before decorating the driveway with a monster RV.

THE DEDICATED GUEST ROOM

It's rare today to have one room reserved for the occasional visitor, since spare space usually gets the office, gym, or giant junk drawer treatment. But if you've got it, baby, flaunt it. Getting the guest away from the household action makes everyone more comfortable.

- Choose a room in a quiet corner of the home. When we built our house eighteen years ago, we located the guest room directly across from the kitchen so it could also function as a handy office. Big mistake, as it turned out, since we have to tiptoe around the kitchen when guests are snoring a few feet away. Now that our kids have their own places, more or less, I'm starting to shunt overnighters to the upstairs bedrooms, where there's peace and privacy.
- Furnish the room with a couple of twin beds rather than one double.

Not all couples want to sleep together, but if they do, two beds can always be pushed into one.

- Slip the comforter into an easily washed duvet. The casing not only saves the comforter, it also can take the place of a top sheet, simplifying bed making.
- Allow at least an eighteen-inch clearance around the bed so no one has to be a contortionist to make it.
- Hang well-lined window coverings for privacy and to shut out drafts and morning light. Blackout drapes may keep guests from wandering around at the crack of dawn.
- Under- rather than overfurnish the room. Guests need plenty of open space for their own belongings.
- Place a sturdy trunk at the foot of the bed as a perch for a suitcase, a bottom, and as storage for extra pillows, sheets, and blankets.
- Slip a bar of sweet-smelling soap in the trunk, to keep linens fragrant.
- Put bedside lights on dimmers or provide a night-light so no one is blinded in the middle of the night. My husband and I once stayed in a Japanese inn where the night-light was *under* the bedside table. It provided just enough light to navigate across the room, but not enough to wake a sleeping roommate.
- Locate a night-light out of reach of dust ruffles, billowing curtains, and other potential flammables.

> "MY ACTUAL RELATIVES CONTINUE TO APPEAR FOR HOLIDAYS AND ODD WEEKENDS THROUGHOUT THE YEAR IN THE OLD-WORLD TRADITION OF WANDERING AND IMPOSING."
>
> —TOM CONNOR AND JIM DOWNEY, **IS MARTHA STEWART LIVING?**

PROCEED AT YOUR OWN RISK

Warning! Use the following ideas only if you really like the guest, and you're willing to risk having him, her, or them burrow in for awhile.

- Give 'em the Ritz treatment. As a flight attendant, Kathi Mallick notices what makes a hotel stay memorable for her and treats her guests accordingly. She hangs a thick terry robe in the closet and provides a "guest only" hair dryer in the bathroom. "Letting guests know they don't have to pack a hair dryer means they can pack another pair of shoes," explains Kathi.
- Make it as self-sufficient as possible with a comfortable reading chair, decent lighting, and a TV. The latter is handy when you want to watch PBS and your guest prefers MTV.

- Spray padded hangers with a favorite cologne, or tack small bags of potpourri to the back of the closet wall.
- Air out a seldom-used room and fill it with fragrant flowers like lilacs, gardenias, or roses just before guests arrive.

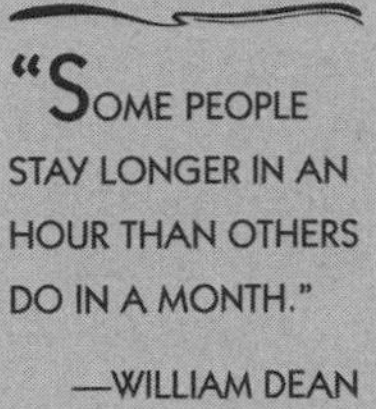

"SOME PEOPLE STAY LONGER IN AN HOUR THAN OTHERS DO IN A MONTH."
—WILLIAM DEAN HOWELLS

- Keep a flower arrangement on the bedside table low and compact so it doesn't get knocked over when guests grope for the alarm clock.
- Place a small, pretty bowl on a dresser or nightstand to hold a watch and other jewelry.
- Find out what visitors like to read and stock up on the genre at a secondhand bookstore. Paperbacks are best since they are easy to transport to the beach, park, or back home on the plane.
- Provide two pillows each, one firm and one soft, as a choice for sleeping, and as props for reading in bed. A baby pillow is a comfy addition and makes a nice little neck roll.
- Dress the bed with fine-quality sheets. The higher the thread count, the better the sheet feels and holds up.
- Consider flannel sheets in winter. They're as warm and cozy as a fuzzy nightgown and come out of the dryer wrinkle-free.
- Fold a quilt, throw, or blanket over the foot of the bed for an afternoon nap, and to pull up on a cold night.
- Stock a guest room basket with a small flashlight, sewing kit, pen, notepad, a bookmark, alarm clock, ear plugs, and a book light. My favorite book light is worn on a strap over the neck, leaving the hands free.

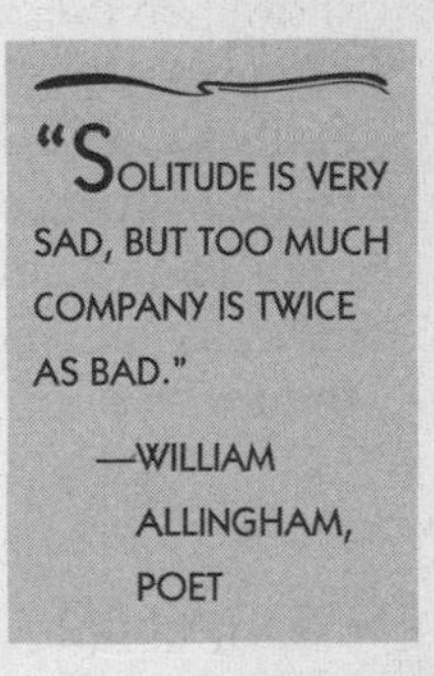

"SOLITUDE IS VERY SAD, BUT TOO MUCH COMPANY IS TWICE AS BAD."
—WILLIAM ALLINGHAM, POET

- Overlay existing framed photos with snapshots of the visiting guest, if you have them. Slip in suitable replacements when the next guest arrives.
- Ready the room for arrival. I once checked into the Prescott Hotel in San Francisco at midnight, weary and grumpy after a grueling work and travel day. I was greeted by a softly lit room, a turned-down bed, fresh fruit on the table, and classical music on the radio. Small gestures that made me feel welcome, soothed, and cared for.

THE BATHROOM

- Provide a basket with small necessities: wrapped soap, razor, toothbrush, toothpaste, cup, shampoo, conditioner, and hand lotion. Not only do these little goodies make us look like heavenly hosts, they prevent guests from getting into *our* personal items.
- Save those airline kits and hotel amenities. The small bottles are just the right size to stock a basket.
- Place a nonskid mat in both the shower and the tub.
- Prevent scalded buns by setting the water heater no higher than 120 degrees.
- Plug in a night-light for safety's sake and so no one is blinded by flipping on the high beams in the middle of the night.
- Keep a squeegee in the shower so guests will, hopefully, wipe down the shower walls and door while they're wet.
- Install a ground-fault circuit interrupter so Aunt Florrie won't fry if she drops her hair dryer into a water-filled sink, tub, or toilet. A GFCI cuts electrical current when it senses a hazard.
- Store at least a couple of rolls of toilet paper in the bathroom so there's no crisis when the holder runs dry.

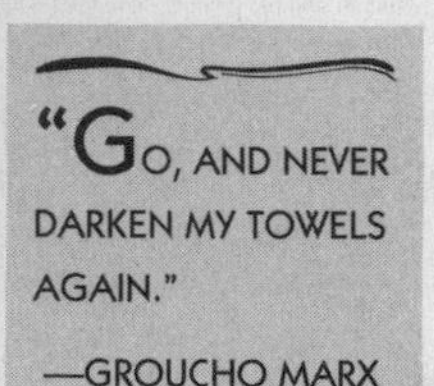

"GO, AND NEVER DARKEN MY TOWELS AGAIN."
—GROUCHO MARX

- Hang an expanding rack on the back of the door for that extra towel, robe, shower cap, and swimsuit.
- Keep a long-handled brush in a caddy next to the toilet bowl so stains can be dealt with immediately.
- Place a plastic bottle of pump soap on the counter and in the tub and shower so there's no melting soap to slime up surfaces.
- Mount a roll of paper towels on an unobtrusive holder so guests can easily wipe a splattered counter or mirror.
- Lock away medicines and cleaning supplies if there are young children in the party. If guests are old enough to know better, keep cleaning supplies accessible. With any luck, they'll clean up after themselves.

ENTERTAINING

- Ask guests, ahead of the arrival date, if they have people to see or other commitments while they're visiting, then plan accordingly.
- Check the local paper or regional magazine's entertainment section to see who and what's in town at the time of the visit.

- Allow for decompression. Travel is tiring, so minimize first-day activities, and plan some quiet R&R time.
- Keep 'em busy. "Plan lots of activities," advised Dr. Joyce Brothers in a *San Diego Union-Tribune* article, "so people can go off, have new experiences, come back and have something to talk about."
- Ask guests what they'd most like to do, but offer an alternative if it's going to qualify you for martyrdom. My seventeen-year-old niece, Cheri, wanted to go to Rodeo Drive in Beverly Hills on her last visit. But since it's a nerve-racking, one-hundred-mile drive, I offered her the alternative of shopping and people watching (euphemism for checking out the University of California guys) in close by but equally chic La Jolla.
- Schedule private time by packing guests off on a bus tour of the area. Most tour companies pick up at local hotels, where one doesn't have to be registered, and may offer half-day, full-day, and sometimes overnight tours. It's an especially useful ploy for carless guests. While they play the tourist, we enjoy a peaceful interlude.
- Check to see if the auto insurance covers guests if you plan to lend the car. Keep the household bikes in good repair, just in case.
- Buy refundable zoo, amusement park, or other local attraction tickets ahead of time to ensure some free time for yourself. "We've just been there," you can say, "you'll love it."
- Plan for bad weather. Museums, galleries, the movies, as well as the VCR and board games, can come to the rescue when the sun doesn't.
- Start a puzzle on a table that can be left undisturbed. Most people find a puzzle in progress irresistible.

WHAT'S FOR LUNCH?

Lunch is the bugaboo of many a host. We may be used to scarfing down peanut butter and jelly or a bean-dripping burrito over the sink, but that hardly seems appropriate for the honored guest. Or does it? According to a Washington Post *survey, the top ten lunch choices for Americans are:*

1. *pizza*
2. *ham sandwich*
3. *hot dog*
4. *peanut-butter-and-jelly sandwich*
5. *steak*
6. *macaroni and cheese*
7. *turkey sandwich*
8. *cheese sandwich*
9. *hamburger*
10. *spaghetti*

FEEDING

- Make cooking count by asking guests what foods they like and dislike, as well as foods they can't tolerate, *before* they arrive. When the response is "Don't worry, I eat anything," and you respond with "Good, I've been wanting to try some really exotic recipes," they'll likely fess up.
- Do the major marketing beforehand and stock up on extra milk, bread, and breakfast foods.
- Cereal is one of the easiest breakfasts to serve. Keep several choices on hand, as well as plenty of bananas or berries.
- Set up a breakfast bar with the coffeemaker, toaster, and food supplies within close range of each other so guests can easily help themselves.
- Stock the freezer with casseroles, soups, and stews. Round them off with a simple salad, a good loaf of bread, and an easy dessert.
- When barbecuing hamburgers, throw something extra on the grill for tomorrow: chicken breasts for a salad, more hamburgers to be crumpled into spaghetti sauce or chili, a fish fillet for fried rice.
- Take Grandma's Sunday-dinner approach: a big roast the first night, then variations on the theme the rest of the week: stir-fry with vegetables, tacos, and finally soup. Intersperse with pizza, pasta primavera, or broiled chicken.
- Make a double or triple batch of rice. Use it to stretch a soup or salad, or make fried rice with leftover veggies, meat, and eggs.
- Hard-cook a dozen eggs at a time. Store them in the original carton and use them in sandwiches, salads, or a "boneless chicken" lunch.
- Steam a bag of tiny new potatoes and keep them in the fridge for soups, oven fries, and frittatas.
- Plan a night of board games or videos and order in pizza.
- Knock 'em out with a nightcap when you're ready for bed and they're still wired. In his book *Restful Sleep,* Deepak Chopra suggests adding a couple of pinches each of ground cardamom and nutmeg to a cup of warm milk to increase its sleep-inducing properties.

KIDS

- If there's a baby in the entourage, consider renting or borrowing a crib, playpen, stroller, and other large equipment, so the parents don't have to haul it all.
- Make sure the crib's mattress fits snugly within the frame and the bars are no more than two and three-eighths inches apart, for safety's sake.

- Have the crib fully made up, so it's ready for landing. Babies are usually tired and cranky at the end of a trip.
- Place a stuffed animal in the crib or on the bed for a visiting child.
- Provide a small child's chair in the living room. It can be pulled right up to the coffee table, and it may keep the kid off the good stuff. You can find charming and affordable little chairs in consignment shops.
- Buy a few puzzles, games, and toys for little visitors. A new stash is always enticing, and may keep curious hands away from the no-nos.
- Check out children's books and videos from the children's department at the local library.
- Investigate fun things to do around town: children's museums, library story hours, miniature golf, and day camps at the local park.
- Make the backyard as inviting as possible with a supervised kiddie pool, badminton, horseshoes, and other furniture and nerve savers. One woman I know sets up tents in her backyard when her four granddaughters visit. "Camping out not only keeps them happily occupied," she reports, "it keeps the house cleaner."

DETAILS

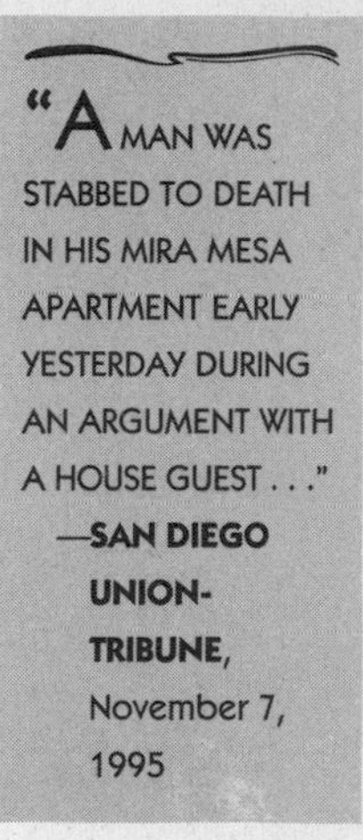
"A MAN WAS STABBED TO DEATH IN HIS MIRA MESA APARTMENT EARLY YESTERDAY DURING AN ARGUMENT WITH A HOUSE GUEST . . ."

—**SAN DIEGO UNION-TRIBUNE,** November 7, 1995

- Silence a chiming clock. We may have gotten used to that mantel piece that gongs every fifteen minutes, but it will likely keep a guest up at all hours.
- Warn guests of wandering pets and other things that go bump in the night.
- Point out the home's idiosyncrasies. I often neglect to tell visitors our hot water system is on a manual timer, till they ask how we put up with such cold showers. This forgetfulness apparently runs in the family. When my daughter Kelley and I stayed at my brother's vacant apartment recently, he called to make sure we took in the view from the rooftop terrace. He forgot, however, to mention that we needed a different key to get back into the building. So on an early Sunday morning, we found ourselves trapped on the 90-degree-and-rising roof. We hollered, we banged on the door, we searched in vain for an escape, but it wasn't till I hung from the rooftop and yelled "Fire" that we were finally rescued by a grumbling tenant.
- Show how to turn off the alarm system if guests accidentally trip the switch.
- Demonstrate how to tune in cable and use the VCR.

- Check for charred spots and bent-out-of-shape wiring in electric blankets to avoid cooking guests.
- Drag out and dust off that gift from visiting Auntie Em or Cousin Vinnie. When writer Lance Johnson's grandmother visits, he always replaces the Ansel Adams poster in his entry with a still life she painted for him. "It's god-awful," he says, "but it makes her so happy to see it displayed."
- Make sure to reciprocate the visit. Doesn't Uncle Buck have a cute little cottage on the Cape?

CHAPTER 15

QUICK CLEANUPS

Guests can leave a mother lode of work in their wake, but with a few defensive moves, a little damage control, and a few shortcuts, we can eliminate a lot of the toil that comes with the territory.

THE DEFENSE

"I CAN'T DEAL
WITH CLEANING UP.
LET'S SELL THE
HOUSE."
—POST-PARTY HOST
MARILYN LOVELL,
IN APOLLO 13

- Distribute plenty of coasters around the home to safeguard any wood tops that are not protected.
- Spray upholstery and table linens with a soil repellent like Scotchgard. Most upholstery fabrics are factory sprayed before they hit the showroom but need a reapplication after every third cleaning. Test-spray on a hidden area of the piece to make sure it doesn't discolor the fabric.
- Avoid using paper plates at stand-up parties since they're easy to overload and spill.
- Strategically place plenty of wastepaper baskets in entertainment zones so guests can easily discard the discardable.

MACHINE DISHWASHING

- If the water supply is hard and the dishwasher is used only occasionally, pour about a cup of distilled vinegar onto its floor to dissolve

hose-clogging mineral deposits. Let it soak for at least a couple of hours, then run the machine as usual.
- Soak pots and pans while scraping and loading plates, cutlery, and glassware.
- Load like items together so unloading goes faster.
- If hard water runs through those hoses, minimize spotting by removing items at the end of the rinse cycle.

HAND WASHING DISHES

- Wear rubber gloves for a better grip, to tolerate the hottest water, and to save your hands.
- Slather hands with a rich lotion before donning gloves. The gloves will slip on easier, and the heat helps the lotion penetrate the skin.
- Use a rubber dishpan to avoid chipping china and crystal against a sink's hard surface.
- Start with lightly soiled items like glassware and silver, followed by plates, with pots and pans last.
- Change the dishwater as it becomes cold, grungy, or sudsless.
- Bring out the sparkle in crystal with a capful of ammonia in the wash water and a half cup of distilled vinegar in the rinse water.
- Never soak cutlery, since the minerals and chlorine found in most water supplies pit sterling, silver plate, and even stainless steel. The Reed & Barton silver company suggests a quick dip, a light scrub, and a *thorough* rinse.
- Don't even *think* about draining silver on a rubber mat. Rubber darkens silver.
- Soak pots and pans that held eggs and starchy foods like rice and oatmeal in cold water.

AFTER THE PARTY'S OVER

There are spots on the sofa
And grease on the floor
The dishes are filthy
But the washer's no more
The party is over
Adios to the guests
They've taken my sparkle
And left me their mess

- Soften a burned coating on a pot or pan by sprinkling it with baking soda. Add water, bring to a boil, then wash as usual.
- Clean the outside bottoms of pots and pans thoroughly. If grease remains, the bottom blackens when heated.
- Rinse dishes in the hottest water possible so they dry quickly.
- Don't dump the trash until all the cutlery is accounted for. It's easy to lose a knife, spoon, or fork in the rush to clean up.

> "I DON'T EVEN WASH DISHES IN THE DISHWASHER. I USE IT TO STORE TO-GO MENUS AND WARRANTIES FOR ELECTRONIC EQUIPMENT."
>
> —PAULA POUNDSTONE

TACKLING THE KITCHEN

- Keep a putty knife in a kitchen drawer to scrape up hardened goop off counters and floors.
- Loosen baked-on gunk in the oven by warming it till it reaches about 150 degrees. Turn it off, spray with oven cleaner, marinate overnight, then wipe it out in the morning.
- Spills and splatters in a microwave absorb energy and slow cooking. Blast them away by nuking a tablespoon of baking soda in a cup of water for thirty seconds, then mop up the fallout.
- Clean stubborn spills in the fridge with a paste of baking soda and water.
- Keep a toothbrush under the sink to tackle nooks and crannies in small appliances like food processors and electric can openers.
- Run a wooden barbecue skewer under the edge of a sink to remove gunk.
- Clean and sanitize cutting boards with diluted chlorine bleach. Rinse and dry thoroughly before storing.

WOOD FURNITURE

- Rub a little furniture oil, mayonnaise, or toothpaste into a white ring stain left from a drinking glass.
- Scrape candle wax from a table by letting it cool, then rubbing it with a credit card in the direction of the wood grain.
- If the table has a wax finish, remove fine scratches with a little paste wax. Apply it in circular sweeps, then buff it dry.
- Attack deeper gouges with a grain-matching crayon. Home centers and hardware stores carry small furniture repair kits that include various wood-colored crayons and liquid scratch polish. Paste shoe

polish or even a broken nut meat (a walnut on a walnut grain, pecan on pecan) may also do the trick.

UPHOLSTERY

- Scoop or towel-blot the spill first, then treat immediately. The longer the stain sits, the more it takes root.
- If the care tag is long gone, try the cleaning product on an inconspicuous spot to avoid making a bigger mess. An acetate fabric, for instance, can dissolve with a product that contains acetone, and dyed cotton, linen, and rayon can bleed when wet.
- Mix up either one tablespoon ammonia diluted in one-third cup water, or one-third cup distilled vinegar diluted in two-thirds cup water. Both are effective stain busters on most fabrics.
- If you prefer a ready-made product, try Blue Coral Dri-Clean Upholstery and Carpet Cleaner, found at auto supply stores. The water-based cleaner tested best out of the eleven products *Consumer Reports* used on a wide range of upholstery fabrics.
- Freeze chewing gum with an ice cube, and let candle wax harden naturally so they're easily scraped off.
- Lightly sponge or spray any cleaner to avoid saturating the fabric.
- Wipe the stain in the direction of the nap with an absorbent white cloth. Avoid scrubbing, since doing so can frazzle fibers.
- Dry the fabric, then gently whisk the nap in both directions with a suede brush.
- Leave stains on suede, aniline-dyed leather, and silk to the pros.
- Find a top-notch pro by getting references from a fine-furniture store, an interior designer, or local dry cleaner.

> "THE DISH TOOK TWO DAYS TO PREPARE, A FULL NINE MINUTES TO EAT, AND THREE DAYS TO WASH UP AFTER."
>
> —ANTHONY LAKE, "LOOK BACK IN HUNGER," **THE NEW YORKER**

TABLE LINENS

- Fight fire with fire. Pour a little white wine over a red wine stain and launder as usual. If you've drunk all the wine, stretch the affected area over a bowl, rub in a paste of salt and cold water, then pour a kettle of boiling water over the spot before laundering.
- If table linens are white, treat stains by wiping them with a cotton swab of chlorine bleach just before they go into the washer.

- Kiss off lipstick, gravy, and other greasy stains with a little dry cleaning solvent and launder as usual.
- Scrape hardened candle wax off a tablecloth with a dull knife or credit card.
- Deal with wax residue by laying a white paper towel or plain brown paper grocery bag over it, and press with a *warm* iron. Repeat until the heat draws the wax into the paper, then launder the cloth.
- If the meal was truly revolting, rinse off the vomit, soak the stain in a lightly diluted enzyme detergent, then add a few drops of ammonia to the wash water.
- If the guests were hostile and the knives sharp, pretreat bloodstains with a paste of meat tenderizer and cold water. Launder as usual.

HARD FLOORS

- Tackle heel marks on wood floors by buffing them with extra-fine steel wool touched with a little floor wax.
- Camouflage scrapes and scratches with a matching shade of shoe polish or crayon. Rub or scrape off the excess so it doesn't get tracked through the house.
- Spot-clean vinyl floors with a little distilled vinegar, window cleaner, or the product the floor manufacturer recommends.

CARPETS AND RUGS

- Attack a spill quickly. Scoop it if it's a solid, blot it with a towel if it's a liquid.
- Sop up a spill with a clean white terry or plain white paper towel, since anything colored may introduce its own stain. (I learned this the hard way by trying to scoop up spilled dip on a white rug with a bright blue napkin.) Give the towel a minute or so to soak up the stain so there's no temptation to rub it in. Then pat dry.
- If you've got pale carpeting, always serve food and drink with white napkins, so helpful and clueless types don't make the above mistake.

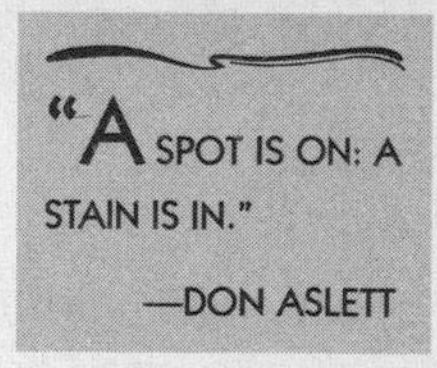

"A SPOT IS ON: A STAIN IS IN."
—DON ASLETT

- If the stain has dried into a hard glob, scrape up as much as possible with a dull blade, a credit card, or the rim of an old spoon, then whisk the spot with a small brush.
- After scraping or blotting the spill, gently sponge it with a little club soda, white distilled vinegar, or cold tap water. Work from the outer edge to the center, so the stain doesn't spread.

- Don't flood the spot. Too much liquid can damage the carpet backing and rot the pad.
- Sprinkle a little cornstarch or baby powder on a greasy stain. Let it set a few hours or overnight, then vacuum. Apply a solvent-based dry cleaner like K2r or Goddard's Dry Clean if a shadow remains.
- Test a product in an inconspicuous area before using it on a noticeable spot.
- Rinse all cleaners thoroughly, since residue attracts more soil.
- Allow the cleaned area time to dry. Walking on it too soon could double the trouble.
- Speed the drying process with a cool fan or an open window, but avoid heat, since it can set residual spots.
- Brush the treated and dried pile with a small brush to bring it back to life.
- Trim out a hopeless stain or burn with a pair of manicure scissors. If the damage is deeper, surgically remove it by cutting around the spot with a sharp utility knife, right through to the backing. Cut a section from a remnant or a hidden area of the carpet, using the damaged piece as a stencil. Glue it with a heavy-duty adhesive, making sure the donor pile is running in the same direction as the existing carpet.
- If all else fails, bring in a pro or rearrange the furniture. Maybe the sofa *would* look better over that spot.

"LADIES, SINCE THIS AIRLINE IS ENVIRONMENTALLY CONSCIENTIOUS, WE ASK THAT YOU WIPE THE LIPSTICK OFF YOUR STYROFOAM COFFEE CUPS SO WE CAN USE THEM ON OUR CONTINUOUS FLIGHT TO ALBUQUERQUE THIS MORNING."

—FLIGHT ATTENDANT/COMEDIAN, SOUTHWEST AIRLINES

STAYIN' ALIVE

- Do not transfer home brews into unmarked bottles or old food containers.
- Open a window when using a dry cleaning solvent, since the fumes can be toxic.
- Never mix chemicals without checking the labels first. The fumes from a brew of ammonia and bleach, for example, can be fatal to the user. It would be *so* embarrassing to die from housework.

STRATEGIES

- Put stragglers to work. "This place is going to take hours to clean. Care to give me a hand?" You'll either recruit them or send them packing. Either way, you win.

- Do as much as possible right after the last guest departs. We may be dead tired, but that mess is going to look worse in the light of day.
- Concentrate on the dishes and kitchen. You don't want any more guests in the morning, especially the crawling kind.
- If you're really bushed, set the kitchen timer for a fifteen-minute attack, then call it a night. It's amazing what can be accomplished in a quarter hour, especially when the ticking keeps us on track.
- Work around a room moving from left to right. It's not only efficient, we can also gauge our progress as we go.
- Simplify the process by using one good all-purpose cleaner like a mix of distilled vinegar and water.
- Fasten a long extension cord to the vacuum cleaner, so there's less need to plug and unplug.
- Slip a jazzy tape into the boom box and get movin'. Music can make cleanup, if not pleasant, at least bearable.

CHAPTER 16

HOW TO BE A GREAT GUEST

We can take all the shortcuts there are on the planet, but playing the guest is always going to be a lot more fun than working as the host. The idea is to get so good at the former, we won't have time to play the latter. Well, maybe that *is* a stretch, but you get the idea. It just boils down to cultivating a few qualities like consideration, enthusiasm, and a little social savvy.

SAVOIR FAIRE

- Answer all invitations promptly. Since food and space need calculating well ahead of time, don't wait to respond till the last minute.
- Forget the "I'll try to make it" replies. Parties can't be planned on "maybes."
- Be true to your word. If you say you'll be there, be there. The only good excuse for flaking is a contagious disease or death. Our own.

"NEVER EAT
MORE THAN YOU
CAN LIFT."
—MISS PIGGY

- Fake it. If we're pooped, we need to perk up. If we're blue, we need to buck up. If we're feeling shy, we need to make the effort. We owe it to our hosts to put on a happy face, dive in, and socialize.
- Volunteer. Offer to pass a tray, answer the door, or hang coats. We're not only helping the host, we're also giving ourselves the freedom to move about and mingle.

- Back off. Learn to take no for an answer if your host doesn't want help.
- Introduce yourself to strangers to take the pressure off the host.
- Spread the wealth. It's bad form to huddle with the same person or small group throughout the party. We have an obligation to touch base with as many people as we can.
- Preserve egos. When it's time to exit one conversation for another, it's best to introduce the person we're bailing to someone close by. If that's not possible, make it a point to carry a half-filled glass so there's always an excuse to "freshen this drink."

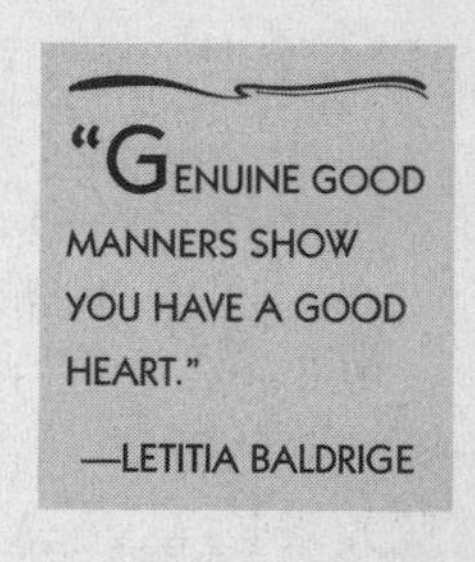

"GENUINE GOOD MANNERS SHOW YOU HAVE A GOOD HEART."
—LETITIA BALDRIGE

- Include wallflowers. If someone nearby is standing alone, it's thoughtful to draw her into the conversation by briefly explaining what is being discussed, and asking her opinion.
- Develop listening skills. The most fascinating conversationalist is usually a fascinated listener.
- Come up for air. Some people rattle on endlessly when they're nervous. But as one social pundit observed, "The time to stop talking is when the other person nods his head affirmatively but says nothing."

DON'T BE A DIP

Land O' Lakes, the butter and dip makers, recently conducted a survey asking guests what they most hated about other people's dipping habits. They came up with the following pet peeves:

1. *Double-dipping—scooping from the community bowl, taking a bite, then redipping.*
2. *Tasting the dip with a finger.*
3. *Digging a submerged chip out by hand.*
4. *Eating straight out of the communal dip bowl.*
5. *Sticking food into someone else's dip on his or her plate.*

POLITICALLY CORRECT DIPPING

1. *Rescue a broken chip with a spoon.*
2. *Instead of hogging the bowl, spoon a little dip onto your plate.*
3. *Never double-dip.*
4. *Eat from your own plate.*
5. *Don't drip the dip.*

- Smoke outside unless it's a cigar convention. Even if someone else is puffing away, ask your host's permission before you light up.
- Leave the bathroom orderly: straighten towels, tissue up hair and splatters, and flush. A party is no time to practice water conservation.
- Cover the damage. When we break something, we're obligated to repair or replace it.
- Offer to be the designated driver if someone drinks too much.
- Call the next day and compliment the host on something specific you enjoyed: the mix of people, the imaginative food, whatever. Morning-after praise carries more weight than parting pleasantries.

SOCIAL MISDEMEANORS

- Don't ask who's coming. It sounds as if we're questioning our host's taste in friends.
- Never arrive early. My husband once opened the door to an early bird just as I had run naked from the shower to my office down the hall to answer the phone. He had to give a tour of our ratty garden just to set me free. However, *we* once made the mistake of arriving a *day* early for a dinner party.
- Don't be more than a half hour late. It's upsetting to schedule an event at 7:00 and have no one show by 7:30. Actor Ben Stein says he can always tell how late a person will be by the responsibilities they shoulder. A busy guest with a good job and lots of commitments will always be on time, he writes in *Reader's Digest.* Someone with a low-level job and few responsibilities will be between fifteen minutes and an hour late. And someone with nothing to do all day will be very, very late, or maybe not show at all.
- Never take a house tour unless invited by the lord or lady of the manor.
- Don't bring an uninvited guest without checking with the host first. If you know someone will be visiting at the time, say so. Responding "I'd love to come, but my brother will be visiting from Boston" gives the host a choice on whether to include you and your guest, or issue a rain check.
- Never ask for a drink that requires more than two ingredients. A martini is fine, but a frozen daiquiri, unless it's offered, is ridiculous.

> "A DINNER INVITATION, ONCE ACCEPTED, IS A SACRED OBLIGATION. IF YOU DIE BEFORE THE DINNER TAKES PLACE, YOUR EXECUTOR MUST ATTEND THE DINNER."
>
> —WARD MCALLISTER, **SOCIETY AS I HAVE FOUND IT** (1890)

- Don't break up the party. When we have to leave early, it's best to do so unobtrusively. Find the host, make a brief explanation, offer your compliments, and slip out quietly.

COME BEARING GIFTS

Bringing a small gift is a thoughtful gesture when visiting, especially if it's attuned to the taste and interests of the host. The offering can be as small as a set of paper cocktail napkins, or if it's a longer visit, food, a cookbook, or a board game for the family. Other possibilities:

- *wine*
- *a small inspirational paperback*
- *a pair of beeswax candles*
- *quality potpourri*
- *boxed notepaper*
- *a flowering houseplant*
- *chocolate truffles*
- *designer vinegar*
- *gourmet preserves*
- *a toy to keep the little terror occupied*

If you're flying in and can't fit a gift into that already bulging bag, either buy the gift at the destination or send something after departure.

NOTE: Avoid bringing gifts of food and drink to a dinner party, since a host may feel obligated to serve them. There's also the potential for embarrassment, as was the case when one host eyed a bottle of wine on her dinner table. She asked her spouse, "Honey, would you please bring in the bottle I brought up from the cellar? Meg deserves better than this." "Darling," replied her husband, "Meg brought *the wine."*

DINNER GAFFES AND GRACES

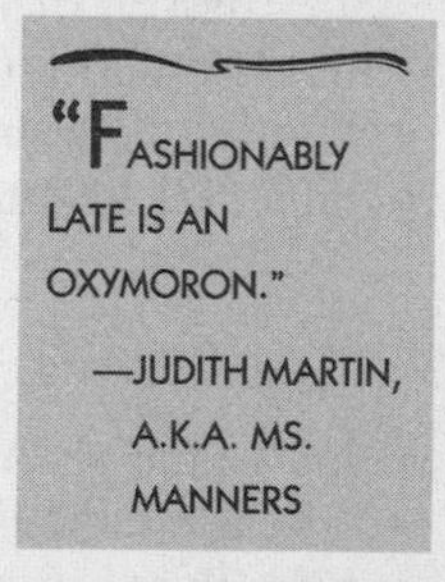
"FASHIONABLY
LATE IS AN
OXYMORON."
—JUDITH MARTIN,
A.K.A. MS.
MANNERS

- Let your host know ahead if you or your partner has any dietary restrictions or food allergies. It's no fun slaving over barbecued steaks to find one of your guests is a vegetarian.
- Show up. When Liz and John Seibold were first married, they invited their boss and his wife to an elaborate dinner Liz took days to prepare. When the guests didn't show at the agreed-upon hour, Liz phoned, only to hear, "Oh, we just didn't feel like going out tonight." "We always declined their invitations after that,"

said Liz. "Not so much out of spite, we just didn't want to hang out with ignorant people."

"YOU HAVE A GREATER IMPACT ON OTHERS BY THE WAY YOU LISTEN THAN BY THE WAY YOU TALK."

—JAMES R. FISHER, JR.

- Never ask if something is made from scratch. Most hosts don't want to admit that the moo shu pork is from the local take-out or the cheesecake came from the grocer's warehouse.
- Sing for your supper. Learn to tell a good joke or an interesting story. "If you can't be funny," advised *New Yorker* founder Harold Ross, "be interesting."
- Don't try too hard to dazzle. "Wit is the salt of conversation," wrote William Hazlitt, "not the food."
- Know your place. Formal dinners can have enough silver to befuddle even a bon vivant, but place settings are based on common sense. Utensils line up so that the outside implements are for the first course, and the rest work their way into the plate for succeeding courses. Dessert utensils are usually placed at the top of the plate.
- Pass dishes to the right at a family-style meal, and the breadbasket to the left. The ritual makes sense when you realize that most people are right-handed and the bread plate is always to the left of the dinner plate.
- Don't freak. If there's a worm in the salad or a bug in the beans, be brave and eat around it. Garden creatures only like what's fresh and tasty, so you're in good company.
- Break bread. Forget slicing and dicing those rolls with a knife. Tear off small chunks by hand and butter them over the bread plate, not the dinner dish.
- Praise the cook. Cooking is a creative effort that requires and deserves accolades.
- Know your cue. The best time to leave is about forty-five minutes after dessert or when the hosts start stifling yawns. Just don't wait till they drop off on the sofa.
- Always thank the host for the "lovely evening" not for the "delicious dinner." The latter sounds as if we just came to fill our bellies.

RESTAURANTS

- Leave the phone at home. It's as intrusive as an uninvited guest.
- Take it off: the hat if you're male, the purse off the table if you're female. Purses (and briefcases) often hang out on car and workplace floors, so plunking them on the dinner table is not only invasive, it's unsanitary.

- Never table-hop. Your best friend may be dining with Tom Cruise at the corner table, but being schmoozed by the standing is awkward for the seated.
- Don't dive. If you drop a utensil, ask the server for another.
- Order conservatively. If your host doesn't drink, think twice before ordering a double Scotch and a bottle of wine.
- Be generous. Offer to split the bill, or at least take care of the tip.

> "GREAT GUESTS ARE THOSE WHO KNOW INSTINCTIVELY THAT THEY HAVE BEEN INVITED TO AMUSE THEMSELVES BY DAY AND THEIR HOST BY NIGHT."
>
> —JULEE ROSSO AND SHEILA LUKINS, **THE SILVER PALATE COOKBOOK**

SLEEPOVERS

- Recognize a reluctant acceptance. When you tell Aunt Minnie you'd like to camp out in her living room for a week, be sensitive to responses like "That's the week of the pig slaughter," especially if she doesn't raise pigs.
- Bring the right clothes. Jeans and sweats might be the most comfortable weekend wear, but they limit our range if our hosts have dressier plans.
- Leave pets at home. Even animal lovers hate someone else's fleas and swirling fur.
- Be prepared to amuse yourself. Bring a good book, a tourist guide, and a car. Most hosts have lives.
- Give time to your hosts. Spending most of the stay visiting others makes hosts feel used and abused.
- Treat the host to lunch, brunch, or dinner at least one day of your stay.
- Don't compare. The weather, baseball team, and school system might be better in our neck of the woods, but our hosts don't want to hear it.
- Give feedback. Guests who answer "I don't care" when asked what they'd like to eat, drink, or do have driven many a host up a wall.
- Use your phone card or call collect if you have to make long-distance calls.
- Childproof your belongings. Keep toiletries, dry-cleaning bags, and medicine away from tiny hands by either locking the suitcase or storing items well out of reach.

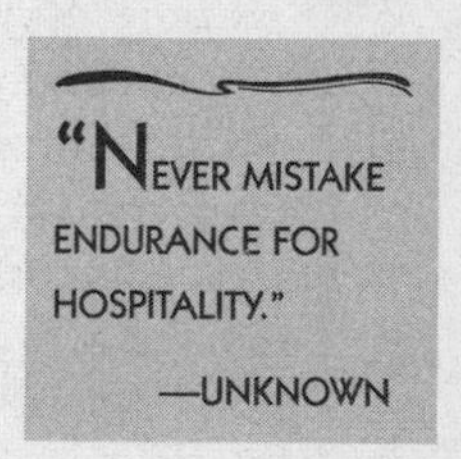
"NEVER MISTAKE
ENDURANCE FOR
HOSPITALITY."
—UNKNOWN

- Childproof your children. Bring or plan to rent a playpen, gate, and/or harness if you use them at home. Familiarize yourself with your kids' play space, set boundaries, and know where they are at all times.

- Pack plenty of opaque, airtight plastic bags for diaper and sanitary napkin disposal.
- Breast-feed in private. It may be the most natural act in the world, but it makes some people uncomfortable.

TEN STUPID THINGS GUESTS DO TO MESS UP THEIR LIVES*

The following blunders are known to have loosened a few rungs on the social ladder.

1. *Neglecting to show. Even at a huge reception, absences are noticed and noted. Hosts are like elephants: they never forget snubs.*
2. *Dressing inappropriately. It may seem trivial, but showing up for a church wedding in low-cut latex, at a snazzy restaurant in a grungy T-shirt, or at a black-tie bash in white frayed shorts may not garner future invitations.*
3. *Hogging the conversation. Personal stories can be entertaining, but "I" statements need to be peppered with queries about the welfare and opinion of others.*
4. *Pigging out. A healthy appetite is one thing, but when a guest hits the buffet table like a shark in a feeding frenzy, it's duly noted.*
5. *Sopping up. Lushes have been known to end up drinking the cooking sherry alone on Saturday nights.*
6. *Showing off. Bragging about or even mentioning parties others weren't invited to won't endear a guest to anyone. Social butterflies must practice discretion if they want to continue flitting.*
7. *Gossiping. Maybe mutual friends* are *being haughty or naughty. But backstabbing over the canapés is never good form.*
8. *Littering. Guests who leave wet towels on the floor, dirty socks on the sofa, and crusty plates on the counter have been known to be murdered in their beds.*
9. *Loitering. Staying on beyond the agreed-upon time, whether the flight is canceled or we're just having a great time, is a no-no.*
10. *Neglecting to say thanks. Compared with the time and trouble the host expends, extending a thank-you call or note takes little effort.*

*With apologies to Dr. Laura Schlessinger.

- Be useful. Play with the hosts' kids, walk the dog, set the table. My sister-in-law Ruth always insists on doing the dishes, contending she loves the job. I've learned to indulge this defect.
- Unless there's a separate guest bath, don't clutter the family bathroom with your own paraphernalia.
- Make the bed every morning, fold the newspaper when finished, and tissue toothpaste out of the sink. In short, be neat, even if it doesn't come naturally.
- Remember to put the toilet seat down, especially at night. No one appreciates a midnight dunk in a cold toilet.
- Keep the stay short and sweet. "Superior people," quipped poet Marianne More, "never make long visits."
- Make it or fake it. Ask your hosts for new sheets so you can make the bed on the day of departure. If they decline, strip and fold the sheets, and make the bed without them. That way the bed looks decent until your host gets around to hauling out new linens.
- Remember that you may be on vacation, but your hosts are probably working their tails off.
- Get in the habit of rounding up personal items at the end of the day, so you don't mislay anything and inconvenience anybody.
- Haul it home. A forgotten item means the host has to hunt down the right-sized box, pack it, wrap it, and take it to the post office. A poem submitted to "Dear Abby" by a friend of its author, the late Ethel Jacobson, says it all:

> "ALWAYS SAY 'THANK YOU,' EVEN IF YOU DON'T MEAN IT."
>
> —FORREST GUMP

LEFTOVERS

Perennial pest
To haunt our nest
Is the featherbrained
Forgetful guest
Who comes for the day
Or a three-month stay
And leaves behind
What she flits away
A scarf, a veil,
Her keys, her kale
Which you must hunt
And wrap and mail.
Her shoes, her comb
Her bubble foam
By post pre-paid

Must trail her home.
Such folk, in fairness
Should be branded
Or travel naked
And empty-handed.

- Send a thank-you note. The gesture has become so endangered, you'll astonish your host.

PART IV

CHAPTER 17

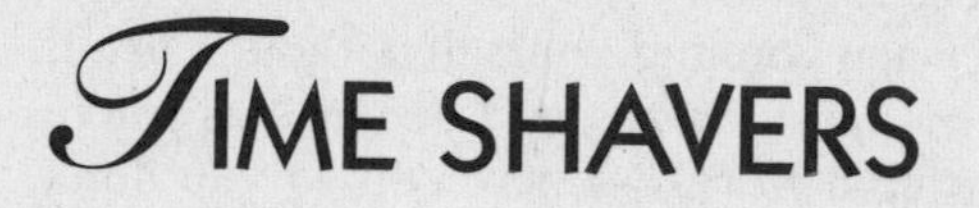

TIME SHAVERS

The following shortcuts are gleaned from friends, family, and food pros, as well as from my own hits and misses.

MARKETING SAVVY

- Limit shopping to one close-range store. Knowing the merchandise, layout, and help is a time saver, while chasing weekly specials around town is energy—and gas—consuming.
- Avoid mega-markets. When we forget the peaches in produce, we shouldn't have to retrace a 5-K by the time we reach the cleaning supplies.

"LIFE IS ENTIRELY TOO TIME CONSUMING."
—IRENE PETER, WRITER

- Ask a checker when the store is least crowded and best stocked. Shopping at midnight doesn't save time if the produce and bakery are depleted, or if the store is hosting a singles' party.
- Avoid shopping on Sunday, since it's the one day markets rarely get meat, fish, bread, and produce deliveries.
- Shop for advertised specials within a few days. They may be on sale for a week, but chances are stock will run out before the ad does.
- Try to shop alone, but if you can't, give tag-alongs coupons and specific items to hunt for.

- Request the bagger load the freezer goods in one bag, fruits and vegetables in another, and pantry items in the rest, so groceries are easier to put away.
- Make multiple copies of a master grocery list and keep one in the glove compartment for milk runs.
- Use a mnemonic technique when you find yourself without a list. If you know you're out of milk, yogurt, onions, and bananas, as you're heading for the store, make up a MYOB-4 acronym so you don't zonk out when confronted by thirty thousand choices.

GOOD CHOICES

- Buy top quality. Simplified cooking relies on fewer ingredients, so items like prime produce, choice meats, and the freshest seasonings are essential.
- Follow your senses. Sniff the berries, thump the melons, squeeze the squash, and pick the brains of the produce stocker to find the perfect peach, the juiciest pineapple, and the crispiest greens.
- Buy in season. Broccoli, Swiss chard, and tangerines are good choices in winter, while corn, tomatoes, and strawberries are at their peak in summer. It *is* possible to buy asparagus in the fall, for instance, but it won't be as tender and fresh as it is in the spring.
- Buy strawberries at the source, if possible. As one of the most delicate fruits, it loses flavor in transit.
- Purchase washed, torn, and bagged salad greens. They're major time savers, and since leaves need no washing, dressings remain undiluted and cling better.
- Take advantage of other convenience cuts and packaging: washed and bagged spinach, shredded carrots, grated cheese, filleted fish, precut poultry and meats.
- Check expiration dates, and choose items stocked from the back of the bin, shelf, or counter since they're almost always the freshest.
- Ask for a sample at the deli before buying something new. Sometimes the best-looking offerings are the biggest flavor disappointments.
- Buy local and seasonal seafood. When the market offers a special—on, say, swordfish—it's usually because the supply is abundant and fresh.
- Rather than asking the seafood seller, "Did the fish come in today?,"

"ARUGULA IS HOW I DEFINE MY CITIES. I GO TO THE GROCERY STORE, AND EITHER YOU CAN GET ARUGULA OR YOU CAN'T. AND I REALLY DON'T WANT TO BE ANYWHERE YOU CAN'T."

—CINDY CRAWFORD

be specific: "When did the salmon come in?" "What's the freshest in the bin?" Also ask for cooking suggestions.

- Cook fish the day of purchase for premium flavor and texture.
- Choose fast-cooking varieties and cuts of fish, poultry, and meats. Scallops, for instance, cook in one to four minutes, depending on their size. Other good bets are clams, shrimp, thin fish fillets such as catfish, boneless chicken breasts, turkey cutlets, boneless pork tenderloin, and thinly sliced beef.
- Minimize slicing and dicing time by buying naturally bite-sized vegetables: button mushrooms, baby beets, shelled peas, pearl onions, and tiny new potatoes.
- For best flavor retention, buy small quantities of oils, dried herbs, and spices. The former turns rancid over time, while the latter lose their flavor and are susceptible to pests.
- If a recipe calls for a small amount of alcohol, buy a wine split or a mini-bottle of liquor or liqueur.
- Leave the cooking wine on the shelf. It's usually salty, bad-tasting, and overpriced.

> **"GROCERY SHOPPING** (GROW*SER*EE SHAH*PING) *N* YOU GO IN LOOKING FOR BREAD, MILK, AND EGGS, BUT COME OUT WITH CHOCOLATE, ICE CREAM, AND **SOAP OPERA DIGEST"**
>
> —MRS. WEBSTER'S DICTIONARY

SMART STORAGE

- Keep a bottle of wine on its side to prevent the cork from drying and shrinking.
- Store wine away from sunlight, heat, and vibrating appliances. A rack in the basement or closet is better than the cabinet next to the fridge.
- Plop freezer-bound foods in heavyweight self-sealing bags. They take up minimal space, prevent foods from drying out, and allow for maximum visibility.
- Use large-enough bags to allow soon-to-be-frozen foods room for expansion. Liquids, particularly, need room to swell.
- Freeze a stew or casserole in a pot or baking dish generously lined with heavy-duty foil. Once the food is frozen, remove it from the container, fold the excess foil over the top, label, and stash it back in the freezer. Return it to the original pot when you're ready to reheat it.
- Keep a few cans of chicken broth in the fridge, so the fat is easily skimmed.

- Store potatoes in air-circulating bins to prolong their freshness.
- Transfer the contents of open cans into lidded plastic or glass containers. When oxygen reacts with metal, it infuses food with a metallic taste.
- Keep a little flour in an old saltshaker to quickly flour a baking pan. Label it so no one flours their popcorn.

COOK IN A FLASH

- Make copies of successful "company" recipes and file them separately so you don't have to paw through the "will trys" and the dishes only the kids like.
- Assemble all necessary components, including seasonings and utensils, to avoid midpoint rummaging. Professional chefs call this time-saving technique *mise en place,* meaning "put in place." "When everything is there," writes Julia Child, "it makes cooking so much faster and easier—and you won't forget to add any special ingredients."
- For a dish that needs a multitude of ingredients, a stir-fry, for instance, place raw, chopped food onto paper plates to cut down on dishwashing.
- Cook in stages. Steam potatoes for tomorrow's potato salad while you're doing the dishes. Sauté onions in the morning, when you're packing lunches, for tonight's pizza.
- Master fast-cooking methods like poaching, sautéing, microwaving, roasting, and broiling.
- Cut meat, fish, and chicken into bite-sized pieces for quick-cooking kabobs, fajitas, and stir-fry dishes.
- Flatten and tenderize fillets for quick-cooking scaloppine dishes. Pound boneless chicken, turkey, or pork between two sheets of waxed paper with a meat mallet until they're uniformly thin.
- Reduce grilling time for steaks and chops by butterflying them first.
- Prevent foods from sticking to the grill by spraying it with vegetable oil before heating.
- Quickly "cook" frozen peas and peapods by placing them in a colander and rinsing them with a kettle of boiling water.
- Buy ready-to-go vegetables like baby peeled carrots, precut celery, and chopped onions.

> "A PARTY AT WHICH THE HOST AND HOSTESS DON'T HAVE A GOOD TIME IS ALMOST INVARIABLY A BAD PARTY."
>
> —MARY RODGERS, AUTHOR, PLAYWRIGHT, DESIGNER, AND DAUGHTER OF COMPOSER RICHARD RODGERS

- Choose pencil-thin asparagus over the fatter kind for a speedy steaming.
- Julienne fresh vegetables for lickety-split steaming, sautéing, and microwaving.
- Don't bother peeling mushrooms. Just rinse them quickly, and trim off any tough ends or bruises.
- Cook in large-enough pans so excess moisture evaporates rapidly and foods cook evenly.
- Invest in an outdoor gas grill. It starts up faster and easier than charcoal, and has better heat control.

NUKE 'EM

- Microwave foods that are naturally high in moisture like vegetables, fruit, poultry, and fish.
- Cooking times vary depending on the age and wattage of the oven and the volume and density of the food. Always check to see if a dish is done before the stated recipe time.
- Place food on round, rather than square containers for even heat distribution. Microwave energy concentrates in the corners of angular pans.
- Since a microwave cooks from the edges to the center, place the thicker parts of food toward the outside of the dish, and stir things up every so often.
- Keep 'em covered. Wraps and lids create tenderizing steam, contain splatters, and speed cooking.
- Avoid cooking in metal-trimmed and lead-crystal dishes. Both can damage the oven. Unglazed pottery is also a no-no since it absorbs moisture from the food.

"HOME IS A
RESTAURANT THAT
NEVER CLOSES."
—UNKNOWN

- Prevent food explosions by piercing potatoes, sausages, egg yokes, tomatoes, and other skins.
- Peel a tomato quickly by zapping it on high for thirty to sixty seconds.
- Flash-dry fresh herbs by placing them in a single layer on a paper towel, and cooking on high from one to three minutes, depending on quantity. Once dry, store them in an airtight container.
- Melt chocolate chips in a glass measuring cup, stirring once before done. Figure one to two minutes per ounce, depending on the size of the pieces.
- Warm dinner rolls in a napkin-lined serving basket or bowl on high

for forty to sixty seconds, depending on the size of the container and the number of rolls.

- Take the chill off a block or wedge of cheese by zapping it on its serving board or dish at half power for about a minute.
- Get more juice out of a lemon or lime by nuking it for about thirty seconds.
- Soften a hardened box of brown sugar by cooking it on high for about one to two minutes.
- Always allow for resting time, since foods still cook internally once the power is off. A cake, for instance, may look underdone, but firms up after sitting on the counter a minute or two.

FASTA PASTA

- Rely on quick-cooking wonders like angel hair, spaghettini, cappellini, and orzo.
- Fresh pasta cooks in less than half the time as dry, but is a little trickier to handle. The Gluck family, pasta specialists and publishers of the newsletter *Pasta Press*, advise letting fresh pasta come to room temperature, then carefully hand-separating it so it doesn't stick together. "Do not," advises Chris Gluck, "rely on the boiling action of the water alone to separate the strands."
- Experiment with flavored pastas. The more taste to the pasta, the simpler the sauce. A basil and garlic rigatoni, for example, only needs a dressing of fresh ripe tomatoes and fine olive oil.
- Stock up on fresh pasta when it's on sale. It can be frozen and cooked with minimal thawing.
- Use a large-enough pot and plenty of water. A pound of pasta needs at least a gallon of water to cook evenly, without clumping.
- Rely on the tongue rather than the timer. Slide a strand down the handle of the spoon or flip a noodle onto the counter and taste for doneness. Package boiling times are always approximate.
- Use curly, wavy, or other textured pasta to trap uncooked tomato sauce. Spaghetti and other smooth strands can be too slick for some sauces to hold.
- Drain pasta well so the sauce stays thick and clings to every strand.
- Simmer the sauce in an oversized skillet so the pasta can be tossed right in it, keeping the serving bowl splatter-free.
- Cook pasta up to a day ahead, then cover it tightly and refrigerate. Bring it to life just before serving by pouring a kettle of boiling water over it.

FAST FIRST AID

- Revive wilted vegetables with a three-minute plunge in ice water.
- Give a bland vegetable or soup a little zing with a spoonful or two of salsa.
- Add body and flavor to a thin or anemic gravy with a little tomato paste, a dollop of sour cream, or a sprinkling of instant mashed potatoes. Add color and seasoning with a little Worcestershire or Kitchen Bouquet sauce.
- Remove fat from soups, stews, and sauces by chilling them in the refrigerator for a few hours. The fat rises to the top and congeals into easily scooped gobs.
- If there's no time for chilling, soak up some of the fat from a hot stew or soup by skimming a piece of bread along its surface.
- Absorb a heavy dose of salt from a soup or stew with a thin slice or two of raw potato. Let the spud simmer till soft, then toss.
- Cut excess saltiness or sweetness in most dishes with a splash of vinegar.
- Freshen stale rolls by placing them in a paper bag with a few water sprinkles and setting them in a 350-degree oven for fifteen minutes.
- Customize a tub of whipped topping by folding in a little ground cinnamon, cocoa powder, or finely ground instant coffee.
- Loosen a stuck wine cork by holding the neck of the bottle under warm water for a minute or two.
- If the cork breaks and falls into the bottle, catch the crumbles by pouring the wine through a tea strainer into the glasses.
- Rescue a pot of weakly brewed coffee by stirring in a teaspoon or so of instant coffee granules, diluted in a splash of boiling water.

KEEP IT FRESH

- Pick garden herbs early in the morning for the best flavor. Like flowers, they build up their nutrients at night.
- Keep garden herbs fresh for days by arranging them like a bouquet in a cup or goblet of water on the kitchen counter. "Refrigerating them in plastic will also keep them in good condition," says commercial herb grower Mary Culver. "But the cold air diminishes their flavor."
- Store a bumper crop of herbs by placing them in a single layer on a cookie sheet, keeping them separate, and freezing for an hour or two. Once they're hard, plop them in self-sealing plastic bags, squeeze out the air, label, and freeze for up to a year.
- Freeze berries and other fresh fruit, using the above method, to blend into sorbets and smoothies.

- Keep fresh berries perky by storing them, unwashed, lightly covered with plastic wrap, and in a single layer in the fridge.
- Prevent fresh ginger from drying out by peeling it, shredding it in the food processor, and refrigerating it in a quality sherry. "The sherry imparts a lovely complementary flavor that doesn't interfere with the taste," says cooking instructor and *Cooking with the Seasons* author, Lesa Heebner. "Best of all, the ginger lasts for years, since the sherry acts as a preservative."
- Don't store dried beans for more than a couple of months. The older the bean, the longer the cooking time.
- Extend the life of an opened jar of red peppers or other marinated vegetable with a splash of vinegar. Figure about a teaspoon for every eight ounces of veggies.

EASY MEASURES

Save measuring and dishwashing time with the following:

- 4 tablespoons = ¼ cup
- 1 stick butter = one cup
- 5 large eggs = approximately 1 cup
- ⅞ cup flour = 1 cup sifted flour
- 1 medium-sized garlic clove = ½ teaspoon freshly chopped or minced garlic or ⅛ teaspoon garlic powder
- 1 medium lemon = about ¼ cup of juice
- 1 medium lemon = 1 tablespoon grated zest
- Measure your caps. I discovered a capful of Schilling flavor extracts equals a scant teaspoon, so I never have to hunt down or wash up a set of measuring spoons.
- When doubling or tripling a recipe, write out the increased amounts on paper before starting. It's easier to do the math in advance than in the midst of whipping and flipping.
- If you find yourself throwing together a feast somewhere without measuring utensils—an underfurnished cabin or your kid's first apartment, for instance—use the following "rules of thumb" from Weight Watchers:
  thumb tip = about 1 tablespoon
  fingertip = about 1 teaspoon
  palm = about 3 ounces cooked meat, poultry, or fish

SMART STAND-INS

- Substitute canned beans for dried ones. It's difficult to detect the difference, and the excess salt rinses easily from colander to drain.
- Use packaged tortilla chips in south-of-the-border soups rather than slicing and frying them.
- Instead of pureeing the small amount of a fruit or vegetable called for in a recipe, use strained baby food.

STRATEGIES

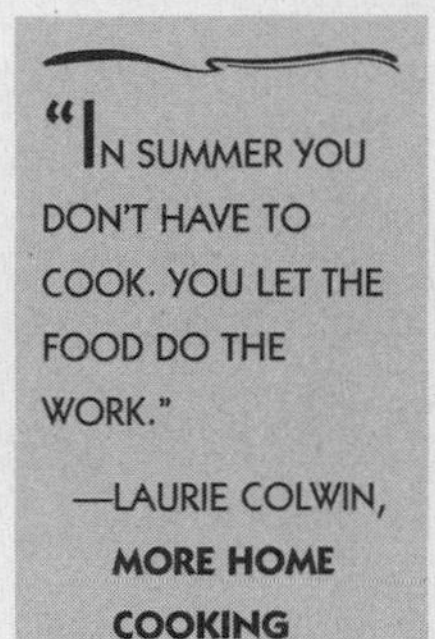

"IN SUMMER YOU DON'T HAVE TO COOK. YOU LET THE FOOD DO THE WORK."
—LAURIE COLWIN, MORE HOME COOKING

- Cook in quantity. Big batches can be easily divided, frozen, and served when time is tight.
- Develop one or two single-pot recipes. A stew, for instance, includes meat, vegetables, and starch, so all it needs is good bread and maybe a salad. One-dish meals are also best when they're made ahead, since their flavors blossom with time.
- Rinse cherry tomatoes, berries, and other produce packed in open-weave plastic right in their baskets.
- Quickly cool a bottle of white wine by submerging it in a sink of ice *and* water. Twenty minutes will do the trick for a room-temperature bottle.
- Toast nuts and seeds on the stove rather than in the oven. The stove is not only quicker, the nuts are also less apt to burn since you can watch them brown.
- Avoid crying into your onions by burning a stick of incense next to the chopping block.
- Pop a soft cheese like mozzarella in the freezer for about fifteen minutes so it's easy to grate.
- Retain the color of green vegetables by cooking until tender, then submerging them in ice water. Serve them cold, or at room temperature, or warm them gently before serving.
- Use a wooden chopstick or barbecue skewer to coax the last smidgen of food out of a can or jar.

WHAT'S YOUR DQ?*

1. *When shopping for fish, you most often:*
   a. buy what looks best and cook it that evening
   b. buy breaded and frozen fish sticks
   c. order fish tacos to go

2. *Your pots and pans come from:*
   a. the best gourmet shop in town
   b. Mom's hand-me-downs
   c. LeRoy's Gently Dented Discounts

3. *When you're asked to bring something to a gourmet potluck, you volunteer:*
   a. the entrée
   b. a six-pack
   c. the paper plates

4. *Who of the following you'd most like to have lunch with:*
   a. Martha Stewart
   b. Heloise
   c. Chef Boy-Ar-Dee

5. *You use your microwave mostly for:*
   a. quickly steaming fresh-from-the-garden vegetables
   b. heating water for instant coffee
   c. rewarming last night's SpaghettiOs

6. *When you separate eggs for a cake, you:*
   a. crack them one-handed on the side of a bowl
   b. crack them carefully with a knife
   c. hard-boil them first

7. *You'd salvage a collapsed cake by:*
   a. slicing, then layering it with fresh fruit, pudding, and whipped cream in a trifle bowl
   b. eating it for breakfast right out of the baking pan
   c. who bakes?

8. *Crème fraîche is:*
   a. something you often have in the fridge
   b. a marital aid
   c. an antidote to Retin-A sensitivity

*Domestic Quotient

9. *Frisee is:*
   a. a salad green cultivated for centuries in France
   b. a breed of dog
   c. a bad perm

Score 10 points for each "a," 5 points for each "b," and 1 point for each "c."

70–90 points: You're a domestic deity.

40–69 points: Your guests may go hungry, but they'll probably go home relaxed.

9–39 points: Consider a course in remedial home ec.

CHAPTER 18

THE JOY OF NOT COOKING

When there's little time and less inclination to cook up a buffet for twenty or even an intimate dinner for two, a little culinary cheating is in order.

GET COZY WITH A COOK

- We don't need to be rolling in dough to enjoy the benefits of the new personal-chef services that are popping up around the country. The chef shops, prepares a two-week supply of dinners in your kitchen in one day, packages and stores them. The catch is you must be a regular client in order to have a feast prepared for a crowd. Cindy Holt, chef and owner of the Posh Pantry in La Costa, California, charges $275 (including grocery shopping and cleanup) for ten days of family dinners, but also handles everything from small receptions to big blowouts. "I do it all, but my clients seem to appreciate the service most when they have houseguests," says Holt. "That way they can enjoy doing things together rather than worrying about what to feed everyone."

"GOURMET COOK (GOR*MAY KOOK) N SOMEONE WITH WAY TOO MUCH TIME ON THEIR HANDS."
—MRS. WEBSTER'S DICTIONARY

TUMS, ANYONE?

Eleanor Roosevelt was one of those people who proved that taking out is often better than cooking in, though few suitable options existed during World War II.

In a New York Times *article, writer Maureen Dowd recounts the tale of the wife of a State Department official who was a frequent guest at the Roosevelt's intimate Sunday-night supper parties:*

"We'd drive our Chevrolet right up to the door of the White House, and then they'd show you up and there was the President in that upstairs study shaking up martinis, which I adored. There would be what he called 'Uncle Joe's Bounty,' a large bowl of fresh caviar sent by Stalin."

The guests filled up on caviar, since Sunday was the cook's night out and the First Lady was, as the guest put it, "the worst cook in the world, you know."

"When she put that chafing dish full of scrambled eggs on the table, they'd be heavier than lead and Mrs. Roosevelt would look so depressed."

MAKE OUT WITH TAKE-OUT

- Check out the deli section of a good grocer. Many markets have gone beyond the shaved turkey, Waldorf salad, and baked-bean bins of the past and are offering more intriguing fare like smoked salmon, stir-fried asparagus with sesame seeds, and fresh roasted red peppers.
- Take advantage of complete dinners offered at markets around major holidays. One Southern California chain offers turkey, ham, and prime-rib dinners ranging from $39.99 to $59.99. The $39.99 dinner includes a roasted twelve-pound stuffed turkey, gravy, mashed potatoes, baked yam casserole, cranberry sauce with apples and pears, and yeast rolls. Once these babies are out of their cartons, on the china, and imaginatively garnished, they're as good (at least in my case) as homemade.
- Think beyond the holidays. Specialty food stores like Honey Baked Hams and Boston Market offer ready-for-the-table roasts as well as all the fixin's year-round.
- Asian restaurants are specialists in the art of take-out, and a whole feast can be built around a dish like Peking duck or Thai beef. My sister-in-law Jean lays out the good china and crystal for family gath-

erings. Once everyone arrives, she takes requests, places the order at our favorite Chinese restaurant, and sends the men out for the kill. It's a win-win situation; no one slaves in the kitchen and everyone gets their favorite dish, as well as a taste of everyone else's.

- Plan ahead. Even if a restaurant isn't known for take-out, most will accommodate orders placed a day or two in advance. A main dish like Hungarian goulash, Spanish paella, or Moroccan lamb stew is easily rounded out with our own salads and condiments.
- Underutilize the pros. Caterers don't have to do the whole show; most can also prepare the main dish, dessert, or any part of the meal in their kitchens. Since labor is the most expensive part of catering, costs come down when we do the picking up and dishing out.

CUSTOMIZE IT

- Serve take-out chili from a bowl nestled in a napkin-lined basket. Surround it with earthenware bowls of chopped avocado, lettuce, onion, tomatoes, chili peppers, sour cream, and shredded cheese.
- Remove frozen lasagna from its disposable aluminum pan and place it in an attractive, ovenproof glass or ceramic dish before baking. Top it with a few sliced tomatoes the last five minutes of baking, so they barely melt into the cheese. Crown it with a healthy sprig or two of basil or oregano just before serving.
- Buy jumbo packs of frozen meatballs from a warehouse market and bake them in a homemade or home-doctored sauce.

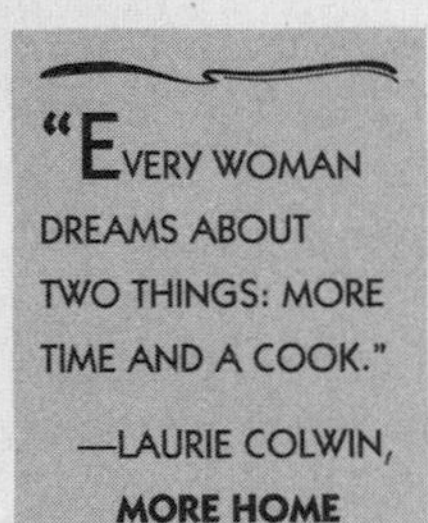

"EVERY WOMAN DREAMS ABOUT TWO THINGS: MORE TIME AND A COOK."
—LAURIE COLWIN,
MORE HOME COOKING

- Add fresh clams, shrimp, and scallops from the seafood counter to a jar of marinara sauce. Splash in a little white wine, a few Italian seasonings, and a bit of tomato paste. Bring to a quick boil, simmer a few minutes, and serve over a bed of pasta.
- Serve smoked fish surrounded by small oyster or clam shells filled with tartar sauce. Garnish with lemon slices and fresh dill.
- Add shrimp to a bottled curry sauce, or present an Indian restaurant's curry over basmati rice surrounded by tiny bowls of shredded coconut, peanuts, chutney, chopped cucumbers, green peppers, cilantro, minced green onions, raisins, diced apples, and yogurt.
- Personalize a French restaurant's boeuf bourguignon with a cookie cutter cutout of frozen puff pastry. My favorite restaurant always tops theirs with a cutout cow. I'd rather not be reminded of Bossy's

salad days, so I crown mine with a heart, star, or closest holiday symbol.

ELEVATE THE ORDINARY

- Chop a ripe tomato and add it to commercial spaghetti sauce for a fresh taste and homemade texture. Water-plumped sun-dried tomatoes also do the trick.
- Freshen the taste and color of store-bought pesto by blending in a little extra basil or parsley in the food processor. The extra herbs displace the excess oil as well.
- Impart a delicate sheen on a loaf of frozen bread dough by brushing it with equal amounts of white vinegar and water before baking.
- Drain a jar of artichoke hearts, serve on lettuce, and top with finely diced sweet red pepper.
- Add crunch and freshness to a jar of marinated bean salad with a little diced celery.
- Jazz up deli coleslaw with chopped apple, whole green grapes, and a little sour cream.
- Slice roasted deli chicken into a salad, soup, or sandwiches.
- Give a prepared chicken salad an international flavor by tossing it with curry powder, defrosted but uncooked petite peas, and a sprinkling of toasted almonds.
- Add texture and color to a take-out potato salad with diced celery, snipped fresh parsley, and chopped hard-cooked egg.

> "IF I HAD MY LIFE TO LIVE OVER, I'D LIVE OVER A DELICATESSEN."
>
> —UNKNOWN

HOW TO DRESS A BAG OF GREENS

Prewashed and torn greens are big time savers when making a salad, but are a bit boring on their own. Give them the gourmet treatment with a sprinkling of edible flowers like nasturtiums, violets, or pansies. Four things to remember about adding flowers to a salad are:

1. Some blooms, like lily of the valley, sweet pea, and azalea, are poisonous, so be sure to research any flower in doubt.
2. Flowers should come from a known garden or supermarket's produce section, not from a florist or nursery where they may be doused with pesticides.
3. Rinse and dry blossoms, and check for hitchhiking critters.
4. Add blossoms *after* tossing the greens with dressing so they retain their color and shape.

Other possible accessories for a well-dressed salad:

- fresh or marinated sweet red and yellow pepper slices
- carrot curls
- designer greens like radicchio, mâche, and arugula
- radish, clover, or sunflower sprouts
- canned baby corn on the cob
- canned asparagus tips
- marinated mushrooms, artichoke hearts, or hearts of palm*
- pitted black or pimento-stuffed green olives
- capers
- snipped sun-dried tomatoes
- jarred baby beets
- sugar snap peas
- halved yellow, red, and orange cherry tomatoes
- sliced chicken, turkey, or smoked salmon to turn it into a main dish

"IT'S RIDICULOUS TO COOK PRETENTIOUS MEALS FOR PARTIES, WHICH ARE SUPPOSED TO MAKE PEOPLE HAPPY, NOT BE A SHOWCASE STAGE FOR THE COOK."

—BARBARA KAFKA, COOKBOOK AUTHOR, FOOD COLUMNIST, AND RESTAURANT CONSULTANT

The following are good toppers *after* the dressing goes on:

- toasted pecans, walnuts, or pine nuts.
- honey-roasted almonds (save those airline packets)
- toasted chow mein noodles
- canned fried onion rings
- crumbled goat cheese
- fresh parmesan shavings

FAST FRUIT SALADS

- Rely on fruits that need little or no peeling, seeding, and hulling, like grapes, blueberries, and bananas.
- Renew a deli mix with fresh grapefruit sections, mint leaves, and a splash of Grand Marnier.
- Pour a little orange or pineapple juice over cut fruit to keep it from browning.
- Doctor a sweet bottled dressing with a pinch of poppy seeds and some finely diced fruit. Fresh mango, papaya, or peaches are especially good.

*Add one part vinegar to three parts of the marinade for a complementary salad dressing.

• Mound and serve fruit in a scooped-out seedless watermelon, cantaloupe, or honeydew melon.

SIX WAYS TO DRESS AN ANGEL

With its low fat and calorie count, angel food cake is a guilt-free dessert everyone loves. It's also a creative canvas for decorating, especially with the distinctive hole that leaves room for all sorts of possibilities.

1. Split and spread the center with vanilla ice cream or frozen yogurt and a layer of sliced bananas. Reassemble, and frost the whole thing with real or tubbed whipped cream. Freeze from two to twenty-four hours, and serve with fresh berries in the middle or a sauce of defrosted berries on the side.
2. Frost with whipped cream, place a tiny bouquet of flowers in the center, and sprinkle with edible petals.
3. Split the cake, spread the center with a half cup of orange curd mixed with an equal amount of sour cream. Reassemble and glaze with a cup of sifted powdered sugar blended with one-quarter to one-third cup orange juice. Fill the center with well-drained mandarin orange segments.
4. Spread with warm honey and sprinkle with crushed pecans, walnuts, or flaked coconut.
5. Pour melted currant jelly over the top so it dribbles down the sides, top with perfect berries, and dust it all with sifted powdered sugar.
6. Create a tropical angel by heating a twenty-ounce can of crushed pineapple mixed with a quarter cup of orange marmalade and two teaspoons of cornstarch. Cool and serve over cake slices.

PERSONALIZE A FROSTED CAKE

• Nuke a handful of chocolate chips or a few squares of baking chocolate in a plastic sandwich bag, snip off a small corner of the bag, and pipe a message or squiggles across the frosting. Designs can also be squeezed onto waxed paper, refrigerated until hard, then used as decorations.

"LET THEM EAT CAKE."
—MARIE ANTOINETTE

• Toss multicolored candy sprinkles over a white or chocolate cake, surround it with two or three colors of curling ribbon, and top it with a sparkler for a birthday or other celebration.
• Place a paper doily or a few maple leaves over fresh chocolate frosting, sift powdered sugar over them, and carefully lift off.

- Paint white or dark melted chocolate over the backs of well-formed camellia or rose leaves. Harden them in the fridge or freezer for an hour or so, then carefully peel off the real leaves and use the chocolate impressions as cake or dessert decorations.
- March animal crackers around the base and top edge of a child's birthday cake.
- Insert birthday candles into Lifesavers candies or pastel miniature marshmallows before placing on the cake.

MORE CAKES

- Poke holes into a thawed pound cake with a skewer. Pour in about a half cup of a favorite liqueur or syrup. Chill for one to twenty-four hours and serve with sweetened whipped cream.
- Jazz up a plain purchased cheesecake with a topping of fresh fruit set in a jewel-like glaze of melted currant jelly. Chicago pastry chef Judy Fairchild is famous for her Independence Day concoction, a plain cheesecake topped with raspberries set in a traced star shape. She then surrounds the star with blueberries to the edge of the cake, leaving a narrow frame of white, and sets it with the melted jelly. "It's our biggest seller all summer," says Fairchild. "But it's the easiest thing in the world to do at home."

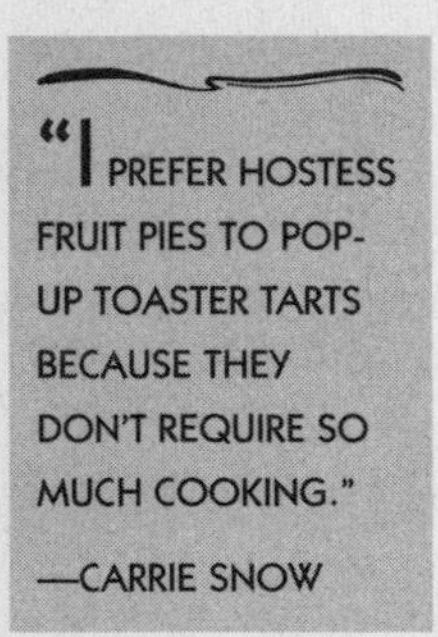

"I PREFER HOSTESS FRUIT PIES TO POP-UP TOASTER TARTS BECAUSE THEY DON'T REQUIRE SO MUCH COOKING."

—CARRIE SNOW

- Layer cubed angel food or pound cake with fresh fruit and prepared vanilla pudding. Top with whipped cream, slivered almonds, and serve in a stemmed glass.

THE INSIDE SCOOP

- Zap a quart of premium vanilla or chocolate ice cream on "defrost" in the microwave for one minute. Whirl it in the food processor with a scant teaspoon of ground cinnamon for fifteen seconds, and scoop it into a pretty mold. Freeze till firm, unmold on a platter, and serve with a sauce.
- Thicken a ready-made chocolate sauce by combining it with a handful of melted chocolate chips. Jazz it up further with a splash of Kahlúa.
- Buy a ready-made meringue or graham-cracker piecrust, transfer it from its disposable pan to a fancy pie plate, and fill it with ice cream or frozen yogurt. Top it with fresh berries, chocolate sauce, or whipped cream.

- Drizzle pure maple syrup over a scoop of vanilla ice cream, top with a few whole toasted walnuts, and serve in a stemmed glass.
- Top a scoop of lime sherbet with fresh raspberries.
- Serve lemon sherbet over a wedge of honeydew melon. Garnish with a tiny cluster of frozen green or red grapes.

SWEET NO-BRAINERS

- Pass around an assortment of fine chocolates or chocolate truffles on a doily-lined silver platter.
- Turn coffee into dessert by serving it with tiny bowls of chocolate curls, whipped cream, citrus peels, cinnamon sticks, liqueurs, or coffee-bar syrup. Torani makes more than forty flavors of nonalcoholic Italian-style syrups that add zing to coffee.
- Serve large stemmed strawberries alongside individual dipping bowls of sour cream and brown sugar.
- Spring the unexpected. Ambassador, congresswoman, and writer Clare Boothe Luce used to take the stiffness out of her formal dinner parties by serving Dove Bars on a stick.

CHAPTER 19

PLAYING WITH FOOD

We don't need to buy tableware at Tiffany's, have the skills of a cosmetic surgeon, or study at the Cordon Bleu to make the most of the flavor and appearance of foods. In fact, some of the most dramatic presentations and remarkable flavors are the easiest to achieve.

The idea is to *enhance* Mother Nature, not make her over.

A POLISHED PRESENTATION

- Develop a few signature dishes, then buy handsome containers to show them off: a great-looking tureen for a specialty soup, a white fluted pan for a trademark lasagna, a pedestal platter for that lemon mousse torte everyone likes.
- Contrast the colors of neighboring foods. Grilled sole and steamed rice benefit from bright vegetables between them.
- Incorporate various shapes on a plate by diagonally slicing carrots into ovals, cutting zucchini into strips, and dividing tomatoes into wedges.
- Avoid puddles and grease spots by thoroughly draining and blotting fried, boiled, and steamed foods before they hit the serving plate.

"IT'S NOT SO MUCH WHAT IS SERVED BUT HOW IT'S SERVED."

—EDITH GILLBERT, WRITER

GARNISHING BASICS

Garnishes are most effective when they're closest to their intended state. Mango hedgehogs, cucumber canoes, and turnip topiaries not only look fussy, they also take an arsenal of surgical implements to execute. "The emphasis is on taste today," says Sarah Stenger, an award-winning chef at Chicago's Ritz Carlton dining room. "Food should be visually appealing," she maintains, "but the look is less structured and more natural than in years past."

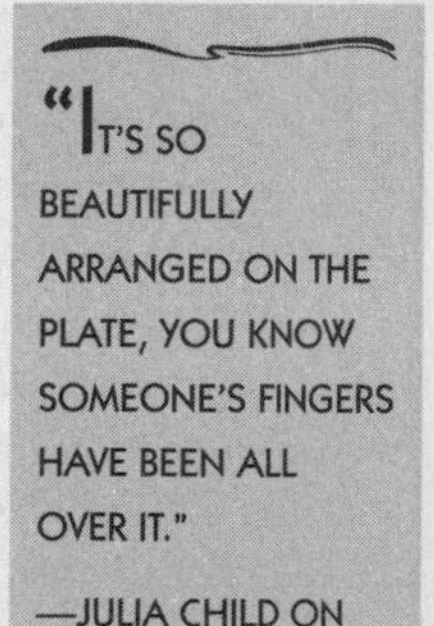

"It's so beautifully arranged on the plate, you know someone's fingers have been all over it."
—Julia Child on Nouvelle Cuisine

- Use only the fresh and unblemished. Brown-tinged greens, bruised fruit, and wilted herbs look better on a compost pile than they do on a platter.
- Prepare garnishes ahead, but add them at the last minute. As Sharon Tyler Herbst advises in *The Food Lover's Tiptionary,* "If you garnish a dish, then let it sit in the refrigerator for several hours, the garnish won't look as good as it should."
- Serve foods on platters large enough to show off the trimmings.
- Garnish with something that's in the dish: a sprig of basil on pesto, a feathery carrot spray on a beef stew, a shaving of dark chocolate over mocha mousse.
- Decorate with garnishes that have a natural affinity for the flavor of the dish: lemon wedges with stuffed grape leaves, charred onion slices with steak, shredded carrots on a vegetable loaf.
- Add something red. Like decorating a room, the color brings any dish to life.

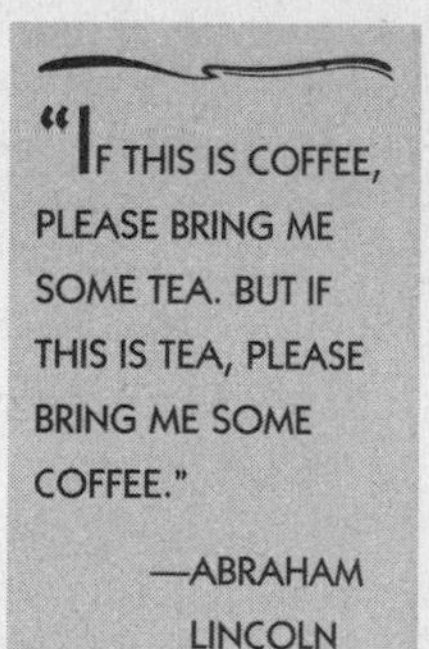

"If this is coffee, please bring me some tea. But if this is tea, please bring me some coffee."
—Abraham Lincoln

JAZZ UP DRINKS

A cool drink in a graceful glass is fine as is, but there are a number of ways to gild the lily.

- Plunk small berries, edible flowers, or mint leaves into ice cube trays, fill with water, and freeze into decorative drink coolers.
- Use bottled or filtered water when making ice cubes if the drinking water is hard. A high mineral content makes for cloudy ice cubes.
- Slice the core of a fresh pineapple into skinny swizzle sticks for fruit drinks.

THE CONNOISSEUR'S GUIDE TO BREWING A BETTER CUP OF COFFEE

- *Start with a scrupulously clean pot. Old oils and soap residue are not the best flavor-enhancers.*
- *Good water brews good coffee, so if that stuff that flows out of the faucet smells like rotting eggs or the local swimming pool, use bottled or filtered water.*
- *Avoid chemically softened water, unless you like a salty brew.*
- *Make it cold. Hot water often has a metallic taste, since it sits in the tank of a water heater.*
- *Buy top-quality beans from a source that has a high turnover.*
- *Find the right grind for your coffee maker. Too fine causes bitterness. Too coarse produces a weak brew.*
- *Grind beans within a few days of purchase, or refrigerate them in an opaque, airtight container for up to a month. "Light, heat, moisture, and age are the enemies of good coffee," says a Starbucks spokesperson.*
- *Experiment with various blends to concoct a personal favorite.*
- *Measure carefully, using one level scoop per cup. A coffee scoop equals two tablespoons, while the cup lines on a pot equal six ounces or three-quarters cup of water.*
- *The standard coffee mug holds twelve ounces, or twice as much as a teacup, so measure accordingly.*
- *For a milder cup, add boiling water to the pot after brewing. Using more or less water in the brewing process deteriorates the flavor.*
- *Hold coffee in a prewarmed thermos rather than on its burner. After twenty minutes, a burner's heat destroys the aromatic oils and makes the brew bitter.*
- *Personalize your own blend by adding a cinnamon stick, orange peel, or a drop of almond, chocolate, or other bottled flavoring to a basket of fresh coffee before brewing.*

- Halve celery or pare a cucumber into edible stirrers for Bloody Marys and vegetable drinks.
- Freeze leftover coffee into ice cubes to cool iced coffee without diluting it.
- Freeze leftover lemonade into ice cubes to sweeten iced tea.
- Dip the damp rims of lemonade glasses into superfine sugar for a frosty crown.

- If there's a fresh layer of snow outside, scoop it up and pack it around a bottle of wine in an ice bucket.

BEAUTIFUL SOUP

- Offer hot soups in individual hollowed-out rounds of sourdough or pumpernickel bread. Pale creamy soups like clam chowder look best in dark breads, while white loaves set off deeper-toned soups like bean and tomato.
- Crown a black bean soup with slim rounds of lemon or lime.
- Use the mother ship. Interior designer Michelle Fuller serves her trademark pumpkin soup from a hollowed-out pumpkin "tureen." She sets it on a silver tray and surrounds it with fall leaves, flowers, and baby pumpkins.
- Serve cold soups cold. Either chill the serving bowls in the fridge for at least an hour, or nest them in larger bowls, surrounded by crushed ice.

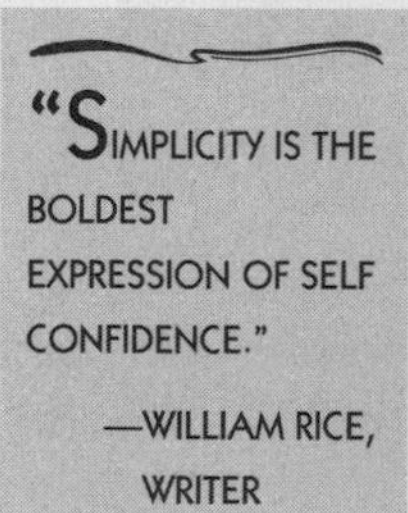

"SIMPLICITY IS THE BOLDEST EXPRESSION OF SELF CONFIDENCE."
—WILLIAM RICE, WRITER

- Contrast textures. Embellish vichyssoise with a sprig of dill, spinach soup with a hard-cooked egg sliver, and a tomato soup with a sprinkling of crushed tortilla chips or popcorn.
- Top a pureed soup with a dollop of sour cream and a bit of the main ingredient: a tiny stalk of broccoli, a slice of a cherry tomato, or a perfect mini-mushroom.
- Fill a plastic sandwich bag with sour cream, snip a corner of the bag, and pipe swirls of the stuff on a smooth and dark soup.

BLAZING SALADS

- Line a bowl with ruffly kale to encompass a chicken, tuna, or other main-dish salad.
- Cap a mayonnaise-based salad with a dollop of mayonnaise and a sprinkling of paprika.
- Give a spinach salad a dusting of yellow by pressing a hard-boiled egg yoke through a sieve.
- Halve cherry tomatoes so they don't squirt when bitten.
- Slice large tomatoes vertically rather than horizontally so they stay firm and don't dilute the dressing.
- Encompass the rim of a bowl of potato salad with a wreath of tarragon, rosemary, or any herb that's doing well in the garden or market.

(NOTE: See additional salad "dressings" in the "Joy of Not Cooking" chapter)

"I BELIEVE IF I EVER HAD TO PRACTICE CANNIBALISM I MIGHT MANAGE IF THERE WERE ENOUGH TARRAGON AROUND."

—JAMES BEARD

SPLENDID ENTRÉES

- Follow the lead of "architectural chefs" and add height to the plate by stacking food or garnishing with vertical elements like long stems of rosemary and tall shoots of chives.
- Drizzle a couple of brilliantly colored sauces in an abstract pattern under a fillet for color and flavor. Squeeze-top ketchup and honey bottlesare perfect squirters for store-bought or homemade sauces.
- Wrap lemon wedges in cheesecloth to contain seeds and wayward juice. The elegant Delicias restaurant in Rancho Santa Fe, California, dresses their lemon wedges in finely woven yellow cheesecloth tied in a twist of leaf-green ribbon.

PAINTING FISH FOR PICASSO

As the companion to writer Gertrude Stein, Alice B. Toklas played co-host at their Paris apartment and salon, where they entertained dancers, writers, artists, and even royalty in the early decades of the 1900s.

Toklas played chef on the cook's day off; and in her cookbook, which includes recipes for the likes of hashish fudge, Toklas tells how she gussied up one dish:

"One day when Picasso was to lunch with us I decorated a fish in a way that I thought would amuse him. I chose a fine striped bass and cooked it according to a theory of my grandmother who had no experience in cooking. . . . She contended that a fish . . . once caught, should have no further contact with the element in which it had been born and raised. She recommended that it be roasted or poached in wine or cream or butter . . . I covered the fish with an ordinary mayonnaise and, using a pastry tube, decorated it with a red mayonnaise, not colored with catsup—horror of horrors—but with tomato paste. Then I made a design with sieved hard-boiled eggs, the whites and the yokes apart, with truffles and finely chopped fines herbes. . . . When it was served Picasso exclaimed at its beauty. But, said he, "Should it not have been in honor of Matisse than of me."

- Quickly sauté a few seedless red or green grapes in a little butter and mass them around servings of fish, poultry, or meat. Sautéing sweetens, gilds, and marbleizes grapes.
- Make a bed of barely cooked greens for broiled chicken or fish. Cooking instructor and food writer Lesa Heebner pours a kettle of boiling water over a colander of fresh spinach, then makes a nest of it on each plate for the entrée. "The spinach wilts without overcooking, and stays bright green," says Lesa. "The only cleanup is wiping the colander dry."

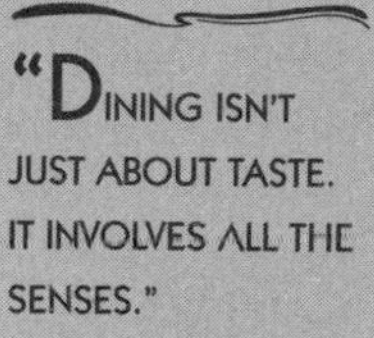

"DINING ISN'T
JUST ABOUT TASTE.
IT INVOLVES ALL THE
SENSES."
—LINDA ELLIS,
FORMER NAPA
VALLEY,
CALIFORNIA,
RESTAURATEUR

SHOW-STOPPING PLATTERS

- Slice open a pomegranate, and sprinkle its edible scarlet seeds around a platter.
- Surround a platter of fish with individual servings of seafood sauce placed in tiny mussel or clam shells. Intersperse them with parsley and lemon wedges.
- Build a nest of crisp greens on a platter for a whole roast. Surround it with fresh or canned peach halves filled with whole cranberry sauce, or bunches of tiny champagne grapes.
- Tie bouquets of herbs like rosemary, sage, and basil with long blades of chives, and tuck them around a whole fish or roast.
- Dunk fresh cranberries in lightly beaten egg white, frost with granulated sugar, and cluster around a roasted turkey or chicken.
- Wipe splatters from the rims of plates and bowls with a tissue or napkin before they hit the table.
- Lightly spray the rim of a platter with nonstick cooking oil, then dust it with finely chopped parsley, dill, or a flurry of paprika.
- Shave a block of room-temperature parmesan into large, loose curls to crown a pasta or main-dish salad.

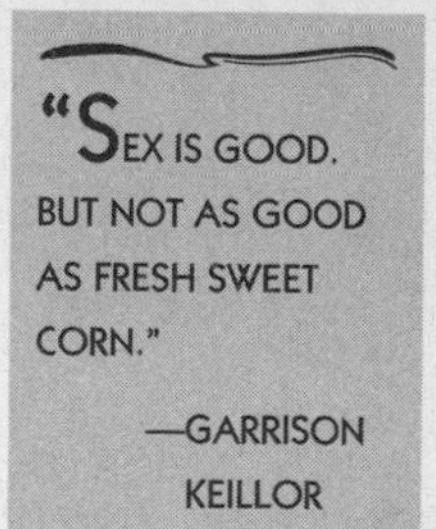

"SEX IS GOOD.
BUT NOT AS GOOD
AS FRESH SWEET

—GARRISON

GLORIOUS DESSERTS

- Fill a squeeze bottle with raspberry, caramel, or chocolate sauce and drizzle a quick pattern across individual plates as a colorful backdrop.
- Serve lemon sorbet or sherbet in large, hollowed-out lemons on doily-lined dishes. Garnish with lemon or mint leaves.

- Layer fruits in a stemmed trifle dish with an eye toward color contrast.
- Tuck a couple of pirouette cookies into a large scoop of ice cream served in a stemmed balloon glass.
- Slice a plump strawberry almost to its top and fan it to garnish a cake, custard, or pudding.
- Team a berry with a sprig of mint for a "just off the vine" look.
- Sprinkle a plain cheesecake with crystallized violets. Crystallized flowers are found in kitchen shops and through mail order gourmet catalogs.
- Top a scoop of ice cream with one perfect pecan, a shard of peanut brittle, or a scattering of chocolate-covered coffee beans.
- Create long, elegant chocolate curls by nuking a thick block of chocolate twenty to thirty seconds (depending on the size of the chunk) at half power. Pare with a vegetable peeler.
- Make chocolate shavings with short, quick strokes against a room-temperature bar of chocolate.
- Pour sparkling wine over perfect strawberries and serve in stemmed glasses.

GOOSE UP FLAVOR

- Seal in taste, moisture, and tenderness by quickly searing meats, poultry, and fish. Finish cooking at a lower heat.
- Roast or grill chicken in its skin. According to the American Dietetic Association, not only are the flavor and juiciness retained, but the fat and calories are negligible when the skin is removed *after* cooking.
- Give zing to grilled foods with a rub of Caribbean jerk, Cajun, or Southwest seasoning.
- For a subtle flavor boost, toss herbs like savory, sage, and rosemary on the coals before grilling.

"BUY OLIVE OIL FOR ITS TASTE, NOT ITS VIRGINITY."
—JULIA CHILD

- Slightly underboil corn on the cob hours before a barbecue, and throw it on the grill the last minute for charred color and flavor.
- Glaze a ham or chicken near the end of baking with the excess syrup from a can of fruit.
- Serve a spoonful of chutney in the curve of a lettuce leaf to wake up the taste of chicken, roast, or curry.
- Poach fish in dry wine for a fast, simple, and delicately flavored dish.
- Season cold foods a little more liberally than those served hot. Cold numbs the flavors of herbs and spices.

- As a rule of thumb, add dried herbs at the start of cooking soups, sauces, and stews, but add fresh herbs near the end.
- Release the flavor of dried herbs by rubbing them between your palms before adding them to a dish.
- Soften the bite of chopped raw onion by giving it a quick soak in ice water.
- Bring out the flavor and color of onions by sautéing them *slowly* in a little butter and oil.
- Add a capful of olive oil to a pot of boiling pasta for a silky texture and richer flavor.
- Bake a whole head of garlic in its skin in a 300-degree oven for about forty minutes. Squeeze the creamy, nut-flavored cloves into pesto, spaghetti sauces, soups, and salad dressings. Baking mellows garlic, so more can be used to the advantage of most dishes.

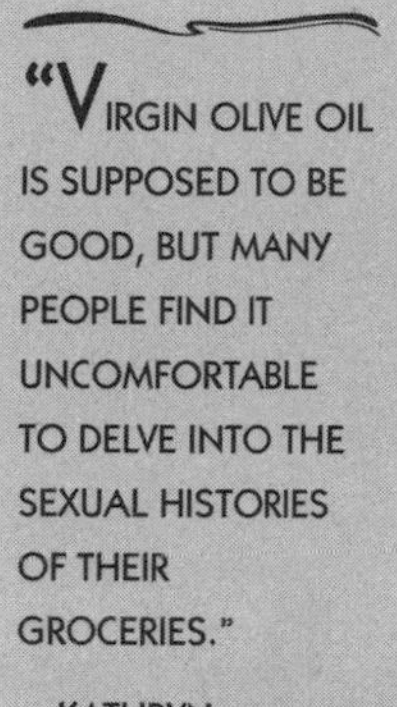

"VIRGIN OLIVE OIL IS SUPPOSED TO BE GOOD, BUT MANY PEOPLE FIND IT UNCOMFORTABLE TO DELVE INTO THE SEXUAL HISTORIES OF THEIR GROCERIES."
—KATHRYN HAMMER, **NATURE ABHORS A VACUUM**

- Substitute part of the water in a tomato-based soup with a can of vegetable juice.
- Jazz up a jar of gravy with meat or poultry drippings and those tasty brown bits at the bottom of the roasting pan.
- Add zing to almost any gravy, stew, or sauce with a splash of balsamic vinegar or red wine.
- Bring out the best in veggies by poaching or stir-frying them in bouillon, white wine, or vegetable juice.

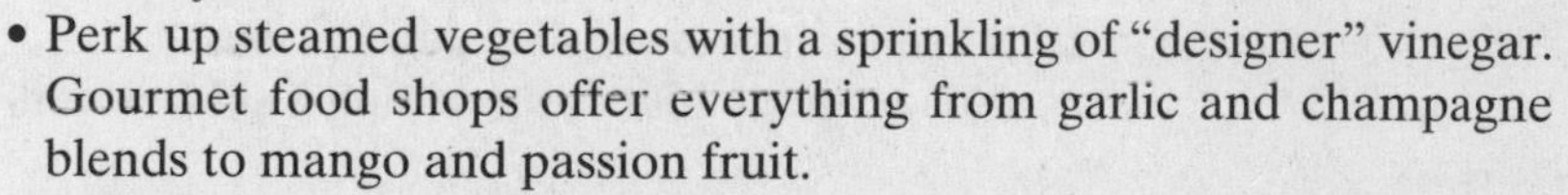

- Perk up steamed vegetables with a sprinkling of "designer" vinegar. Gourmet food shops offer everything from garlic and champagne blends to mango and passion fruit.
- Enhance the taste of sautéed mushrooms with a pinch of marjoram or thyme.
- Top green vegetables with a sprinkling of toasted nuts, sesame seeds, or crumbled goat cheese.
- Dress boiled potatoes, destined for potato salad, with a little vinegar before adding mayonnaise.
- Add zip to mashed potatoes with a smidgen of horseradish.

CHAPTER 20

HOW NOT TO POISON THE GUESTS

When guests overstay their welcomes and generally drive us nuts, we may be tempted to poison them, especially when salmonella, *E. coli,* and botulism are so easy to come by.

But it may take days for the effects to show up, and it's embarrassing to fill out those hospital forms, then have the victims reject that homemade goody we took the trouble of smuggling in just for them.

Besides, we might fall victim to our own dirty deed. So just to be on the safe side, follow these basic guidelines for avoiding food-borne illness.

POULTRY

The USDA estimates that about a third of poultry is contaminated with salmonella, but a number of private sources insist that figure is higher. So precautions are in order.

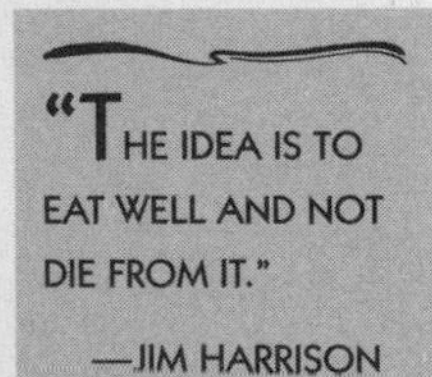

"THE IDEA IS TO EAT WELL AND NOT DIE FROM IT."
—JIM HARRISON

- Cook poultry within one or two days of purchase.
- Thaw frozen birds in the refrigerator. Figure about five hours per pound for whole fowl.
- Rinse thoroughly under cold running water to wash off bacteria. Some Asian chefs douse raw poultry with vinegar as a further precaution, as well as to enhance its flavor.

- Trim off as much fat as possible, since this is where toxins settle.
- Wash hands, the cutting board, knife, and anything else that has come in contact with the bird in hot soapy water.
- Cook parts like thighs, breasts, and wings until juices run clear and the meat is no longer pink.
- Roast whole poultry until the meat thermometer registers at least 170 degrees in the breast, or 180 degrees in the thigh.
- Cook the stuffing separately or pack the cavity lightly with cold dressing just before roasting. An early bird may get worse than worms.
- Remove and separately pack all stuffing before refrigerating the cooked carcass.
- Cut the cooked meat from the bones before refrigerating.

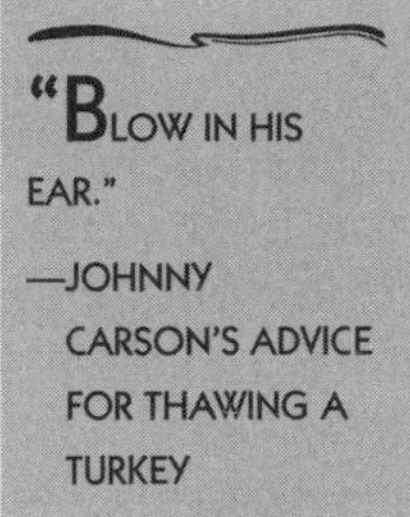

"Blow in his ear."
—Johnny Carson's advice for thawing a turkey

EGGS

- Avoid buying unrefrigerated eggs.
- Forget the suggested expiration date. The important number to check, according to the American Egg Board, is the two- to three-digit packing number on the side of the carton. An "01" means the

LIFE IN THE FRIDGE

The USDA recommends the following shelf life for refrigerated foods:

FOOD	STORAGE TIME
bacon	*one week*
eggs, fresh	*three to five weeks*
eggs, hard-cooked	*one week*
cheese, hard	*two to three months*
cheese, soft	*two weeks*
chicken, cooked and uncooked	*one to two days*
lunch meats, unopened	*two weeks*
lunch meats, opened	*three to five days*
mayonnaise	*two months*
milk	*five days after expiration date*
stews and soups	*three to four days*
tuna, egg, or chicken salad	*three to five days*

eggs were packed on January 1 of the current year. A "365" means they were packed on December 31. Refrigerated eggs stay fresh for four to five weeks, but the older the egg, the more subject it is to bacterial growth.

- Open the carton and nudge each egg, two at a time, with the thumb and forefinger to see if they move easily. A stuck egg means a cracked shell, and a cracked shell means trouble.
- Refrigerate eggs in their cartons. Not only do opened eggs spoil faster, they also dry out, and absorb the smells of neighboring foods.
- Salmonella can lurk inside the freshest eggs, so cook them until both the whites and yokes are firm. Sunny-side up, soft-boiled, and even soggy French toast can shelter bacteria.
- Avoid serving foods containing raw eggs, like Caesar salad, Hollandaise sauce, and eggnog.
- Don't make ice cream with raw eggs. Freezing will not kill salmonella.

FISH

- Find a savvy source that has a quick turnover. One market in my area has fresh seafood delivered every day, while the others have deliveries only once or twice a week.
- Request the fish be packed in ice if it's going to sit in the car trunk for more than twenty minutes.
- Return limp or "fishy"-smelling fish to the vendor. Fish should spring back when touched and smell like an ocean breeze, not mud flats at low tide.
- Avoid buying fish at a temporary road stand or from the back of a

P. J. O'ROURKE'S GUIDE TO FOOD SPOILAGE

- *Bibb lettuce is spoiled when you can't get it off the crisper without Comet.*
- *Fresh potatoes do not have roots, branches, or dense leafy undergrowth.*
- *. . . Any canned goods that have become the size or shape of a basketball should be disposed of. Carefully.*

—*From* The Bachelor's Home Companion: A Practical Guide to Keeping House Like a Pig

truck. There's no way of knowing how it's handled or who or what it's been hanging out with.

- Cook fish the day it's bought for best flavor and texture as well as for safety.
- Avoid trendy pan searing, when the fish is browned on the outside and left rare on the inside. According to the FDA, parasites lurk in undercooked fish.
- Measure the thickest part of the fish, and cook at about 450 degrees, ten minutes for each inch. The flesh should be opaque and flake with a fork.

FISH IS ANOTHER
MAN'S POISSON."
—LOIS PHILLIPS

- Avoid serving ceviche, an appetizer made with raw seafood, unless you're certain the fish is commercially frozen first. Contrary to popular belief, the requisite lime juice doesn't "cook" the fish, it only makes the parasites tastier.
- Leave sushi making to the masters. Professional sushi chefs commercially flash-freeze fish, slice it paper-thin, then hold it to the light to check for worms. A home freezer cannot dip to the below-zero temperatures required to kill those worms.

SHELLFISH

- Steer clear of the raw stuff. Oysters, clams, and mussels often harbor hepatitis and other diseases, since they readily absorb waste from offshore dumping of toxins and raw sewage.
- Always buy in-the-shell fish live for safety and best flavor.
- Check for signs of life by tapping the shells. Live ones open and close. Dead ones don't.
- Store live shellfish in ventilated containers rather than in airtight plastic bags and cartons.

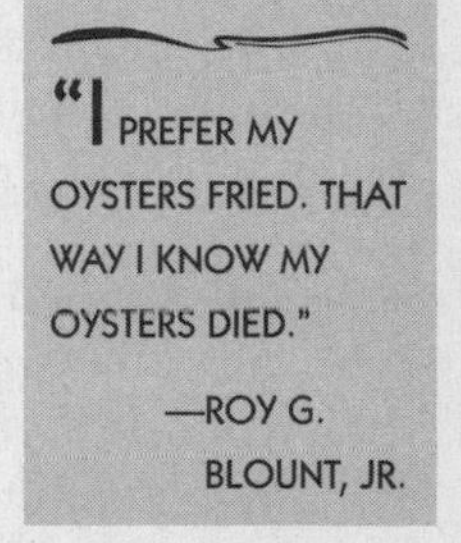

"I PREFER MY
OYSTERS FRIED. THAT
WAY I KNOW MY
OYSTERS DIED."
—ROY G.
BLOUNT, JR.

- Boil shellfish like clams and mussels for three to five minutes, or steam them from four to nine minutes. Toss any whose shells don't open.

MEAT

- Boned, stuffed, rolled, and tied roasts are highly susceptible to bacterial growth, so cook them within a day of purchase.
- Don't store ground beef in the refrigerator for more than two days.
- Cook ground beef till the juices run clear and there's no trace of redness.

- Be especially careful cooking frozen patties, since they can remain red on the inside while the outside looks perfectly browned.
- Liquid forms naturally in a package of hot dogs, but if it turns cloudy, chuck them.
- Make sure that mail-order meats are sent with a cooling element. If they arrive warm, send them back, pronto.
- Get in the habit of using a meat thermometer. Pork roasts should read 160 degrees for medium and 170 degrees for well-done. Beef roasts should register 145 degrees for medium-rare, 160 degrees for medium, and 170 degrees for well-done. Rare is risky, but brown is beautiful.

PRODUCE

Other than the garden variety pesticides we have to put up with, fruits and vegetables are not usually the culprits in food poisoning. However, there's always a chance of contamination when food is shipped in from developing countries, since raw manure is the fertilizer of choice.

- Avoid bruised and split fruits and vegetables. Dents and cuts allow bacteria to penetrate.
- Scrub the outside of all fruits, including those with inedible skins like pineapple, melon, and grapefruit. When the knife hits the skin, it also touches the flesh, carrying the germs with it.
- Wash hands before and after handling all fruits and vegetables.
- Pare eyes and green spots from potatoes. They contain heat-resistant toxins.
- Avoid picking mushrooms in the wild no matter how tempting or harmless they may look. "There are bold mushroom hunters," goes the saying, "but there are no old mushroom hunters."

TEST YOUR FOOD-SAFETY SAVVY

1. *Refrigerate warm leftovers in:*
   a. deep, stackable plastic.
   b. almost any material, as long as it's wide and shallow.

2. *Hot and cold foods can sit at room temperature for:*
   a. three to four hours
   b. no more than half an hour
   c. two hours

3. *Cracked wood cutting boards are best repaired with:*
   a. Shoe Goo
   b. wood sealer
   c. nothing

4. *The most effective sterilizing setting on the dishwasher is:*
   a. normal wash
   b. pot scrubber
   c. drying cycle

5. *True or False: Rinse slimy chicken and fish for two minutes before cooking.*

6. *True or False: The "scratch and sniff" test is a good indication of food spoilage.*

7. *True or False: Toss all moldy foods.*

8. *True or False: Take-out food is best kept warm in a 150-degree oven.*

9. *True or False: Milk is best tossed on its "sell by" date.*

ANSWERS:

1. b. Warm leftovers cool quickest in wide, shallow containers.
2. b. It's best to refrigerate cooked foods as soon as possible, but most remain safe at room temperature for up to two hours.
3. c. All kinds of nasty organisms lurk in wood fissures, so it's best to toss and replace the cutting board with a plastic model that won't crack and can be sterilized in the dishwasher.
4. c. Dry heat is most effective in the war against bugs.
5. False. Slimy foods need a quick burial.
6. False. Some types of bacteria are so sneaky they cannot be detected with the eye or nose. So when in doubt, throw it out.
7. False. According to the FDA, hard cheeses, salamis, and dry cured hams are safe once the mold and one inch of the surrounding area are scraped off.
8. True.
9. False. As long as it's refrigerated properly, milk remains fresh four or five days after the "sell by" date.

CANNED GOODS

- Boycott any signs of botulism: bulging cans, cracked jars, and swollen lids. Just a tiny taste of the bacteria can knock 'em dead.
- Eat canned meats and fish that accidentally freeze within a day or two. But if the can's seams have rusted or opened, chuck 'em.
- Rotate canned foods so they're eaten before the can deteriorates. High-acid foods like tomatoes and citrus can eat away at the metal after a few years on the shelf.

SHOPPING

- Shop at a high-volume market that replenishes its stock rapidly.
- Pick up the perishables like milk, meat, and eggs after filling the carriage with produce and canned goods.
- Avoid buying deli and other ready-to-eat foods displayed next to raw meats and fish.
- Look for the latest "sell by" date on all packages.
- Buy rock-hard frozen foods and avoid dribbles, odor, or other signs of thawing.
- Ask the bagger to pack frozen goods in one bag so they stay cold.
- Keep a cooler in the car trunk in case the weather is hot and the drive is long.

STORAGE

- Don't pack the refrigerator to the gills. Foods need a healthy circulation of cold air.
- Store meats and poultry on the lowest shelf of the refrigerator so juices don't drip and contaminate other foods.
- Avoid placing milk, meat, fish, and eggs on the door since it's vulnerable to warm air each time it's opened.
- Thaw meat, fish, and poultry in the fridge rather than on the counter. Or zap it in the microwave.
- Quickly cool a large pot of refrigerator-bound soup or stew by submerging it in a sink of ice and water. Stir till it stops steaming, then transfer it into smaller containers.
- Don't panic if the power fails. A freezer stays safely chilled from one to two days, and a refrigerator for four to six hours, depending on the kitchen temperature. Just resist opening the door to check things out.

> "IN THE OLD DAYS, FOOD STORAGE WAS SIMPLE. YOU KILLED A MASTODON AND STORED IT IN THE CORNER OF THE CAVE. AS LONG AS IT DIDN'T SMELL TOO BAD, YOU ATE IT."
>
> —JANE SNOW, KNIGHT-RIDDER NEWS SERVICE

- If the power hasn't come on in a day, stash dry ice in the freezer, and block ice in the fridge.

PICNICS

- Avoid serving creamed foods, stuffed poultry, and egg-based dishes at warm-weather picnics or buffets.
- Keep cold foods cold by insulating them well, and packing them with commercial or homemade ice packs. Frozen containers of juice or fruit cocktail do double duty.
- Don't freeze sandwiches with fillings that contain mayonnaise since it separates when thawed. Make sandwiches with frozen bread instead to keep fillings cold. Bread thaws quickly once unpacked.
- Substitute a mayonnaise spread with mustard or an avocado ripe enough to slather.
- Thoroughly cook all meat, then chill it before packing.
- Keep hot foods hot in preheated vacuum bottles. Fill the bottles with hot water, drain, then load with anything from soup to hot dogs.
- Pack food in clean-as-a-whistle containers. Old spills can create new problems.
- Bring along packaged, premoistened wipes to clean hands before and after working with food.

NINE LIVES

The following tale may or may not be true, but it's a good one:

Leonore Hudson put the finishing touches on a tuna salad she was serving to her bridge group that afternoon. After filling the water glasses, she stepped back into the kitchen to find her cat up on the counter, eating the tuna from the bowl. She swatted the cat out the backdoor, carefully scraped off the top of the salad, and served it without anyone the wiser.

Clearing up for cards, she took out the garbage, and to her horror, found the cat dead on the back step. She rushed back into the house, hurriedly explained the situation to her guests, and advised everyone to hightail it to the hospital for a stomach pumping.

When she returned exhausted that night, her neighbor knocked on the door. "I'm sorry I hit your cat this afternoon," he said. "I didn't want to upset you with all your company, so I laid it on the back step."

PREPARATION

- Always wash hands in hot, soapy water before preparing foods and after changing diapers, using the toilet, and handling pets.
- Marinate meat, fish, and poultry in the refrigerator, not on the counter.
- Cook food without interruption. A roast turkey for example, whose recipe calls for an initial blast of high heat, then a long sit in a turned off oven, could send guests to the nearest clinic.
- Set the freezer at 0 degrees and the fridge at 40 degrees.
- Designate one area of the kitchen for meat, poultry, and fish preparation to avoid cross-contamination.
- Microwaving can leave cold spots in food, so use a probe or meat thermometer to ensure thorough cooking.
- Never return cooked meat, fish, or poultry to the plate that held it raw without first washing the plate in hot, soapy water.
- Boil a marinade that's been steeping raw meat, poultry, or fish for at least two minutes before turning it into a sauce.
- Always use clean utensils to scoop or spear items from a jar.

CLEANUP

- Wash all utensils that have come in contact with raw foods before using them again.
- Sponges are often chambers of bacteria, which can then be spread throughout the kitchen. Sterilize sponges regularly in the dishwasher or dunk them in a gallon of water mixed with a couple of capfuls of chlorine bleach.
- Disinfect food preparation surfaces with bleach and water.
- Wash dish towels frequently, especially if they're used to wipe down counters and the sink.

CHAPTER 21

RECIPES AND MENUS

The following recipes possess the four virtues that I look for when entertaining: simplicity, speed, good looks, and great flavor.

SMALL BITES

> "COOKING NEED NOT BE THE FRAUGHT, PERFECTIONIST, SLIGHTLY PARANOID STRUGGLE THAT IT HAS LATTERLY BECOME."
>
> —ANTHONY LANE, **THE NEW YORKER**

HUMMUS

(Makes about 3 cups)

If you're only making one hors d'oeuvre, make it this. It's fast, foolproof, and universally liked. Use any leftovers as a sandwich spread. It keeps for weeks.

Two 15½-ounce cans garbanzo beans, drained and rinsed
4 cloves minced garlic
1½ cups sesame oil
½ cup freshly squeezed lemon juice
1 teaspoon salt
1 teaspoon finely chopped fresh parsley

Blend all ingredients except for the parsley in the food processor or blender until smooth. Pour into a decorative bowl. Allow flavors to develop in the refrigerator from a few hours to a few days. Sprinkle with parsley, and surround with triangles of pita bread and/or vegetable sticks.

TUSCANY BREAD

One 22-inch-long baguette, split horizontally
One 7-ounce purchased or homemade container of basil pesto
One 8.5-ounce jar of sun-dried pesto
¼ pound sliced Muenster cheese

Spread the green pesto on 1 half-loaf, and the red pesto on the other. Top with cheese, and broil 4 inches from the heating unit for 3 minutes, or until cheese starts to bubble and brown. Cool slightly. Using a sharp knife, cut into 1-inch-diagonal slices.

JAMAICAN SHRIMP SPREAD

(Makes about 4 cups)

1 pound medium shrimp, sliced into fourths
Juice from half a lemon
2 cups mayonnaise
1 cup green onions, finely snipped
1 cup flaked coconut
1 teaspoon cayenne

Combine all ingredients. Serve in a ramekin surrounded by cocktail crackers.

> "PASTA AND POTATOES ARE MOTHER NATURE'S PROZAC."
>
> —SARAH BAN BREATHNACH, **SIMPLE ABUNDANCE**

TUXEDO POTATOES

Caviar may seem extravagant, but when it's domestic and used as garnish, it won't bust the budget. If you decide to double the recipe, buy 1 jar of black and another of red for a nice play of color.

24 tiny red-skinned potatoes, boiled and cooled
½ cup sour cream
One 2-ounce jar caviar
1 small bunch of parsley

If potatoes are 1½ inches or less in diameter, slash and pinch the tops. If they're larger, cut them in half. Top with a dollop of sour cream, a ¼ teaspoon caviar,* and finally a teeny sprig of parsley.

DRINKS

CAPE COD PUNCH

(Makes 32 cups)

With so many weird conglomerations of fruits and syrups out there, punch is often regarded with suspicion. However, this jewel-toned blend is so elegantly crisp and simple that it makes a perfect self-service refresher for a crowd. Spike it with a cup or so of vodka if you want to give it kick.

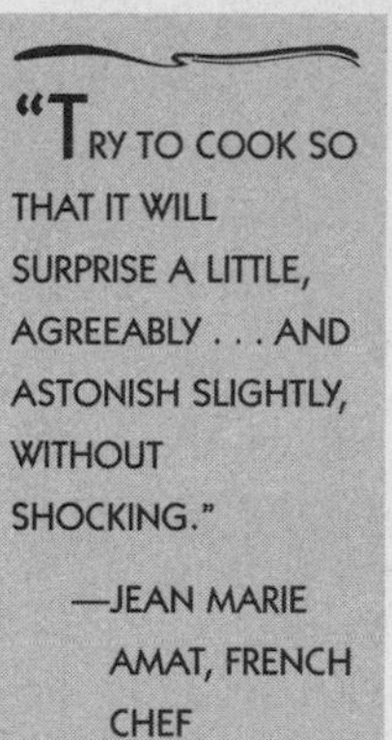

"TRY TO COOK SO THAT IT WILL SURPRISE A LITTLE, AGREEABLY . . . AND ASTONISH SLIGHTLY, WITHOUT SHOCKING."
—JEAN MARIE AMAT, FRENCH CHEF

Three 64-ounce bottles cranberry juice cocktail
Green grapes
Two 2-liter (64 ounces) bottles ginger ale

Fill a Bundt pan or other ring mold with some of the cranberry juice and a few tiny bunches of green grapes. Freeze till solid. Unmold in punch bowl. Fill the bowl with the rest of the cranberry juice. Add the ginger ale just before serving for maximum fizzle.

SPARKLING SANGRIA

(Serves 6 to 10)

There are so many variations of this Spanish concoction, the only way to go wrong is to use a wretched wine. The rule is, if you wouldn't drink the wine straight, don't mix it.

One 750-millimeter bottle Rioja red wine, chilled
½ cup brandy
1 cup fresh-squeezed orange juice, strained
1 large orange, sliced into thin disks, and then into halves
1 liter bottle club soda

*Spoon it carefully, so the delicate eggs don't break.

Combine and chill the first 4 ingredients from 1 to 24 hours. Mix in club soda just before serving. Pour from a clear glass pitcher over ice cubes into stemmed glasses.

SOUPS

It's not necessary to mess with carcasses, scraps, and prolonged simmerings when we want a flavorful soup. The following are good examples of what can be done with fresh vegetables, interesting seasonings, and quick cooking techniques.

ROASTED TOMATO SOUP

(Serves 8 to 10)

Olive oil spray
2 pounds onions
4 pounds tomatoes
1 teaspoon salt (or to taste)
Two 15½-ounce cans chicken broth
Sprigs of rosemary, basil, or parsley, for garnish

Preheat oven to 300 degrees. Spray olive oil over a large roasting pan. Horizontally slice the onions, and place them in the roasting pan. Slice the tomatoes horizontally, and lay them over the onions. Spray with more oil. Roast about 45 minutes. Scrape into food processor (in a couple of batches) with a spatula. Add salt and blend about 30 seconds. Pour into a large pot. Stir in chicken both. Bring to a boil, turn down heat, and simmer for 2 minutes. Garnish each serving with a sprig of rosemary, basil, or parsley.

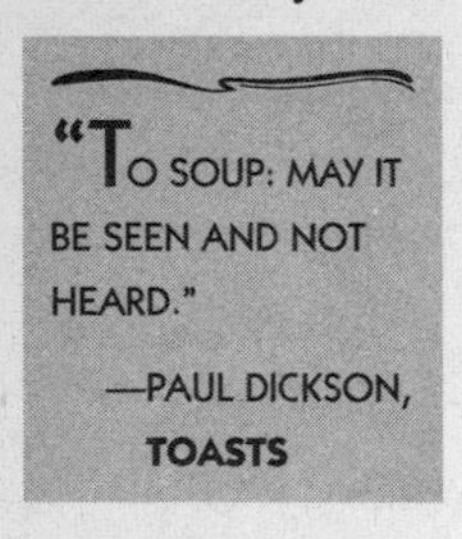
"TO SOUP: MAY IT BE SEEN AND NOT HEARD."
—PAUL DICKSON, **TOASTS**

SWEET POTATO BISQUE

(Serves 8 to 10)

I found this creamy, rich-tasting yet fat-free soup a few years ago in *Sunset* magazine. (*Sunset* is a great source for innovative and reliable recipes.) The formula is one of the few I've not needed to fiddle with, and everyone seems to love it.

4 to 6 medium-sized sweet potatoes (about 2 pounds)
Two 14½-ounce cans chicken broth
One 6-ounce can tomato paste
1 teaspoon curry powder
2 tablespoons fresh lemon or lime juice
Salt to taste
Sour cream (optional)

Steam potatoes till soft, about 10 to 15 minutes. Peel and place into food processor in batches with the chicken broth and tomato paste. Puree. Pour mixture back into pan along with the curry powder and lemon juice. Bring to a boil while stirring. Reduce heat and simmer and stir for 3 minutes. Add salt. Ladle into serving bowls and top with a tablespoon of sour cream.

"CUISINE IS LIKE COUTURE: SOUP TO NUTS ONE YEAR, FOCACCIA TO TIRAMISÙ THE NEXT."
—DAVID COBB CRAIG, WRITER, LIFE

ICED GAZPACHO

(Serves 6)

This Andalusian "liquid salad" was thought so exotic in the mid-nineteenth century, a French traveler to Spain wrote, "Strange as it may seem, the first time one tastes it, one ends by getting used to it and even liking it." Gazpacho has wide appeal today, especially when days are hot and vines are heavy.

4 large peeled and seeded tomatoes
2 small peeled and sliced cucumbers
1 large chopped and seeded red pepper
2 tablespoons red wine vinegar
2 cups V-8 juice
2 cloves minced garlic
Cucumber slices for garnish

Mix all ingredients in food processor or blender. Chill till cold. Serve in a wide-mouth stemmed glass, topped with a thin cucumber slice.

POSH POULET AND PASTA SOUP

(Serves 6 to 8)

With cooked chicken and pasta on hand, this hearty soup is as easy to throw together as it is scrumptious to eat.

1 medium onion, chopped
2 teaspoons butter or margarine, divided
5 medium stalks of celery, sliced
5 midsized carrots, sliced thin
1 teaspoon poultry seasoning
1 teaspoon Extra Spicy Mrs. Dash Salt-Free Seasoning
Three 14½-ounce cans chicken broth
2 broth cans of water
1½ cups sliced or torn cooked chicken
2 cups cooked tortellini, or any bite-sized pasta
3 tablespoons finely chopped parsley

Sauté onion in 1 teaspoon of the butter or margarine in a big pot over low heat till it's soft and golden, about 15 minutes. Remove from pot and set aside. Sauté celery, carrots, and seasonings in the rest of the butter or margarine on medium heat about 5 minutes. Add broth, water, chicken, and sautéed onions. Bring to a boil. Lower heat and simmer gently about 5 minutes. Add pasta and parsley, bring to a simmer again. Turn off heat and serve.

BROCCOLI SOUP

(Serves 6)

A friend brought this winner back from the Tucson National Resort and Spa, so it's not only flavorful, it won't pack on the pounds.

2 cups finely chopped broccoli
2 tablespoons chopped onion
½ teaspoon curry powder
Two 15½-ounce cans chicken broth
Sour cream for garnish

Steam broccoli in a large pot about 5 minutes or until tender. Combine with onion, curry powder, and some of the chicken broth in a food processor or blender. Puree till smooth. Pour back into the pot with the rest of the chicken broth. Bring to a boil, then stir and simmer 2 minutes. Serve warm or chilled with a dollop of sour cream.

COLD SALADS

KYOTO COLE SLAW

(Serves 6)

My sister-in-law Ruth once spent the weekend with us with her friend Ruth Nako. As it is the Asian custom to arrive bearing gifts, Ms. Nako brought this offering. I've been making a variation of it ever since.

1 large head green cabbage
½ cup chopped green onions
4 tablespoons sesame seeds
One 2-ounce package sliced almonds
Two 3.55-ounce packages ramen soup noodles

Dressing
¼ cup sesame oil
¼ cup salad oil
6 tablespoons rice wine vinegar
4 tablespoons sugar
½ teaspoon freshly ground pepper
½ teaspoon salt

Shred cabbage in the food processor or with a sharp knife. Toss with green onions and salad dressing. Toast sesame seeds and almonds in a skillet, watching carefully, till they just start to brown. Remove from heat. Break noodles into small pieces. Toss noodles, nuts, and seeds with salad just before serving.

MANDARIN SPINACH SALAD

(Serves 6 to 8)

Two 6-ounce bags washed baby spinach leaves
Two 10½-ounce cans mandarin orange sections, drained
Two 2-ounce bags whole pecans, lightly toasted

Celery-Seed Dressing
(Makes about 2 cups)

⅓ cup sugar
1 teaspoon dry mustard
2 teaspoons celery seed
Salt and pepper to taste
3 tablespoons grated onion
1 cup salad oil
⅓ cup red wine vinegar

Measure sugar, mustard, celery seed, salt, pepper and onion and pour into a blender or mixer. Gradually add oil and vinegar in a steady stream, beating constantly. Toss spinach and oranges with about ⅓ cup of dressing. Sprinkle with pecans just before serving.
(Refrigerate the remaining dressing for future salads.)

PISTACHIO PEA SALAD

(Serves 6 to 8)

One 1-pound freshly shelled peas *or* one 1-pound package of petite frozen peas, defrosted, drained, and patted dry
1 cup thinly sliced celery
½ cup chopped green onions (optional)
½ cup mayonnaise
1 cup pistachio nutmeats

Mix peas, celery, and onions with mayonnaise. Toss with pistachios just before serving.

TABOULE

(Serves 5 to 6)

This popular Middle Eastern dish holds up well for a buffet or picnic.

One 5¼-ounce package taboule
1 cup cold water
1 tablespoon olive oil
1 cup diced fresh tomatoes
½ cup peeled and diced cucumber
2 tablespoons fresh lemon juice

Combine the grain and the packaged spices in a large bowl. Stir in the water and oil. Allow the grain to absorb the liquid for 30 minutes. Add the tomatoes, cucumber, and lemon juice. Mix well, cover, and marinate from 4 hours to overnight. Fluff with a fork, and serve on a bed of fresh greens.

CAL-A-VIE DRESSING

(Makes ½ cup)

I once spent a blissful week at this Southern California spa, where the food was so flavorful and virtuous, Oprah Winfrey absconded with Rosie Daley, the chef. I'm including the dressing not only for its "no regrets" quality, but also for its tangy flavor.

2 tablespoons concentrated apple juice
2½ tablespoons apple cider vinegar
1 tablespoon water
1 large shallot, coarsely cut
2 teaspoons Dijon mustard
1 teaspoon dried tarragon
6 to 8 small sprigs fresh parsley
Freshly ground black pepper to taste

Blend all ingredients in a blender or processor. Toss with fresh greens.

HOT VEGETABLES

KILLER ASPARAGUS

(Serves 4)

Another *Sunset* magazine adaptation, the balsamic vinegar gives this a rich, full-bodied flavor, while the raspberry vinegar imparts a slightly sweet tang.

1 tablespoon peanut oil
1 pound pencil-thin asparagus
2 tablespoons balsamic or raspberry vinegar

Preheat oven to 450 degrees. Spread oil in a large cast-iron frying pan. Place the oiled but otherwise empty pan in the oven for 5 minutes. Trim tough ends from asparagus. Remove pan from oven, and roll asparagus in the hot oil.* Place the pan back in the oven and roast for 5 minutes. Remove pan from oven, pour the vinegar over the asparagus.*

ROASTED VEGGIES

(Serves 6)

Vegetable cooking spray
6 plum tomatoes, quartered
One 8-ounce package whole mushrooms
One pint basket small white onions
1½ tablespoons olive oil
1½ tablespoons balsamic vinegar, divided
½ teaspoon dried thyme

Preheat oven to 425 degrees. Lightly oil a baking pan with the cooking spray. Toss veggies in a bowl with the oil, vinegar, and thyme. Evenly spread vegetables in the pan. Roast on upper rack for 20 to 25 minutes (check frequently so they don't overdarken) or until tender.

GRILLED SUMMER VEGETABLES

(Serves 4 to 6)

1 each large red, yellow, and green peppers, sliced into ½-inch strips
1 large onion, sliced into ⅛-inch-thick disks
3 medium zucchini, sliced lengthwise into ½-inch strips
¼ cup bottled Italian or other clear oil-based salad dressing

Toss vegetables into a plastic bag with the dressing. Shake to cover vegetables. Pour on grill. Separate with tongs. Grill on one side, watching carefully, till vegetables just start to char. Turn and continue grilling till done.

*Be careful. Both the hot oil and vinegar splatter.

MAIN DISHES

CHICKEN SCALOPPINE

(Serves 8)

8 boneless, skinless chicken breasts
4 tablespoons freshly grated parmesan cheese
½ cup packaged seasoned bread crumbs
1 teaspoon dried thyme
3 tablespoons butter or margarine
½ cup sherry
1 large bunch slightly steamed spinach or chard

Ask the butcher to pound the chicken breasts thin and flat. Rinse chicken in colander. Combine cheese, bread crumbs, and thyme in a shallow pan or dish. Dredge moist chicken through crumb mix. Melt butter in large, heavy skillet over medium-low heat. Brown breasts about 5 to 7 minutes (depending on thickness) on each side. Remove to serving plate; cover to keep warm. Pour sherry into skillet. Bring to a boil, scraping up browned bits, till the wine is reduced to about half its volume. Pour the glaze over chicken. Serve on a bed of barely steamed greens accompanied by white rice.

SEOUL SALMON

(Serves 6)

The following marinade is from my Korean-born and ace-cook sister-in-law Marion. It's meant for bulgogi, a thinly sliced, barbecued beef that is a staple of Korean menus and *was* my signature company dish. However, now that meat is no longer politically correct, I've found the marinade works beautifully on almost any fish that's firm enough to be broiled or grilled.

3 tablespoons soy sauce
3 tablespoons sesame oil
3 tablespoons water
3 tablespoons sugar
3 tablespoons green onion, thinly sliced
1 fat clove of garlic, minced
2 tablespoons sesame seeds
6 salmon steaks or other firm fish fillets

Mix the first 7 ingredients in a jumbo zip-lock bag. Add fish, one at a time, making sure each piece is moistened. Marinate 30 minutes to 2 hours. Grill or broil for 10 minutes per inch of thickness.

CAJUN CATFISH

(Serves 4 generously)

My favorite fish seller gave me this "secret" recipe before he retired to his rowboat and reel.

- 8 catfish fillets
- 2 tablespoons freshly squeezed lemon or lime juice
- ¼ cup bottled Italian or Caesar salad dressing
- 4 tablespoons Cajun's Choice Blackened Seasoning

"A FILLET OF FISH IS A COOK'S BEST FRIEND."
—LAURIE COLWIN, MORE HOME COOKING

Place the catfish in a wide, shallow pan. Mix lemon juice with the dressing, and pour it on both sides of the fish. (The dressing should just moisten the fish, not drown it.) Sprinkle the seasoning over each piece, rubbing it in. Marinate for 30 minutes to 2 hours. Grill approximately 5 minutes on each side (figuring 5 minutes each side, per inch). Garnish with lemon wedges and parsley. Serve with white rice, grilled vegetables, and a big green salad.

PALERMO PASTA SALAD

(Serves 6)

This adaptation of a Planter's Peanut Oil recipe is a favorite standby when I have to feed a crowd. It can be made ahead, doubled easily, and is best at room temperature.

- ¼ cup peanut oil
- 2 cups small broccoli flowerets
- ¾ teaspoon dried basil
- ½ teaspoon salt
- 2 cloves garlic, minced
- ¼ cup sliced green onions
- ½ pound fusilli (spiral) or farfalle (bow tie) pasta, cooked and drained
- One 1-pint basket cherry tomatoes, halved
- ½ cup freshly grated parmesan or Romano cheese

Heat oil in a large, heavy skillet over medium-high heat. Add broccoli, basil, and salt, and cook and stir for 3 minutes, or until broccoli is tender-crisp. Add garlic and onions, cook and stir for 1 more minute. Remove from heat. Toss with the warm pasta, tomatoes, and cheese. Serve warm, cold, or in between.

FRESH PESTO

This quick, no-cook sauce has many uses: it can be tossed with warm pasta, spread on a pizza shell, stirred into soup, or painted on a tomato-topped bagel. Since it's so rich and intensely flavored, a little goes a long way.

> "THE TROUBLE WITH EATING ITALIAN FOOD IS THAT FIVE OR SIX DAYS LATER YOU'RE HUNGRY AGAIN."
>
> —GEORGE MILLER

2 cups fresh basil leaves (remove the bitter stems)
¾ cup freshly grated parmesan
¼ cup pine nuts
4 cloves minced garlic
Pinch of salt
½ cup olive oil

Puree basil, cheese, nuts, garlic, and salt in a food processor or blender. Gradually add the oil through the feeding tube, blending until the mixture is the consistency of mayonnaise.

CARAMELIZED-ONION PIZZA

Innovative cook and heavenly host Pam Barnett came up with this winner. (She also developed the above Tuscany Bread and Jamaican Shrimp Spread recipes.)

1 tablespoon olive oil
1 tablespoon unsalted butter
2 jumbo onions (about ¾ pound each) sliced about ⅛ inch thick
1 teaspoon sugar
½ cup fresh basil leaves, chopped
One 12-inch prebaked pizza shell or pita round
⅓ cup shredded Gruyère cheese
2 tablespoons crumbled goat cheese

Heat oil and butter in a large skillet over low heat (200 degrees, if using an electric skillet). Add onions and cook until they begin to soften, stirring occasionally, about 15 minutes. Add sugar, continue to cook and stir until golden, about another 10 minutes. Remove from heat. Stir in basil, and spoon onto bread shell. Place on round pizza pan, sprinkle first with Gruyère, then with goat cheese, and bake in a 450-degree oven for 10 minutes.

ENSALADA DEL SOL

(Serves 8)

My friend Janice and I developed this dish for a charity luncheon and house tour. We had to close off the kitchen, however, since we didn't want guests to see us tossing their salads (we served over one hundred) in jumbo garbage bags.

1 small head Boston lettuce, torn into bite-sized pieces
1 small head red leaf lettuce, torn into bite-sized pieces
4 chicken breasts, cooked and shredded
1 cup chopped green onions
4 medium tomatoes, cut in wedges
2 large avocados, peeled, and sliced lengthwise
½ cup sliced black olives
½ cup each jack and cheddar cheese
2 hard-cooked eggs, sliced horizontally

Toss the first 6 ingredients with celery-seed dressing (see page 202). Garnish with the olives, cheese, and egg slices. Serve in fluted tortilla bowls on dinner plates along with a side of seasonal fruit.

> "PUT A POT OF CHILI ON THE STOVE TO SIMMER. LET IT SIMMER. MEANWHILE BROIL A GOOD STEAK. EAT THE STEAK. LET THE CHILI SIMMER. IGNORE IT."
>
> —RECIPE FOR CHILI FROM FORMER TEXAS GOVERNOR ALLAN SHIVERS

FLUTED TORTILLA BOWLS

We made these originally by lining a soup bowl with a paper towel, placing a cup over a tortilla, and zapping them one at a time in the microwave. They were crispy enough, but rather pale and anemic tasting. The following method, adapted from *Sunset* magazine instructions, makes a prettier and tastier shell.

Vegetable oil
1 package 10-inch flour tortillas

Preheat oven to 450 degrees. Place 3 empty 14½-ounce to 19-ounce soup cans on a baking sheet.

Top each with a 12-inch square of aluminum foil. Fill a pizza pan with water and add a few drops of vegetable oil. Dip tortillas in water, one at a time, and shake off excess moisture. Place tortillas over cans. Bake for 7 minutes. Remove each carefully from can. Allow to cool. Store in airtight plastic bags for up to a week. Fill with salad.

COMPANY OMELET

(Serves 2)

Omelets are fast and simple, and are best made separately in 1 or 2 servings. The following, however, can be doubled, tripled, or quadrupled. Just don't try to feed a crowd with it or you'll be flipping over a hot stove all night.

1 teaspoon butter or margarine
2 whole eggs
3 egg whites
2 tablespoons water
½ small avocado, peeled and chopped
1 teaspoon sun-dried tomato shavings
2 tablespoons crumbled goat cheese
1 small plum tomato, finely diced

Melt the butter or margarine in a 10½-inch skillet over medium heat. Break and separate the eggs in a bowl, add the water, and beat with a fork until well blended. Pour the eggs into the pan when the butter starts to bubble. Cover for about half a minute. When eggs are set, sprinkle with the avocado, sun-dried tomatoes, plum tomato, and cheese. Fold the omelet over on itself. Take the pan off the burner. Let the omelet set for 1 minute. Serve.

CHARLIE

(Serves 4)

Since this homey dish can be pulled almost entirely from the pantry, it's just the thing around the third or fourth day of a visit, when you just can't stand to make another grocery run.

Two 6-ounce cans fancy albacore tuna
2 tablespoons finely chopped green onions or chives
2 tablespoons Worcestershire

¼ teaspoon Tabasco sauce
4 heaping tablespoons (more or less) of mayonnaise, divided
1½ cups cubed bread
1 teaspoon sesame seeds
Pinch of dried thyme, basil, and oregano

Combine the first 4 ingredients along with 3 tablespoons of the mayonnaise in individual baking shells or an eight-inch- to twelve-inch-wide shallow ovenproof dish. Toss bread with the remaining mayonnaise and top tuna mixture. Sprinkle sesame seeds and herbs over bread cubes and bake at 350 degrees for 20 minutes. Serve with baked potatoes and a salad.

BREADS

HARVEST PLUNKS

(Makes about 24)

I bake these dense babies in the fall, when nuts and dried fruits are at their flavor peak and affordable. They keep well and are good to have on hand through the holidays.

Vegetable cooking spray
3 cups dried apricots, quartered
1 cup golden raisins
1 cup dark raisins
1½ cups whole almonds
1½ cups whole pecans
¾ cup all-purpose flour
¾ cup sugar
½ teaspoon baking powder
3 eggs
1 teaspoon vanilla

Preheat oven to 275 degrees. Coat miniature-muffin pans with spray oil. Combine fruits and nuts in a large bowl. In a separate bowl, mix flour, sugar, and baking powder together. Dump into fruit-and-nut mixture. Beat eggs with the vanilla and stir into the rest of the ingredients. Bake around 25 minutes, or until a toothpick or skewer comes out clean.

SKY HIGH POPOVERS

(Makes 6)

Butter-flavored vegetable oil spray
2 eggs
1 cup buttermilk
1 cup all-purpose flour

Preheat oven to 450 degrees. Spray 3 muffin tins with cooking oil. Whirl eggs, buttermilk, and flour in blender or food processor till thoroughly blended, stopping to scrape down the sides once or twice. Pour batter to the top of every other cup (to give them space to rise). Bake 20 minutes.(Be sure to turn off preheat element first.) Without opening the oven door, lower the heat to 350 degrees and bake 15 more minutes. Immediately pierce each popover with a thin skewer or toothpick to release the steam. Serve at once.

BEER BREAD

(Makes 1 loaf)

Who needs a bread-making machine when there's a brew on hand? Baking dissipates the alcohol, so don't worry about Granny slipping under the table.

3 cups whole wheat flour
1 teaspoon baking powder
½ teaspoon baking soda
3 tablespoons honey
One 12-ounce can beer
Vegetable oil spray
Butter or margarine

Preheat oven to 350 degrees. Mix the dry ingredients in a large bowl. Add honey and beer. Stir mix until moistened. Spoon into an oil-sprayed loaf pan and bake 55 minutes. Remove from oven. Cool on wire rack 10 minutes. Run a knife around the sides of the pan and dump on a plate. Rub the top and sides with butter. Eat while warm.

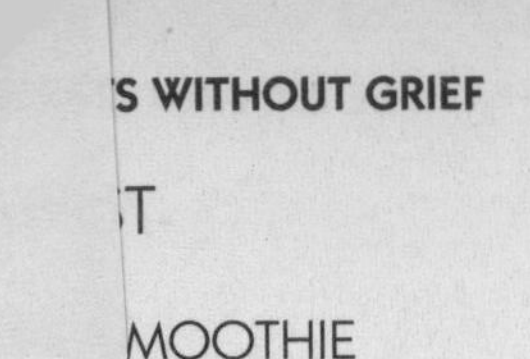

'T

MOOTHIE

(Serves 2)

The secret to a cold and creamy smoothie is a frozen banana. Freezing not only sweetens the fruit, it also thickens the drink.

2 cups orange juice
1 banana
One 6-ounce carton plain yogurt

Peel and slice the banana onto a plate. Freeze overnight. Scrape it into the blender in the morning with the juice and yogurt. Blend on high for 20 seconds. Pour into glasses and serve.

COTTAGE PANCAKES

(Makes about 24 thin pancakes or 4 generous servings)

Save these for the last day of the stay. Otherwise, houseguests may never leave.

1 teaspoon butter or margarine (or butter-flavored spray)
4 eggs
2 cups cottage cheese
½ cup all-purpose flour

Melt the butter or margarine in a large skillet over medium heat. Combine the rest of the ingredients in a blender or food processor. Whirl about 20 seconds till smooth, stopping to scrape down the sides once or twice. Pour into 6-inch rounds in the skillet. Flip them over when their air bubbles break, and cook 3 minutes more. Serve with a shaker of powdered sugar and lemon wedges, or fresh fruit preserves.

FRESH FRUIT SAUCE

Puree an abundance of berries, peeled peaches, apricots, or plums in the blender or food processor with sugar to taste. Serve with Cottage Pancakes, or over most anything, including the following bombe.

SWEET THINGS

This is so easy, yet so impressive-looking, it's almost (but not completely) embarrassing to collect the compliments.

BRAINLESS BUT BEAUTIFUL BOMBE

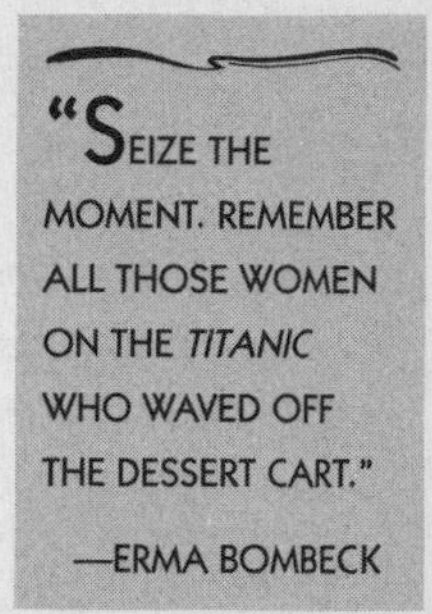
"SEIZE THE
MOMENT. REMEMBER
ALL THOSE WOMEN
ON THE *TITANIC*
WHO WAVED OFF
THE DESSERT CART."
—ERMA BOMBECK

1 quart premium vanilla ice cream or frozen yogurt, packed in a round carton
One 3-ounce package 3-inch-long lady fingers

Chill footed cake platter. Run knife around the inside edge of the ice cream carton. Cut carton on the seam and peel it away. Invert ice cream on platter. Smooth it with a spatula or wide knife. Press split lady fingers into the sides and top of the ice cream until it's completely covered. Freeze a couple of hours. Serve with pureed fruit and whipped cream.

CHOCOLATE MARBLED CHEESECAKE

Piecrust

1 cellophane packet cinnamon graham crackers (or 22 squares)
⅓ cup melted butter or margarine

Buzz crackers in a blender or food processor. Dump into a bowl, and mix in the butter or margarine. Pour crumbs into a 9-inch pie pan. Press another same-sized pan on the crust to make it perfectly even. Chill at least 1 hour.*

Filling

2 eggs
Four 3-ounce, or 1⅓ 8-ounce packages cream cheese, softened
⅓ cup sugar
1 teaspoon vanilla
Four 1.55 Hershey's chocolate bars or four 1.30-ounce Dove chocolate bars

Preheat oven to 325 degrees. Beat eggs, cream cheese, sugar, and vanilla until smooth. Pour into chilled pie shell. Break chocolate into pieces

*If the crust isn't thoroughly cooled, the filling may break it up in the oven.

and microwave 2 minutes at half power. Stir any remaining chocolate pieces until melted. Drop by teaspoons into 4 evenly placed circles over the filling. Lightly swirl the chocolate through the filling with a sharp knife. Bake in a 325-degree oven for 20 to 25 minutes or until the center appears set. Refrigerate, but bring to room temperature about 30 minutes before serving.

APPLE PUDDING CAKE WITH CALVADOS SAUCE

(Serves 6)

This winner is the signature dish of The Lodge in Riggins, Idaho. "It's the most requested item on the menu," says co-owner Kate Bradbury. "And it's so easy to throw together, it's virtually idiotproof."

2 large (about 1 pound) Granny Smith apples, quartered, cored, and peeled
1 cup brown sugar
¼ cup butter, softened
1 egg
1 cup flour
¼ teaspoon salt
1 teaspoon baking soda
½ teaspoon cinnamon
½ teaspoon nutmeg

Finely chop apples in food processor, and dump into large mixing bowl. Blend sugar and butter in processor and blend off and on until they're fluffy. Add egg and continue to process until well blended. Add flour, salt, baking soda, and spices and process about 30 seconds. Scrape mixture out of the processor onto the apples in the bowl and stir until blended.

Bake at 350° in buttered, unpapered muffin tins, about 25 minutes. Remove from tins when slightly cooled. Invert 1 on each serving plate, and serve warm with the sauce.

Calvados Sauce
1 cup powdered sugar
1 cup heavy cream
½ cup butter
2 tablespoons Calvados or other apple brandy (bourbon may be substituted)

Place all ingredients in a heavy saucepan, and stir over medium heat until sauce is creamy and well blended. Do not boil. Pour warm sauce over cakes.

SMART COOKIES

(Makes 3 to 4 dozen)

This no-bake recipe is for 1 batch of cookies, but 3 batches, each made with chocolate, butterscotch, and white chocolate, make an even prettier and more delectable presentation.

> "REMEMBER YOU'RE ALL ALONE IN THE KITCHEN AND NO ONE CAN SEE YOU."
>
> —JULIA CHILD

One 12-ounce package chocolate, butterscotch, or white chocolate chips
One 6-ounce package chow mein noodles
¾ cup chopped pecans, walnuts, or almonds

Microwave chips on half power 2½ to 3 minutes in a large bowl. (Chips will look whole, but will melt when stirred.) Fold in noodles and nuts. Drop by heaping teaspoons onto a waxed paper–lined tray. Refrigerate for an hour or so.

SUGGESTED MENUS

HOLIDAY COCKTAIL PARTY

Creamy hummus, crunchy bread, spicy-sweet shrimp, lusciously stuffed potatoes, crisp, brightly colored vegetables, fragrant, warm almonds, rich Brie; this good and plenty spread satisfies all the senses.

Hummus with Pita Triangles and Vegetable Sticks
Tuscany Bread
Jamaican Shrimp Spread
Tuxedo Potatoes
Brie with Water Crackers
Whole Roasted Almonds

A MIDSUMMER'S EVE COOKOUT

Whether it's a hibachi on the fire escape or a gas grill by the pool, appeal to your partner's primal need for grilling on an open fire in the great outdoors.

Sparkling Sangria
Cajun Catfish
Couscous
Grilled Vegetables
Angel Food Cake with Fresh Strawberries and Vanilla Ice Cream

BUFFET LUNCH

This simple buffet is a palate pleaser whether you run with vegetarians or carnivores. Make the pasta salad a day ahead, and slice the melons in the morning. Since the pasta is at its flavorful best served at room temperature, there's no messing with hot plates, electrical cords, or smelly chafing dish fuel.

Cape Cod Punch
Palermo Pasta Salad
Thin Slices of Cantaloupe and Honeydew Melon
Dense Flourless Chocolate Cake (from the best bakery in town)

SIT-DOWN DINNER FOR EIGHT

The robust flavors of the Mediterranean make this fuss-free combo a universal favorite.

Gourmet Greens with Marinated Artichokes and Goat Cheese in Cal-A-Vie Dressing
Chicken Scaloppine
Tortellini with Pesto
Lemon Sorbet with Fresh Raspberries

PACIFIC RIM DINNER

Asian food is light, elegant, and easy to prepare. Fresh fruit is the traditional dessert choice, but I figure with all those calories saved, it's a golden opportunity to splurge on something decadently Western.

Mandarin Spinach Salad
Kyoto Cole Slaw
Seoul Salmon
Steamed White Rice
Brainless But Beautiful Bombe

FIRESIDE SOUP AND PIZZA FEAST

Light the fire, break out the mugs, and pop the pizza in the oven while everyone is enjoying their choice of steaming soup.

Roasted Tomato Soup
Broccoli Soup
Caramelized Onion Pizza
Chocolate Marbled Cheesecake
or
Coffee, Cognac, and Conversation

"TO EAT IS HUMAN, TO DIGEST DIVINE."

—MARK TWAIN

ACKNOWLEDGMENTS

HOW I GOT SO SMART

In addition to those listed in the text, thanks to the following designers, food pros, vintners, sages, and ace hosts who fed me enlightenment, inspiration, and advice: Nancy Blandford of Built in Design, the Chino Family at the Vegetable Shop, Jean Chung, Marion Chung, Ruth Chung, Pat Finlayson, Vicki Gibbs, Deborah Harding, Diane Jaffari, Vicky Jans of D'Ashley & Jans Entertainment, Lisa Jhung, Ellie Johns, Ann McKinney, the Robert Mondavi Winery, Patti Phillips, Barbara Riccio, Julia Sweeney, Debra Trevino, Jane Wenman, Carol Yalam, and Yasko Zimmerman.

HOW I GOT SO LUCKY

I owe it all to the encouragement of my agent, Sandra Dijkstra, the foresight of my mentors Diane Gage and Kathy Saideman, the wisdom of my editor, Betsy Radin Herman, the proofreading of Barbara von Rosen and Kelley Jhung, and the patience, fortitude, and digestion of my husband, Larry.

INDEX